EDITORIAL RESEARCH REPORTS

Consumer
Protection
gains and setbacks

Timely Reports to Keep
Journalists, Scholars and the Public
Abreast of Developing Issues, Events and Trends

Published by Congressional Quarterly, Inc.
1414 22nd Street, N.W.
Washington, D.C. 20037

About the Cover

The cover was designed by Staff Artist Terry Atkinson, under the supervision of Art Director Richard Pottern.

PRINTED IN THE UNITED STATES OF AMERICA
MARCH 1978

Editor, Hoyt Gimlin
Associate Editor, Sandra Stencel
Editorial Assistants, Barbara Cornell, Diane Huffman
Production Manager, I.D. Fuller
Assistant Production Manager, Maceo Mayo

Library of Congress Cataloging in Publication Data

Congressional Quarterly, Inc.
    Editorial research reports on consumer protection.

    Bibliography: p.
    Includes index.

    1. Consumer protection—United States. I. Title. II. Title:
Consumer protection
HC110.C63C596   1978   381'.3   78-2927
ISBN 0-87187-130-0

Contents

Foreword

For more than a decade the consumer movement has been a pervasive force in American life. Consumer affairs offices now exist in all Cabinet-level departments of the federal government, as well as in most independent agencies from the Civil Aeronautics Board to the Small Business Administration. At least one office or division dealing with consumer affairs has been set up in each of the 50 states. The consumer movement has been responsible for passage of legislation requiring truth in lending, fair credit reporting, toy safety and the banning of cyclamates, red dye No. 2 and other dangerous and toxic substances.

In recent years consumer advocates have turned their attention to much broader issues, including job health and safety, media standards, oil company divestiture and genetic research. Perhaps the most significant achievement of the consumer movement has been an attitudinal change in the public. People are more aware of their consumer rights, more willing to complain about shoddy goods and services, and more careful about where and what they buy in the first place.

In spite of these positive signs, the consumer movement has faced some serious setbacks in the last few years. By far the biggest disappointment has been Congress's refusal to enact legislation setting up a federal consumer protection agency. This has been the No. 1 goal of the consumer movement since the mid-1960s. One factor thought to have contributed to the bill's latest defeat is a problem that has plagued the consumer movement from its beginnings 15 years ago—the movement's inability to present a united front on most issues. Marc Leepson writes in this book's opening report that "the consumer movement, almost by its definition, is as fragmented as the myriad needs the consuming American public has."

The 10 reports included in this book reflect the ever broadening concerns of American consumers and how the nation's policymakers are responding to them.

Sandra Stencel
Associate Editor

March 1978
Washington, D.C.

Consumer Protection: Gains and Setbacks

by

Marc Leepson

**Feb. 17
1978**

CONSUMER PROTECTION: GAINS AND SETBACKS

T HE AMERICAN CONSUMER movement has grown from virtually nothing 15 years ago to an established force for change today. There have been notable successes, such as the many federal laws and regulatory-agency rulings on consumer matters. But the movement also has been frustrated by a number of setbacks in recent years, including Congress's refusal to enact legislation setting up a federal consumer protection agency. In light of the setbacks, some wonder whether the consumer movement will ever again be as powerful and effective as it was in the late 1960s and early 1970s. "To assess such an amorphous thing as the consumer movement is not easy," Arthur E. Rowse, editor of *Consumer Newsweekly,* wrote recently. "There is no yardstick of progress. One can merely list gains and losses while trying to spot causes."[1]

Many consumer advocates say that Jimmy Carter's election has been a significant gain for the consumer movement. Carter spoke out strongly for consumer issues during the presidential campaign. He stressed his support for a strong government agency to represent consumers. In his presentation to the Democratic Party Platform Committee at the nominating convention, Carter called for "major reforms to protect the consumers of this country." A nationwide program of consumer education and vigorous enforcement of the nation's antitrust laws were two other Carter campaign promises.

During his first year in office, Carter placed some 60 former consumer and public interest activists in important positions in the government, a move highly praised by consumer groups (see p. 16). In his State of the Union Address, delivered Jan. 19, 1978, Carter again said he was "strongly committed" to legislation creating a federal consumer protection agency. But despite White House support, the House voted down the measure on Feb. 8 (see p. 6). White House Press Secretary Jody Powell said the following day, "It was a case of the best efforts on the part of the administration not being able to overcome some very organized and effective opposition" from business groups. Powell promised that "administration efforts on behalf of the consumer...will continue and intensify."

[1] Rowse, former executive director of the White House Consumer Office, writing in *The Washington Post,* Dec. 25, 1977.

Another positive sign is the growth of consumer offices in state and local governments throughout the country. According to the Office of Consumer Affairs of the Department of Health, Education and Welfare, at least one office or division dealing with consumer affairs has been set up in each of the 50 states, the District of Columbia, Guam, Puerto Rico and the Virgin Islands. The total is 141.[2] The number of county consumer offices has grown markedly in the last few years—from only 18 six years ago to 150 today. City consumer departments have grown from 53 in 1971 to 67 today. *The Christian Science Monitor* reported recently that "more than 600" local, county and state government consumer protection agencies are in operation—"a figure that has doubled in the past two years."[3]

New Jersey has one of the most comprehensive state consumer programs. The New Jersey Division of Consumer Affairs works with some 100 county and municipal consumer offices throughout the state. This Consumer Affairs Local Assistance Network handles consumer complaints, corrects frauds and conducts educational programs. In May 1974, the state created the nation's first Cabinet-level Department of Public Advocate with wide powers to sue in the public interest. The Public Advocate office has rolled back rent increases in state-run housing units and helped get voting rights for mentally retarded persons in state institutions.

Among the most successful of the newer county consumer programs is the Los Angeles County Department of Consumer Affairs, which started operations in April 1976. The agency has received some 80,000 telephone inquiries since that time, and has investigated some 10,000 consumer complaints. Many cities across the nation—including Chicago, Honolulu, Boston, Detroit, Atlanta, Houston and Columbus, Ohio—have complaint centers to hear consumer grievances about city services. Local consumer agencies are "gaining more authority all the time," *Business Week* magazine commented recently, "and the scope of consumerist activities at the state and county levels is growing accordingly."[4]

Public Perception of Consumer Movement

Consumer affairs offices exist in all Cabinet-level departments of the federal government, as well as in most independent agencies, from the Civil Aeronautics Board to the Small Business Administration. In addition, the government operates the Federal Information Center which provides citizens

---

[2] Office of Consumer Affairs, U.S. Department of Health, Education and Welfare, "Directory of Federal, State & Local Government Consumer Offices," Aug. 1, 1977, p. 8.
[3] *The Christian Science Monitor,* Jan. 27, 1978.
[4] "Local Muscle for Consumers," *Business Week,* Sept. 26, 1977, p. 146.

with information about the government and helps with specific consumer problems. Located in major cities across the country, the offices are run by the General Services Administration and the Civil Service Commission.

There are other, less tangible, signs of the consumer movement's imprint on American life. A national opinion survey conducted by Louis Harris and Associates for Sentry Insurance indicated that most Americans believe the consumer movement has significantly improved conditions in the marketplace in the last 10 years. Seventy-two per cent of those polled in the February 1977 survey said they believed their shopping skills had improved in the last 10 years; 70 per cent felt that labeling and product information had gotten better; and 60 per cent believed that the safety of most products had improved.

The study also indicated a large measure of distrust of business. Exactly half of those questioned said that consumers do not get a better deal in the marketplace than they did 10 years ago; 61 per cent believed the quality of most products and services has grown worse in the last decade. The main consumer concerns were the high price of products, the high cost of medical and hospital care, the poor quality of products, and the failure of many products to live up to advertised claims. The survey concluded: "In the next few years [the business community] can expect to be vigorously attacked by both consumer activists and elected representatives. And it will be more severely regulated unless there are major changes within the business world."[5]

Recent Defeat of Consumer Agency Bill

There have been other gains in the consumer movement in recent years. Increasing numbers of federal, state and local consumer protection laws and regulations have been implemented. Budgets and working capital for consumer groups—both private and governmental—have generally risen, as has the number of persons actively working in consumer groups. Many newspapers and television and radio stations have hired consumer affairs experts. And some businesses have taken voluntary steps to help consumers. Many grocery stores provide open-dating of perishable products.[6] Some give comparative prices for different sizes and brands of the same items. Some food processors exceed government requirements for ingredient and nutritional labeling. Other manufacturers offer expanded guarantees and warranties.

---

[5] "Consumerism at the Crossroads," Louis Harris Research Study, May 1977, pp. 6-7.
[6] Open-dating means that the date by which a product should be sold to ensure freshness is clearly marked on its container.

In spite of these positive signs, the consumer movement has faced some setbacks in the last several years. By far the biggest disappointment has been Congress's unwillingness to enact legislation creating a consumer protection agency. Legislation to establish such an agency was introduced for the first time eight years ago.[7] In spite of a heavy lobbying effort by consumer groups, the House of Representatives Feb. 8 rejected creation of a federal consumer protection agency by a 227-189 vote. The vote came on a considerably scaled-down version of previous consumer agency bills. The legislation nevertheless would have given the agency power to represent consumers in government proceedings. Observers believe that the House vote reflected congressional unhappiness with setting up yet another federal agency as much as it did anti-consumer sentiment.

Some laws passed by Congress in recent years have had unintended effects that have hurt the consumer cause. Several of them, in the words of Arthur E. Rowse, "have boomeranged or failed to come close to original expectations." The Truth in Lending Act of 1968 is one example. It was intended to give consumers useful information about loan and credit charges. But some businesses that had not imposed credit charges took advantage of the law's complicated and ambiguous wording and began to do so. Others increased credit charges. The Senate Banking Committee recently began considering ways to simplify the law.

Another law that has not worked as intended is the 1974 Employee Retirement Income Security Act. Marjorie Boyd has called the act, which was designed to simplify private pension plans, "perhaps the most complicated piece of regulatory legislation ever devised."[8] In order to comply with the law, some small businesses have been forced to make costly investments to set up employee pension plans. Boyd wrote that within two years after the measure became law, some 10,000 companies dropped their pension plans rather than comply with the law's complicated provisions.

The 1975 Magnuson-Moss Warranty Act[9] is another case in point. The measure gave the Federal Trade Commission power to set standards for written warranties on products priced at more than five dollars. The law's vague language, some claim, allowed furniture and appliance manufacturers to stop issuing

---

[7] The Senate passed a bill in 1970 but it was blocked in the House Rules Committee. The House passed a bill in 1971, but the Senate version was killed by a filibuster in 1972. Consumer protection agency bills were nearly enacted in the 93rd (1973-74) and 94th Congresses, but the opposition of Republican administrations and business groups proved too powerful. See Congressional Quarterly's *Congress and the Nation*, Vol. IV, p. 434.

[8] Marjorie Boyd, "The Protection Consumers Don't Want," *The Washington Monthly*, September 1977, p. 30.

[9] Named for Sen. Warren G. Magnuson (D Wash.) and Rep. John E. Moss (D Calif.).

some warranties and weaken existing ones. Other consumer-oriented rulings have proved unpopular with the public and, according to Chuck Fager, they "have produced, or have been manipulated to produce, widespread skepticism about the federal government's capacity to write effective consumer legislation in many areas."[10]

A Department of Transportation regulation requiring auto manufacturers to install interlock systems that prevented cars from being started until seatbelts were fastened was widely criticized. Congress passed legislation in 1974 overruling the department's order. The bill stipulated that the interlock system would no longer be mandatory and that existing systems could be legally dismantled. The Food and Drug Administration proposed a ban on saccharin, the only artificial sweetener available in the United States, in March 1977. The announcement drew angry protests from consumers and representatives of the food industry. The FDA ban was based in part on Canadian tests that showed rats fed high dosages of saccharin developed bladder cancer. In November 1977, Congress voted to delay the ban 18 months until further tests were completed by the National Academy of Sciences.

Criticism of Product Safety Commission

Consumer unhappiness with government-run programs can perhaps best be illustrated by examining the Consumer Product Safety Commission, an independent agency set up by Congress in 1972. The agency is headed by a five-member commission and has the authority to set safety standards for consumer products and to ban products presenting an unreasonable risk of injury. When the commission was established in 1972, it received widespread support from consumer groups.

Since then, the agency has come under wide-ranging criticism. Its chairman, S. John Byington, submitted his resignation Feb. 8 in the face of complaints that the commission does not act quickly or efficiently.[11] Howie Kurtz, a Washington, D.C., investigative reporter, wrote recently that the commission has "been such an abysmal failure that it is at least as responsible as any other government agency for the plummeting popularity of consumer protection."[12] Jo Thomas of *The New York Times* wrote that the commission "is almost universally regarded as feeble, tardy and reluctant in banning or recalling dangerous products and in setting Federal safety standards."[13]

---

[10] Writing in the newsweekly, *The Boston Phoenix*, Jan. 10, 1978, p. 7.
[11] Byington will leave office June 30, 1978, four months before his term expires.
[12] Howie Kurtz, "The Consumer Product Safety Commission and Asbestos," *The Washington Monthly*, December 1977, p. 29.
[13] *The New York Times*, Jan. 30, 1978.

Strong indictments of the Consumer Product Safety Commission also have come from government investigatory units. A General Accounting Office (GAO) report[14] took the commission to task for not developing and issuing safety standards promptly. During its first four years, the commission issued standards for only three products—swimming pool slides, architectural glass and matchbooks. The GAO report said that the commission took an average of 834 days to develop those standards, far more than the 330 days Congress specified in the 1972 legislation setting up the agency.

A report by the U.S. Civil Service Commission[15] also was highly critical of the consumer commission. The report found that it "violated personnel laws, regulations and requirements" in 30 cases by giving preferential treatment and personal favoritism to hired consultants. The report blamed Commission Chairman Byington and his former top administrative aide, Albert Dimcoff, for the violations.

A third highly critical report was made public Feb. 1, 1978, in *The Washington Post*. The newspaper reported that a 170-page internal commission report said that the commission had been ineffective in performing its main function—reducing product-related injuries to consumers. "Overall, consumer product-related injuries requiring emergency medical treatment have increased by 44 per cent in the CPSC's five-year history," the report stated. Several factors were cited for the commission's poor performance, including "political or leadership disagreements among the commissioners...tensions between staff and commissioners...staff performance...[and] the effects of having no permanent Executive Director for so long." The report did praise some of the commission's work, especially the development of toy safety and crib construction standards.

Consumer Product Safety Commission officials have defended the agency. Byington said recently that "the critics overlook the fact that the very existence of the agency has been a positive factor in terms of improved safety. There have been dramatic improvements in the whole area of outdoor power equipment.... The standards adopted by the industries have been tightened substantially. Toys are another area where the industry itself has made dramatic improvements."[16]

Two rulings by the commission have been particularly unpopular. The first, in 1972, required that children's sleeping gar-

---

[14] "The Consumer Product Safety Commission Needs to Issue Safety Standards Faster," Dec. 12, 1977.
[15] "Merit System Investigation in the Consumer Product Safety Commission Headquarters, Washington, D.C.," Jan. 12, 1978.
[16] Interview published in *U.S. News & World Report*, Oct. 24, 1977, p. 34.

ments be treated with flame-retardants. Then, in 1977, the agency banned use of one of the chemical retardants, Tris, after determining that it could cause cancer. The two actions angered both manufacturers and consumers. Parents faced higher prices for children's sleepwear in 1972 when the chemical flame retardants were added. Manufacturers protested the ruling that allowed purchasers of Tris-treated garments to have their money refunded. Sleepwear producers say the costs of developing new flame retardants will mean even higher prices.

The commission also has been criticized for not moving quickly against asbestos, which some tests indicate can cause cancer. The agency recently issued a ban on the asbestos coating on artificial fireplace logs. But it took two years to do so. Asbestos is an ingredient in many other products, including children's modeling clay and papier maché. Some time this year the agency is scheduled to issue safety standards for power lawn mowers, gas space heaters, Christmas lights, contact adhesives, communications antennae and baby rattles. The agency also plans to hold regional hearings to let consumers around the country have some voice in influencing rulemaking. But criticism continues and the Consumer Subcommittee of the Senate Commerce, Science and Transportation Committee will be looking into the agency's operations in hearings scheduled for Feb. 24 and 27.

Activities of Nader Groups

C ONSUMER CONSCIOUSNESS is due in large part to the activities of Ralph Nader, a 43-year-old lawyer who was virtually unknown to the public only 12 years ago. "If I were to do a social history of the 1960s and 1970s, I'd write it in terms of Ralph Nader," Carol Tucker Foreman, Assistant Secretary for Food and Consumer Services at the U.S. Department of Agriculture and former head of the Consumer Federation of America, said recently. "He influenced more people than anyone else."[17]

David Ignatius, who worked as a Nader lobbyist in 1973, has written that Nader's career can be divided into four stages. A look at these stages reveals some of the successes and failures of the U.S. consumer movement since the mid-1960s. Nader's career as the nation's foremost consumer advocate began in November 1965 with publication of his book *Unsafe at Any Speed: The Designed-in Dangers of the American Automobile.*

[17] Quoted in *The Washington Star,* Jan. 1, 1977.

Although he attacked the whole Detroit automobile industry for emphasis on profits and styling over safety, Nader concentrated his fire on the Chevrolet Corvair, "one of the nastiest-handling cars ever built." The book became a best-seller, and the demise of the Corvair was attributed to its influence.

Meanwhile, congressional support was growing for passage of auto-safety legislation, and Nader testified on behalf of such a bill early in 1966. On March 6, 1966, newspapers published Nader's complaint that he had been under investigation by private detectives hired by the auto industry. Three days later, General Motors conceded that it had initiated a "routine investigation" of Nader to find out if he had any connection with damage suits that had been filed against the company because of defects in the Corvair.

In a nationally televised hearing on March 22, GM President James M. Roche told the Senate Subcommittee on Executive Reorganization that there had been "some harassment," and publicly apologized to Nader. Final passage of the National Traffic and Motor Vehicle Safety Act of 1966 came five months later. After the General Motors apology, Ignatius wrote: "The Nader legend was born. An aroused citizen had waged a successful guerrilla campaign against the world's most powerful corporation."[18]

The second phase of Nader's career lasted from 1968 to 1970. An organizational period, it featured the opening of the parent Nader organization, the Center for the Study of Responsive Law, in June 1969. The center is a Washington-based tax-exempt organization. It operates on a yearly budget of some $300,000, much of it provided by foundations. The center is perhaps best known as a staging area for the activities of "Nader's Raiders"—groups of young people who gather in Washington during the summer months to ferret out information from government and business groups for subsequent reports.

The Center for the Study of Responsive Law has produced reports on the Federal Trade Commission, the Interstate Commerce Commission, the Food and Drug Administration and on antitrust enforcement, occupational safety and health laws, air pollution, airline safety, nursing homes and the medical profession—among others. The exposés of waste and inefficiency that some of the reports documented won Nader and his raiders the title of modern-day muckrakers. The successes of Nader's organization helped the consumer movement in general to grow rapidly.

---

[18] David Ignatius, "Stages of Nader," *The New York Times Magazine,* Jan. 18, 1976, p. 9.

Nader and Congress

Ralph Nader has never been shy about criticizing those who he believes act contrary to the interest of American consumers. When the proposed consumer protection agency bill failed in Congress last year, Nader spoke out harshly against some liberal House members for their lukewarm support.

This year for the first time Nader's major lobbying organization, Congress Watch, will be working in congressional districts throughout the country during the 1978 House campaigns. Congress Watch Director Mark Green said recently that the local groups "will be a way to get information on to people...about what their representatives are really doing, as opposed to what they may say they're doing and to mobilize public support for our issues.... We're still thinking about whether to make formal endorsements; we might."

Nader summed up his position on politics in this way: "Liberal *versus* conservative is no longer the real dividing line in politics; the actual distinction is between the 'corporatists,' those who support and expand the power of corporations, and 'consumerists,' those who are working to expand the power of the people. The abuse of power by large corporations is the number-one issue in our society and we intend to make it the major political issue in 1978."

During the third phase of his career (1970-1972) Nader began the push for federal legislation setting up a consumer protection agency. Congress's unwillingness to do so, after months of intense lobbying by the Nader organization, led to a second major Nader undertaking: the formation in November 1971 of a 1,000-member team to conduct a yearlong study of Congress. The authors of the Congress Project set out to rate each member of Congress running for re-election in 1972. Nader characterized the effort as "the largest study of [Congress] ever conducted—an effort to share with citizens a better understanding of how the members and committees of our national legislature operate both among themselves and in relation to outside forces working on the Congress."[19]

"Everyone who had anything to do with it—Ralph Nader included—now admits the Congress Project was something of a boondoggle," Ignatius, who himself helped with some of the profiles, wrote. The main problems were the large volume of work and the short time to complete it. All the work was scheduled to be released before the November 1972 elections and the massive effort to complete the project was further hampered by administrative and organizational problems.

---

[19] Ralph Nader and Robert Fellmeth, writing in the introduction that accompanied the profiles, "Ralph Nader Congress Project, Citizens Look at Congress," August 1972.

Little new information was contained in the profiles. There were no sensational revelations or charges. *The New York Times* commented [20] that the profiles were "unlikely to furnish any damaging information that could not have been obtained elsewhere with a little digging."

The other significant undertaking during the "third phase" of Nader's career was the establishment of the Public Interest Research Group (PIRG) in 1970. The PIRG, which has been described as Nader's public-interest law firm, has satellite organizations on 145 college and university campuses with some 500,000 student members. Aside from student fees at the various colleges, the organization's budget is met by Nader's lecture fees and book royalties. Nader also donated the proceeds from an out-of-court settlement on an invasion-of-privacy suit against General Motors—estimated at some $270,000 after taxes and attorney fees.

Litigation, Lobbying and Organizing

The fourth phase of Nader's career began in 1972 and lasted into 1976. Ignatius described the period as one in which Nader embraced "the traditional tools of interest-group representation: litigation, lobbying and grass-roots organizing." Nader succeeded in setting up a relatively smooth bureaucracy, Ignatius wrote, "with a sensible delegation of authority, leaving him free to ruminate on the future."

In 1972, Nader established the tax-exempt Public Citizen, an umbrella-group, which directly supports four other Nader organizations: (1) the Citizen Action Group, which includes the Public Interest Research Group; (2) Congress Watch, a full-time lobbying office with a yearly operating budget of $145,000 and seven full-time lobbyists, which succeeded the Congress Project; (3) the Public Citizen Litigation Group, set up with a staff of eight attorneys to act in legal suits for consumers, especially in Freedom of Information suits; and (4) the Health Research Group, which studies and researches health issues.

Headed by Dr. Sidney Wolfe, the Health Research Group has petitioned the Food and Drug Administration to act against certain drug manufacturers and it was successful in helping ban the artificial food coloring, red dye No. 2. The Health Research Group conducts policy-oriented research on such issues as unnecessary surgery, comprehensive health planning, hospital construction and operation, mental illness, nutrition, drugs, pesticides and carcinogens, dental health and the education and training of health professionals.

Since 1976, articles in national news magazines and major

---

[20] Oct. 22, 1972.

newspapers have examined Nader's career and questioned his effectiveness and power and that of the entire consumer movement. The debate over Nader's effectiveness was sparked by the 1976 publication of the book *Me & Ralph: Is Nader Unsafe for America?* by David Sanford, then managing editor of *The New Republic.* In his self-described "rare and controversial view" of Nader,[21] Sanford conceded that Nader had done an admirable job working for American consumers, especially in influencing Congress to pass important consumer legislation. But the book concentrated on Nader's personal life—his personality, living habits and financial affairs. Sanford presented an overwhelmingly negative picture of Nader, accusing him of acting in his own self-interest rather than for consumers.

Some Nader supporters said the book was part of a personal vendetta against Nader. Theodore Jacobs, a Nader aide, wrote that Sanford's "allegations about...Nader are based on double and triple hearsay and consequently suffer from inaccuracies and misrepresentations."[22] Mark Green, the director of the Congress Watch project and a long-time Nader associate, called it a "pastiche of gossip, innuendo and error about Ralph Nader." Nader himself termed the book "a dirty trick." "One of the things that was so irritating," Nader said, "was his [Sanford's] faking a close association with us. I've talked to him less than three hours in the last nine years."[23]

Debate Over Nader's Influence and Power

Questions about Nader's effectiveness and speculation that he had lost influence and power continued through 1977. Two incidents fueled the controversy. The first was the largely negative reaction by political commentators and sports columnists to the formation of FANS—the Nader-sponsored Fight to Advance the Nation's Sports. The purpose of the group, Nader wrote,[24] was to allow sports fans to "exercise some fundamental consumer rights to know and to shape the product or service they are buying." Among the issues to be confronted were the high and growing cost of tickets, the high-priced, low-nutrition junk food sold at sports arenas and television blackouts. Nader said FANS eventually would focus on bigger issues, such as excesses by sports corporations and the over-extension and overlap of schedules of different sports.

"The owners and the players each have their own protection organizations. It's time the fans have one of their own," Nader

---

[21] David Sanford, *Me & Ralph* (1976), p. xii. Sanford currently is managing editor of *Skeptic* magazine.

[22] Writing in the letters column of *The Washington Post*, Aug. 11, 1976, in response to a letter Sanford wrote about the book.

[23] Quoted in *The Washington Star*, Jan. 1, 1977.

[24] In his nationally syndicated column, published June 11, 1977, in *The Washington Star.*

said as he and lawyer Peter Gruenstein announced the formation of the organization Sept. 27, 1977, in Washington. An editorial in *The Washington Post* Sept. 29 criticized FANS' formation, saying that Nader was overextending himself: "The idea that organizations can speak for groups of people is getting out of hand.... [B]eing a sports fan, after all, is a little different from being a food buyer—or a taxpayer. You don't have to be one if you don't want to."

Newspaper columnist George F. Will also attacked the organization. "FANS is like many organizations that are concocted by 'consumerists' skillful at making work for themselves," Will wrote. "It is the assertion, by a few persons who have appointed themselves to speak for many strangers, of concerns that few consumers share...."[25] Television commentator Eric Sevareid chided Nader for concerning himself with food at ballparks. Sevareid said Nader "would drive out the odor of peanuts and popcorn from ballpark and football stadium and spray the joints with astringent fumes of the germicide called Social Responsibility."[26]

The controversy over FANS is not crucial in terms of assessing the strength of the entire American consumer movement. But the reaction to its founding illustrates that Ralph Nader—who for much of his career had been extremely popular and rarely criticized except by conservative supporters of big business—can no longer count on general public acceptance of his every move.

Another round of anti-Nader criticism followed soon afterward. The uproar came after Nader publicly upbraided Joan Claybrook, head of the National Highway Traffic Safety Administration, who had been one of Nader's closest associates when she served as his chief congressional lobbyist.[27] Nader charged that Claybrook had "etched a trail of averted or broken promises" and demanded her resignation in a long letter made public early in December 1977. He accused her of betraying consumers by supporting a Carter administration decision to give auto manufacturers six more years to install air bags in cars.

Nader's outburst drew wide attention. Ross K. Baker, a professor of political science at Rutgers University, wrote that Nader's attack on Claybrook and other outbursts at government officials was symptomatic of Nader's unwillingness to realize that the federal government must be responsive to all in-

[25] Writing in *The Washington Post*, Oct. 2, 1977.
[26] Quoted in *The Wall Street Journal*, Dec. 13, 1977.
[27] Former Congress Watch lobbyist Nancy Chasen described Claybrook in 1976 as "undoubtedly [Nader's] most trusted employee—more so than anybody. She has extremely direct access to him. There is no issue that she is left out of." Quoted in Sanford, *op. cit.*, p. 80.

14

terests—not just to consumers. "Having succeeded to a remarkable degree in placing people identified with consumerism and public-interest activity in the Carter Administration," Baker wrote, "the zealots on the outside are attacking and repudiating their erstwhile colleagues for their moderation in the pursuit of reformist objectives."[28]

Has Nader's overall impact been significantly reduced by the Sanford incident, the creation of FANS and the Claybrook attack? Nader denies that he has lost any power. "There are two ways you can judge it," Nader said recently. "First, consider who we are up against. If we can come up neck and neck against the biggest coordinated lobby of trade groups ever, as we did on the consumer protection agency bill last fall, that's real power.... Second, you judge by whether a group wins its battles, and achieves what it's aiming at; or if you lose, by how close you come. And in those terms we've also been doing well."[29]

Rep. Toby Moffett (D Conn.), one of the leading voices for consumers in Congress, said recently that although Nader himself may be losing some influence, his lobbyists are becoming more effective. What Nader is doing, Moffett said, "is creating what I call an information stalemate. Ten years ago, you had information pouring in from the special interests but nothing to counter it. What Nader has done is even up the odds on information...."[30] While there may be disagreement on whether Nader himself has lost power and influence, there can be no doubt—as Moffett indicated—that the Nader organization is an established, effective voice for consumer causes.

Future of American Consumerism

PRESIDENT CARTER came to office last year with wide support from the nation's consumer leaders. Ralph Nader described Carter's views on consumer issues as "a breath of fresh air" compared to those of Presidents Nixon and Ford. Nader met with Carter Aug. 7, 1976, and pronounced Carter's positions on consumer issues "better than [those of] any candidate that has achieved the nomination of any major party in recent decades."[31] Speaking at a Nader-sponsored Public Citizen Forum in Washington, D.C., two days later, Carter said he wanted to challenge Nader "for the title of top consumer ad-

---

[28] Writing in *The New York Times*, Dec. 8, 1977.
[29] Quoted in *The Boston Phoenix*, Jan. 10, 1978, p. 7.
[30] Quoted in *National Journal*, Dec. 31, 1977, p. 1995.
[31] Quoted in *The Washington Post*, Aug. 8, 1976.

vocate in the country." Other national consumer leaders, including Kathleen O'Reilly, executive director of the Consumer Federation of America, also praised Carter's positions on consumer issues, especially his support for the proposed consumer protection agency and class action lawsuits by citizens. A group called Consumers for Carter, which included Bess Myerson, former New York City consumer affairs commissioner, formed to help the Carter presidential effort.

After the election, Nader's support for Carter faded somewhat. Nader found fault with Carter's initial Cabinet appointments, especially Energy Secretary James Schlesinger, and Treasury Secretary W. Michael Blumenthal. Nader accused Schlesinger of favoring nuclear energy at the expense of solar energy and conservation. Blumenthal, Nader told reporters, is not "someone who has had a record of strong commitment...to using the Treasury Department as something other than a plantation for bankers, trying to get genuine tax reform and trying to use the leverage of monetary policy and the Treasury's resources for housing and other purposes."[32] Nader did praise some of Carter's appointments, including Secretary of Labor F. Ray Marshall, Secretary of Health, Education and Welfare Joseph A. Califano Jr. and Secretary of Agriculture Bob Bergland.

Public Interest Activists in Government

Generally, there has been high praise from other consumer leaders for the large number of appointees with consumer backgrounds in the Carter administration. Important positions have gone to former public-interest lawyers, consumer advocates, civil-rights workers and environmental activists. Juan Cameron reported that some 60 former public interest advocates hold important positions in the federal government.[33]

One of the former consumer advocates in the Carter administration is Peter Schuck, HEW's Deputy Assistant Secretary for Planning and Evaluation, who previously served as Washington director of Consumers Union *(see p. 19)*. Schuck said recently that he, like many others newly appointed to government positions, faced problems with the vast size and procedural difficulties within the government bureaucracy. "It's a very stimulating experience, but it has also confirmed my worst suspicions about how difficult it is to get things done in a bureaucracy," Schuck said recently. "There are just so many bases to touch, so many groups to be conciliated."[34]

---

[32] Interviewed on "Face the Nation," (CBS-TV), Dec. 26, 1976.
[33] Juan Cameron, "Nader's Invaders are Inside the Gate," *Fortune*, October 1977, p. 252.
[34] Quoted in *Newsweek*, Jan. 12, 1978, p. 22.

Carter's Consumer Crusaders

Carol Tucker Foreman
Assistant Secretary of
Agriculture for Consumer
and Nutrition Services

Michael Pertschuk
Chairman, Federal
Trade Commission

Esther Peterson
Special Assistant
to the President for
Consumer Affairs

*"I want to challenge
Ralph Nader for the title of
top consumer advocate
in the country."*

—President Carter
Aug. 9, 1976

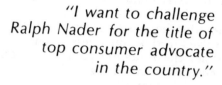

Joan Claybrook
Administrator,
National Traffic Safety
Administration

Robert Greenstein, a former lobbyist for the Community Nutrition Institute, now is a special assistant to Agriculture Secretary Bergland. As a public-interest advocate, Greenstein worked to liberalize food stamp laws. He was assigned the same task when he entered government. "I never dreamed I would get involved in this, much less be one of the principal advisers on the new [food stamp] legislation," Greenstein said last fall.[35] He is credited with writing an important change in the new food stamp law that allows qualified recipients to receive stamps without paying for them.

Changes at the Federal Trade Commission

The former consumer advocate with perhaps the most potential to influence the marketplace is Michael Pertschuk, chairman of the Federal Trade Commission. As chief of staff of the Senate Commerce Committee, Pertschuk earned a reputation as a campaigner against unfair business practices and for consumer rights. Pertschuk has promised to make the FTC, which enforces the antitrust laws either through voluntary compliance or court action, a voice for consumers. "We want to make sure consumers are better off than they were before as a result of our actions," Pertschuk said recently.[36]

Pertschuk took over as FTC chairman in May 1977. He has instituted several changes since then. The commission now allocates funds to consumer group representatives to attend FTC rule-making hearings, something the groups had not been able to afford to do in the past. Pertschuk has overseen a general reorganization of FTC procedures aimed at enabling the commission to move quickly to obtain injunctions and get penalties by direct court action.

Pertschuk has been criticized by both business and consumer representatives. Consumer groups say the commission has not moved quickly enough under Pertschuk and that the commission has not significantly aided the consumer cause since he took over in May 1977. On the other hand, businesses generally do not like his pro-consumer outlook. "We are not happy with him," Barry A. Friedman of the U.S. Chamber of Commerce said recently. "He's taken a strong pro-consumer position..." that potentially could harm business.[37]

The future of the American consumer movement hinges on many factors. The pivotal question, Arthur E. Rowse of *Consumer Newsweekly* wrote recently, is whether organized consumers can "ever build up enough power to forge significant im-

---

[35] Quoted by Juan Cameron, *op. cit.*, p. 253.
[36] Quoted in *The New York Times*, Jan. 19, 1978.
[37] Quoted in *The New York Times*, Jan. 19, 1978.

provements in the marketplace and society." One measure of the consumer movement's strength is the fate of the Consumer Protection Agency Bill. Many agree with the assessment of Rep. Benjamin S. Rosenthal's (D N.Y.), "I think we have heard the last of it, at least for a time," Rosenthal, a sponsor of the bill, said Feb. 9. "The margin of defeat was significant, and I don't see any basis for us to recover...."

Size and Shapelessness of the Movement

One thing that contributed to the bill's failure is a prob-problem that has plagued the American consumer movement from its beginnings 15 years ago—the movement's inability to present a totally united front on most issues. The consumer movement, almost by its definition, is as fragmented as the myriad needs the consuming American public has. The Nader organization, with 100 people working full-time in Washington on a yearly budget of some $1.1 million, is the closest thing to a national consumer organization. But the principal Nader organization, Public Citizen, is involved with many different issues and does not directly involve the public.

Lee Richardson, former president of the Consumer Federation of America and now head of HEW's Office of Consumer Affairs, said recently that ultimately "we may need a national membership organization. Without one, it is a little bit scary. Other interests such as labor and women have built up solid constituencies with chapters and affiliates across the country. We are a long way from the kind of organization consumers need."[38]

There are several national consumer groups, but none represent the constituency of which Richardson speaks. The National Consumers League, Common Cause, Consumers Union of the United States and the Consumer Federation of America are the principal national consumer groups. The largest one, the Consumers Union, has been active since 1936, publishes the magazine *Consumer Reports* and has some two million members.

There is no question that the consumer movement has had an important impact on the American marketplace in the last 15 years. While there is no unified national consumer organization, there is a large and growing number of federal, state and local consumer-oriented government offices. And the Carter administration has proven to be very responsive to consumer demands. These signs strongly indicate that today's consumer movement will remain an important voice for change for years, if not decades.

---

[38] Quoted in *The Washington Post*, Dec. 25, 1977.

Books

Buckhorn, Robert F., *Nader: The People's Lawyer,* Prentice-Hall, 1972.
Cohen, Manuel F. and George J. Stigler, *Can Regulatory Agencies Protect Consumers?* American Enterprise Institute, 1971.
Gardner, John W., *In Common Cause,* W.W. Norton, 1972.
Gorey, Hays, *Nader and the Power of Everyman,* Grosset and Dunlap, 1975.
McCarry, Charles, *Citizen Nader,* Saturday Review Press, 1972.
Mintz, Morton and Jerry S. Cohen, *Power, Inc.,* Viking, 1977.
Sanford, David, *Me & Ralph,* New Republic Book Co., 1976.
Peterson, Mary Bennett, *The Regulated Consumer,* Nash, 1971.

Articles

Boeth, Richard, "The Outsiders Move Inside," *Newsweek,* Jan. 2, 1978.
Boyd, Marjorie, "The Protection Consumers Don't Want," *The Washington Monthly,* September 1977.
Cameron, Juan, "Nader's Invaders Are Inside the Gates," *Fortune,* October 1977.
Cross, Mercer, "Carter Leads Push for Consumer Agency Bill," *Congressional Quarterly Weekly Report,* June 4, 1977.
Fager, Chuck, "Nader Takes on the 'Mushy Liberals,' " *The Boston Phoenix,* Jan. 10, 1978.
Glass, Gene V., "Nadir is to Nader as Lowest is to," *National Review,* July 8, 1977.
Ignatius, David, "Stages of Nader," *The New York Times Magazine,* Jan. 18, 1976.
"Is Nader Losing His Clout?" *U.S. News & World Report,* Dec. 19, 1977.
Kurtz, Howie, "The Consumer Product Safety Commission and Asbestos," *The Washington Monthly,* December 1977.
"Local Muscle for Consumers," *Business Week,* Sept. 26, 1977.
"Nader: Success or Excess?" *Time,* Nov. 14, 1977.
Rothman, David H., "Phony Consumer Groups," *The Nation,* Sept. 17, 1977.
"What the Government Can—and Cannot—Do to Protect the Public," *U.S. News & World Report,* Oct. 24, 1977.

Reports and Studies

"Consumerism at the Crossroads," Louis Harris Research Study, May 1977.
"Directory of Federal, State & Local Government Consumer Offices," Department of Health, Education and Welfare, Office of Consumer Affairs, Aug. 1, 1977.
Editorial Research Reports, "Directions of the Consumer Movement," 1972 Vol. I, p. 21; "Consumer Protection," 1960 Vol. I, p. 157.
"The Consumer Product Safety Commission Needs to Issue Safety Standards Faster," General Accounting Office, Dec. 12, 1977.

Access to Legal Services

by

Sandra Stencel

July 22
1 9 7 7

ACCESS TO LEGAL SERVICES

A CCORDING TO the basic laws of economics, excess supply usually results in lower prices and greater accessibility to a product. Conversely, high prices along with growing difficulty in obtaining the product should indicate an inadequate supply. But the law of supply and demand does not always function smoothly, as the current state of legal services in the United States demonstrates.

In the past 10 years, law has become the country's fastest growing profession. There are now approximately 445,000 lawyers in the United States. The nation has one lawyer for every 484 persons—a higher ratio than in any other country except Israel. Despite the number of attorneys, there appears to be a significant demand for legal services that has not been met. The problem, according to a *Trial* magazine editor, Barbara A. Stein, revolves around two factors: (1) the public's ignorance of how to find an attorney as well as the kind of services lawyers provide, and (2) an apparent inability of the legal profession to deliver services at prices that are reasonable.[1]

A recent survey by the American Bar Association and the American Bar Foundation underscored the magnitude of the problem. Only about one-third (35.8 per cent) of the adults who were surveyed had ever consulted a lawyer, and only about a quarter (27.9 per cent) had actually retained a lawyer. One reason so many people appear to avoid lawyers is the perceived cost of their services. Over 60 per cent of the respondents to the survey agreed to the statement: "Most lawyers charge more for their services than they are worth."

In addition, more than a quarter of the respondents said that "lawyers needlessly complicate clients' problems." The survey indicated that many people do not know where to turn for legal advice or how to determine a lawyer's competence. Nearly half of the people questioned said that if they needed to choose a lawyer they would ask friends, relatives or neighbors to recommend one. The telephone book was the next most frequently mentioned source.[2]

[1] Barbara A. Stein, "Legal Economics," *Trial*, June 1976, p. 12. *Trial* is published by The Association of Trial Lawyers of America.

[2] Survey results published in *alternatives: legal services & the public*, Vol. 3, No. 1, January 1976. *alternatives* is a bimonthly newsletter of the ABA Consortium on Legal Services and the Public. Research for the survey was conducted by the ABA's Special Committee to Survey Legal Needs in collaboration with the American Bar Foundation.

In the past, discussions of access to legal services generally centered on the problems of people too poor to pay any legal fees at all—people who constitute about 20 per cent of the population. Although much more needs to be done before a truly effective or comprehensive legal services program is available to persons in the lowest economic brackets, legal aid programs financed by the government and private sources have begun to meet the legal needs of the poor. At the other extreme, people in the upper 10 per cent of the economic spectrum have sufficient funds to take care of even very high legal costs.

Caught in the middle are perhaps 140 million Americans who do not qualify for free legal aid and who cannot afford standard legal fees, which now average $40 to $50 an hour in urban areas. The legal needs of the middle class "have been greatly overlooked," said a Philadelphia lawyer, Robert T. Richards.[3] In recent years the legal profession has begun to rectify this oversight. Programs designed to improve the availability of legal services to people of moderate means have sprung up across the nation.

Introduction of Pre-Paid Legal Insurance

One answer to the problem of providing low-cost legal services is pre-paid legal insurance. Under such plans, which are similar to Blue Cross and other health insurance programs, individuals or someone acting on their behalf contribute regularly to a fund for legal services that the individuals may need or use in the future. By spreading the cost of services over a large number of people over a period of time, the expense to the individual client is kept relatively low. Pre-paid plans are "probably the best way for the majority of Americans to be able to assure themselves of legal assistance when they need it," according to James Fellers, a former president of the American Bar Association.[4]

In addition to providing reasonably priced legal services, pre-paid plans encourage members to practice "preventive law"—to seek legal advice before they get into trouble, not just afterward. The ABA survey indicated that in only three situations—(1) the making of wills, (2) serious difficulty with a former spouse about alimony and child support, and (3) difficulties with custody of children[5]—did the majority of Americans consult with lawyers. When faced with other legal problems—such as the acquisition of property, personal injuries, landlord-tenant disputes, serious problems with a creditor, or denial of constitutional rights—most people either consulted a non-legal resource, handled the problem themselves, or did nothing about it.

---

[3] Quoted in *The New York Times*, May 2, 1977.
[4] Quoted in "Pre-paid Legal Services," a pamphlet published by the Resource Center for Consumers of Legal Services.
[5] Inexplicably, divorce itself was not among the situations listed.

Lawyer Surplus

Current problems with the delivery of legal services exist side by side with a growing surplus of lawyers. Since 1968, enrollment in the nation's law schools has doubled to approximately 125,000 students. Women have accounted for much of this increase. Today about 23 per cent of all law students in the United States are women, up from 8.5 per cent in 1971.

Nearly 30,000 students graduate from law school each year, but according to the latest figures from the Bureau of Labor Statistics, there are only about 21,000 jobs awaiting them in the legal profession. Nearly one-third of all law school graduates must seek jobs in other fields. By 1985, the Bureau of Labor Statistics estimates, there may be as many as 100,000 surplus lawyers.

Some of the graduates who do find jobs are prospering as never before. Starting salaries at top New York law firms average $25,-000 a year. Outside of New York, starting salaries at top firms run about $5,000 less. The median income for lawyers in private practice is slightly under $30,000—considerably less than the median income of the nation's doctors, which is above $50,000.

According to the ABA there are now about 150 full-scale pre-paid legal insurance plans operating in the United States, covering approximately two million people. Lillian Deitch and David Weinstein estimate that such plans may cover 10 million to 20 million subscribers by 1985.[6] Prepaid plans vary widely according to how they are run, how much they cost, who operates them and what benefits they provide. Most plans now operating in the United States are sponsored by labor unions and are funded through collective bargaining agreements or from union dues. Other plans are administered by state and local bar associations, credit unions, insurance companies and other private businesses. One of the newest providers is Blue Cross, the nation's biggest health insurer. Its western Pennsylvania unit started writing legal insurance policies in May, selling to individuals as well as groups—a major innovation, according to Sandy DeMent, executive director of the Resource Center for Consumers of Legal Services.[7]

The cost of pre-paid legal insurance ranges from $25 to $300 a year, typically falling between $40 and $90. Benefits vary greatly, from fairly modest amounts of advice, office work and litigation services to coverage of almost every legal need that might arise. Some plans even provide for "major legal" expenses

[6] Lillian Deitch and David Weinstein, *Prepaid Legal Services: Socioeconomic Impacts* (1976), p. 6. Deitch is an economist and Secretary of the Futures Group. Weinstein is an independent consultant in matters concerning the administration of justice and protection of personal property.

[7] The Resource Center for Consumers of Legal Services is a tax-exempt, nonprofit organization that was established in 1975 in Washington, D.C., to analyze, produce and promote the most effective techniques for developing legal services plans.

just as health plans cover "major medical" problems. Most plans, however, do not provide coverage when lawsuits are initiated by the insured, an exclusion designed to discourage trigger-happy litigants.

Pre-paid legal insurance dates only from the early 1970s, and it has spread considerably in the last four years. A 1973 amendment to the Taft-Hartley Act allowed legal services to be a subject for collective bargaining. At its 1973 convention, the AFL-CIO recommended that pre-paid plans be incorporated into the collective bargaining programs of all affiliated national and international unions. The pre-paid movement achieved an important breakthrough in February 1975, when the ABA, after intense debate, adopted rules for the establishment, operation and promotion of pre-paid plans. Such plans also received a boost from last year's tax reform law, which put legal insurance on a par with health insurance, granting tax exemptions both for employers' premium payments and for the dollar value of services provided under insurance coverage.

Critics of legal insurance say such programs could lead to higher, not lower, legal costs. They cite the tendency of health care costs to rise under health insurance programs such as Blue Cross and Blue Shield. If legal insurance becomes widespread, the critics say, lawyers will feel free to raise prices, as doctors have done, confident that the insurance companies will pay whatever they charge.

Legal Clinics for Middle-Income Americans

Another alternative to traditional methods of providing legal services is the legal clinic. Patterned after low-cost medical clinics, legal clinics provide basic legal services for substantially lower prices than those charged by most lawyers. Most clinics also let clients pay in installments or with credit cards. Legal clinics are able to keep prices down by handling a high volume of cases and by making use of "paralegals" *(see box, p. 28)*, standardized forms and procedures, and other money-saving efficiencies.

Persons who oppose legal clinics argue that they provide unfair competition that will drive out individual lawyers and small law practices. Clinic advocates say that competition is healthy for any business. They add that clinics do not take potential clients away from existing lawyers, but instead draw people who otherwise would not seek legal advice. Legal clinics were never intended as a panacea for every legal problem, Denver lawyer Karen Metzger wrote in *Trial* magazine. Rather, they were viewed as a means of handling routine matters such as uncontested divorces, individual bankruptcies, consumer problems, traffic questions, landlord-tenant disputes, wills, and real estate transactions.[8] Generally, legal clinics are not prepared to pursue big cases pushed by consumer, environmental or other public interest groups—most of these are handled by "public interest" law firms financed through foundation grants.[9]

The country's first legal clinic was set up in Los Angeles in 1972 by two young lawyers, Stephen Z. Meyers and Leonard D. Jacoby. Today, Meyers and Jacoby have four offices in the Los Angeles area which serve about 350 clients a month. Despite their success only about 10 other legal clinics are known to be operating around the country. The slow growth of legal clinics, according to Meyers and Jacoby, is due to the opposition of the organized bar, which, they say, feels "economically threatened by such a successful attempt at delivering high-quality, low-cost legal services."[10] On the other hand, the ABA itself is sponsoring an experimental legal clinic in Philadelphia. Fees at the eight-month-old clinic range from $10 for the initial visit to $350 for an uncontested divorce.

Supreme Court's Decision on Advertising

The number of legal clinics in the United States is expected to increase significantly now that the Supreme Court has lifted restrictions on advertising legal fees and services. The court ruled June 27 that state laws and bar association rules against advertising by lawyers violated the First Amendment right to free speech. Supporters of legal clinics had long maintained that the clinics needed to advertise to attract enough business to offer low rates.

The ruling reversed a decision by the Arizona Supreme Court. The Arizona court last year upheld the public censure of two young attorneys, John Bates and Van O'Steen, who had placed an ad in a Phoenix newspaper, the *Arizona Republic,* to publicize their legal clinic. The censure was rooted in an advertising ban originated by the ABA in 1908 and subsequently adopted in all of the states, either by statute or court-imposed regulation. Defenders of the ban said it helped protect consumers from unscrupulous lawyers, discouraged needless lawsuits, and preserved the dignity and standards of the legal profession.

But the Supreme Court rejected these arguments. Justice Harry A. Blackmun, writing for the majority, said: "It is at least somewhat incongruous for the opponents of advertising to extol

---

[8] Karen Metzger, "Legal Clinics: Getting into the Routine," *Trial,* June 1976, p. 32.
[9] Public interest law generally is defined as legal representation for persons and groups that have been unrepresented or underrepresented. *(See p. 565.)*
[10] Quoted in "Legal Clinics: Lawyers in Storefronts," *Consumer Reports,* May 1977, p. 287.

Use of Paralegals

Some traditional law firms, as well as legal clinics and public interest law firms, have turned to non-lawyers —paralegals—to help them with their work. Lay persons have been involved in the practice of law since colonial times, when no special training was required to assume the role of attorney or judge. But according to Constance D. Capistrant, executive director of the National Alliance of Paralegal and Consumer Interests, it was not until the 1960s that paralegals were employed extensively to perform "lawyer tasks."

Today paralegals perform a wide variety of tasks. They may interview clients and witnesses; prepare case histories and do legal research; assist in preparing depositions, motions and pleadings; preparing wills and materials for divorce, custody and adoption proceedings, real estate transfer closings and incorporation filings.

Training of paralegals is almost as varied as the types of work they do. Some paralegals are trained on the job—some through experience as legal secretaries. Others hold degrees in paralegal studies from two- or four-year colleges. Still others are trained in special paralegal institutes, some of whose programs accept persons with only a high school diploma.

the virtues and altruism of the legal profession at one point, and, at another, to assert that its members will seize the opportunity to mislead and distort." Blackmun went on to say: "Bankers and engineers advertise, and yet these professions are not regarded as undignified. In fact, it has been suggested that the failure of lawyers to advertise creates public disillusionment with the profession. The absence of advertising may be seen to reflect the profession's failure to reach out and serve the community."

In a dissenting opinion, Justice Lewis F. Powell[11] said he was "apprehensive" that the decision "will be viewed by tens of thousands of lawyers as an invitation to engage in competitive advertising on an escalating basis." Powell did not oppose all advertising by attorneys, but decried price advertising: "It has long been thought that price advertising of legal services inevitably will be misleading because such services are individualized...and because the lay consumer of legal services usually does not know in advance the precise nature and scope of the services he requires.... The type of advertisement before us will inescapably mislead many who respond to it. In the end it will promote distrust of lawyers and disrespect for our own system of justice."

---

[11] Others dissenting were Chief Justice Warren E. Burger, Justices Potter Stewart and William H. Rehnquist. Joining Justice Blackmun in the majority opinion were Justices William J. Brennan Jr., Byron R. White, Thurgood Marshall and John Paul Stevens.

The majority opinion made clear that the decision was a narrow one concerning the newspaper advertising of routine services and fees, and that there remained a large area in which such attorney advertising could be curtailed or regulated. "There may be reasonable restrictions on the time, place and manner of advertising," Blackmun wrote. Advertising that was false, deceptive or misleading was subject to restraint, as well as advertising focusing on the claimed quality of service or involving in-person soliciting of clients. The decision left unclear whether television and radio ads would be acceptable.

It is too early to assess the impact of the Supreme Court ruling. Most observers say that it will principally benefit young attorneys just starting out in the business, smaller firms and legal clinics. For the moment, most big law firms appear to be adopting a wait-and-see attitude. There is much disagreement as to how legal costs will be affected by advertising. In the majority opinion, Blackmun wrote: "It is entirely possible that advertising will serve to reduce...the cost of legal services to the consumers." But others contend that the added expense of advertising will be shifted to clients, thus diluting whatever consumer savings might result from increased competition.

There also has been some concern expressed that the expense of advertising will bear hardest on the new members of the profession rather than on established law firms. James G. Reardon, president of the Massachusetts Academy of Trial Lawyers, said last year: "[Advertising] would be most unfair to those least able to afford it—the young practitioner just launching his career who has no allowance in his budget for an expensive campaign. Those firms whose volume of cases makes it possible for them to absorb such cost would have no need to hype an already successful office."[12]

Public Interest Law Movement

NEBRASKA LAWYER Roscoe Pound, who later would become America's foremost legal educator, delivered an address entitled "The Causes of Popular Dissatisfaction with the Administration of Justice" to the House of Delegates of the American Bar Association at its 1906 meeting in St. Paul, Minn. Pound told his fellow jurists: "The law does not respond quickly to new conditions. It does not change until ill effects are felt; often not until they are felt acutely." Those familiar with the

[12] Quoted by Barbara A. Stein, "Is Professional Advertising Unprofessional?" *Trial*, June 1976, p. 37.

history of public interest law have little reason to question Pound's words. A study undertaken in the 1970s by F. Raymond Marks for the American Bar Foundation concluded that the organized bar was "slow to recognize the consequences of the inequality of access to legal representation." Marks wrote:

> Although early views of a lawyer's responsibility to represent all who sought representation did include reference to the unpopular cause or client, they failed to include any recognition of a duty to represent those who lacked the lawyer's price.[13]

To a great extent, the legal profession was simply reflecting the attitudes of the broader community where, before the beginning of the 20th century, little formal attention was directed to the needs of the poor.

The access of the poor to legal services was further restricted by the emergence of a minimum fee concept which prevented lawyers from basing their charges on the client's ability to pay. Paradoxically, however, the adoption of minimum fee schedules forced the legal profession to face up to the problems of the poor. "If attention had not been paid to those who could not afford minimum fees," Marks wrote, "the bar would have been open to community charges and to self-admission that law and justice were for the rich and not the poor."

This new concern led to the establishment of legal aid societies to assist those who could not pay for legal advice. Legal aid services were available in New York City as early as 1876, and by 1916 there were 41 legal aid organizations in the United States, according to Emery Brownell.[14] The following year, the first national conference of state and local bar associations adopted a resolution urging the associations to help in forming and administering "Legal Aid societies for...the worthy poor." In 1922, the American Bar Association recommended that every state and local bar association appoint "a Standing Committee on Legal Aid Work."

One reason for the organized bar's growing interest in legal aid work was the publication in 1924 of Reginald Heber Smith's classic work, *Justice and the Poor.* Smith wrote that legal aid societies were "relieving the bar of a heavy burden by performing for the bar its legal and ethical obligation to see that no one shall suffer injustices through inability, because of poverty, to obtain needed legal advice and assistance." For Smith, legal aid work was a professional duty and not a charitable option. Most lawyers, however, did not share Smith's outlook. To them, Marks observed, "legal aid work was something that was out-

---

[13] F. Raymond Marks, *The Lawyer, The Public, and Professional Responsibility* (1972), pp. 15-16.
[14] Emery Brownell, *Legal Aid in the United States* (1951), p. 11.

side of professional pursuits—in fact, as organized, it was done by others, by staff lawyers considered marginal by the bar generally...." He added: "This is not to say that individual lawyers did not contribute money to legal aid, or, as a matter of charity, render assistance to 'deserving poor' on a no-fee or a reduced fee basis; they did. It is simply to say that the bar as a whole did not assume this responsibility."[15]

Court-Required Counsel; Poverty Programs

One aspect of poverty law did command growing attention—the problem of the indigent criminal defendant. One explanation for this, according to Marks, is that since relatively few lawyers made their living as defense attorneys, "the notion of professional responsibility to include free legal counsel in that area would bring little threat to the economic self-interest of the bar as a whole." But even more significant "was the awareness that the Sixth Amendment of the Constitution provides that a person accused of a crime shall be entitled to the assistance of counsel." Gradually the courts adopted the position that when defendants could not afford a lawyer, the courts would appoint one to represent him without charge.

In 1932, the Supreme Court extended the right to counsel to indigent defendants in state cases involving the death penalty.[16] This right was applied in 1938 to all federal felony cases and in 1963 to indigents in all felony cases.[17] The Supreme Court in 1966 established the suspect's right to counsel during police questioning, and in 1967 it ruled that juvenile courts must provide youths with counsel, even though these court proceedings are considered civil rather than criminal.[18]

Legal aid came into its own in the mid-1960s during the civil rights movement. *Fortune* magazine writer Peter Vanderwicken traced the legal activism of the 1960s to the summer of 1964 when some 400 law students and young lawyers went to Mississippi to defend civil rights workers who were registering blacks to vote. "They discovered there," Vanderwicken wrote, "that the blacks' problems were compounded by their inability to get legal advice and protection."[19]

President Johnson made access to legal services an important part of his war on poverty. When the Office of Economic Opportunity was established in 1965, it included legal services in the Community Action Program. The inadequacies of privately funded legal aid programs had been described the previous year

---

[15] Marks, *op. cit.*, pp. 18-19.
[16] *Powell v. Alabama*, 287 U.S. 45 (1932).
[17] *Johnson v. Zerbst*, 304 U.S. 458 (1938) and *Gideon v. Wainwright*, 372 U.S. 335 (1963). For a discussion of events leading to the *Gideon* decision, see *Gideon's Trumpet* (1964) by Anthony Lewis.
[18] *Miranda v. Arizona*, 384 U.S. 436 (1966) and *In re Gault*, 387 U.S. 1 (1967).
[19] Peter Vanderwicken, "The Angry Young Lawyers," *Fortune*, September 1971, p. 77.

31

by the president of the National Legal Aid and Defender Association. In the organization's 1964 annual report, he said: "Too often troubled people find that legal aid does not really exist in their communities or that it is fenced off from them by too stringent eligibility rules, anachronistic policy on the type of cases handled, lack of publicity, insufficient staff personnel or unconscionable delay in services."

Within a year of OEO's establishment, its budget for legal services ($20-million) was nearly double that of the legal aid societies affiliated with the National Legal Aid and Defender Association ($11.7-million). During fiscal year 1967, the anti-poverty agency boosted the funds allocated to legal services projects by $5-million. By the end of 1967, according to Sar A. Levitan, the legal services program was funding 250 projects, providing legal assistance in 48 states, employing nearly 2,000 lawyers in 800 neighborhood law offices, and devoting 49 other projects to research, training and technical assistance. OEO lawyers helped poor people fight creditors and landlords in court, obtain divorces and declare bankruptcy.[20] The 1968 *Report of the National Advisory Commission on Civil Disorders* commended the legal services program for making "a good beginning in providing legal assistance to the poor."[21]

The legal services program became mired in controversy in succeeding years. Conservative critics charged that its interests were social activism rather than helping poor people. The Nixon administration, opposed to much of Johnson's anti-poverty program, sought to dismantle the Office of Economic Opportunity and its legal services program. Supporters of legal services for the poor sought to preserve the program by placing it in an independent, quasi-private corporation. Nixon, in 1971, vetoed one bill to create a legal services corporation and threatened to veto another the following year, thereby effectively killing the measure.[22] A Senate filibuster blocked a similar bill in 1973. Legal services legislation in 1974 became embroiled in Watergate pressures, but was passed and signed by Nixon a few days before his resignation.

The Legal Services Corporation Act established an 11-member board to govern the corporation, with the members appointed by the President and subject to Senate confirmation. The law restricted the activities of legal services lawyers in several ways. For example, they were prohibited from handling cases involving such controversial matters as school

---

[20] Sar A. Levitan, *The Great Society's Poor Law: A New Approach to Poverty* (1969), p. 179.

[21] The commission was set up by President Johnson on July 27, 1967, after riots erupted in Newark, Detroit and several other cities. The commission was instructed to find the underlying causes of the riots and to recommend courses of action.

[22] See Congressional Quarterly, *Congress and the Nation*, Vol. III, p. 608.

desegregation, abortion and draft evasion. The act also contained a provision intended to eliminate "back-up centers"—outside "poverty law" research centers doing work for legal services programs.

Bills to lift some of these restrictions were approved in May 1977 by the House Judiciary Committee and the Senate Human Resources Committee but have not received floor action.[23] The president of the Legal Services Corporation, Thomas Ehrlich, testified in favor of removing all restrictions on legal services attorneys, a position supported by the American Bar Association. "Poor people should not be prevented from vindicating their rights through lawful means simply because a given issue may be politically unpopular," Ehrlich told the Senate Subcommittee on Employment, Poverty and Migrant Labor on April 25.

Ralph Nader and the Citizen Law Movement

While legal services lawyers concentrated on individual cases and client needs, other public interest lawyers litigated issues affecting broad segments of the public, such as consumer and environmental protection. Nearly 100 public interest law centers now operate in the United States, according to a recent study conducted by the Council for Public Interest Law.[24] Mitchell Rogovin, co-chairman of the council, wrote recently in the *American Bar Association Journal:*

> These centers were established in response to the problem that policy formulation in our society is too often a one-sided affair, a process in which only the voices of the economically or politically powerful are heard.... Ordinary citizens, because they are poorly organized and without financing, are unable to purchase the legal representation necessary to make their interests known, too.... Public interest law centers, by giving voice to citizen views in public policy deliberations, have made great strides in correcting this imbalance and assuring that government works for everyone, not just the rich and powerful.[25]

Ralph Nader is probably the country's best-known public interest lawyer. His career in consumer advocacy drew national attention with the publication of his book *Unsafe at any Speed* in November 1965 and General Motors' mishandled attempt to investigate his private life.[26] Although Nader attacked the entire U.S. automobile industry for emphasizing profits and styl-

---

[23] See *CQ Weekly Report*, June 4, 1977, p. 1104.

[24] Council for Public Interest Law, *Balancing the Scales of Justice: Financing Public Interest Law in America* (1976). The Council for Public Interest Law was set up in January 1975 under the sponsorship of the American Bar Association and the Edna McConnell Clark Foundation, the Ford Foundation and the Rockefeller Brothers Fund.

[25] Mitchell Rogovin, "Public Interest Law: The Next Horizon," *American Bar Association Journal*, March 1977, p. 336.

[26] The GM-sponsored investigation by private detectives drew a public apology from the corporation's president, James M. Roche, at televised hearings before the Senate Subcommittee on Executive Reorganization, March 22, 1966. Roche acknowledged that the investigation entailed some "harassment" of Nader.

ing rather than safety, he concentrated his fire on the Chevrolet Corvair. Chevrolet's subsequent decision to stop making the car and Congress's passage of the National Traffic and Motor Vehicle Safety Act of 1966 were both attributable to the book's influence.

Having won his initial victory on auto safety, Nader turned his attention to other areas where he felt the public interest was threatened. These included health hazards in mining, safety standards for natural-gas pipelines, the lot of American Indians, and indiscriminate use of X-rays in dental examinations. In the past decade Nader has greatly expanded the scope of his activities on behalf of consumers. To this end he has set up a number of organizations staffed largely by idealistic young people who receive small salaries and work exceptionally long hours—as does Nader himself.

The parent Nader organization is the Center for the Study of Responsive Law, based in Washington, D.C. Other important Nader groups are the Public Interest Research Group and the Corporate Accountability Research Group. Under the umbrella of a group called Public Citizen Inc., Nader sponsors seven public interest groups: Congress Watch, Critical Mass (an environmental group), Health Research Group, Freedom of Information Act Clearinghouse, Litigation Group, Tax Reform Research Group and the Public Citizen Visitors Center.

One of the earliest public interest law firms in the nation is not connected with the Nader organization. It is the Washington-based Center for Law and Social Policy, which engages in consumer affairs, environmental issues, health care, foreign affairs, women's rights, occupational safety and health, mine safety and media access. The Mental Health Law Project, an offshoot of the center, is devoted entirely to protecting the rights of mental patients. Some public interest groups, such as the Natural Resources Defense Council and the Sierra Club Legal Defense Fund are devoted to environmental issues.

Although the practice of public interest law is centered in Washington, such firms are now operating across the nation. Public Advocates, a San Francisco firm, is involved in education, employment, women's rights and the environment. The Women's Law Fund in Cleveland specializes in sex discrimination issues. Others are found elsewhere.

Problem of Funding Public Interest Firms

Over the years, public interest law has had a continuing problem: the lack of adequate and stable sources of funding. The principal source of funding has been foundation grants. But some persons fear this source may soon dry up. This fear was in-

Legal Conduct and Competence

Responding to a growing number of malpractice suits against lawyers, the American legal community has mounted a campaign to rid the profession of dishonest and incompetent members. In the past four years, there has been a 172 per cent increase in disciplinary actions taken against lawyers by professional legal groups. More than $8-million a year now is being spent on lawyer discipline—most of it by the legal profession itself.

Not everyone is satisfied with lawyers' efforts to police themselves. A recent report commissioned by Public Citizen, a Ralph Nader group, concluded that lawyers' self-regulation attempts had failed to provide adequate disciplining either of lawyers or judges. Although clients filed more than 37,000 complaints against lawyers in 1976, only 1,757 lawyers were disciplined, according to the American Bar Association.

In recent years the public has begun to take a more active role in judging legal competency. Herbert S. Denenberg, a former Pennsylvania insurance commissioner, has written "The Shoppers' Guide to Lawyers," a pamphlet now included in the *Shoppers' Guide Book.* The ABA advises the public not to hesitate to discuss fees with a lawyer. A good lawyer, the association said, should be able to provide a reasonably exact estimate of the costs for his services.

creased by the economic recession of 1973-74, which reduced the assets of most private foundations, inducing them to cut back on their grants. The Ford Foundation, for example, announced a 20 per cent across-the-board decrease in its support for public interest law.[27] Foundation funding presents other problems as well. Along with the money comes an Internal Revenue Service prohibition on lobbying by tax-exempt organizations.

The funding problems of public interest law firms were aggravated by a 1975 Supreme Court decision, *Alyeska Pipeline Service Co. v. Wilderness Society,*[28] which brought a halt to the widespread practice of awarding attorney's fees to the winning side in public interest cases. Striking down an award of attorney's fees to environmental groups which had challenged construction of the Alaska oil pipeline, the Supreme Court held that federal judges could not make such awards unless Congress expressly authorized them to do so.[29]

The congressional response to the *Alyeska* decision was the Civil Rights Attorney's Fees Awards Act of 1976. This act authorized fee awards, in the discretion of the courts, to victorious parties in cases brought under federal civil rights laws;

[27] See Carlyle W. Hall Jr., "In the Public Interest," *The Center Magazine,* January-February 1977, p. 31.

[28] 421 U.S. 240 (1975).

[29] A number of environmental and civil rights statutes provide for fee awards and were not affected by the *Alyeska* decision.

fee awards already available under other laws were left intact. Although most public interest advocates applauded the new law, Howard Lesnick, a law professor at the University of Pennsylvania, expressed concern that the foundations might seize on it to justify a further decrease in their support of public interest law firms.[30]

One funding proposal is to increase the contributions of the organized bar—perhaps through a system of voluntary checkoffs from annual bar association dues. A checkoff system for the benefit of legal aid has been in effect for many years in Chicago, and recently the Arizona State Bar established a dues checkoff for public interest firms in that state. The Council for Public Interest Law has proposed creation of a National Fund for Public Interest Law, to help finance public interest law efforts nationwide, especially in localities where resources are not readily available. The council has proposed that the ABA develop a voluntary dues checkoff system for this national fund, a plan supported by Supreme Court Justice Thurgood Marshall, among others.[31]

Another proposal is to let the government provide citizen advocates. They are already provided in a number of state attorneys general offices, and New Jersey is now operating a public advocate office as a separate state agency. "Placing the representation of the public in the hands of the state gives the public interest lawyer a secure base he or she has never enjoyed before," wrote Barbara Stein.[32] However, such plans pose problems. "Because public interest law centers are so heavily involved in the monitoring of government," argued Mitchell Rogovin of the Council for Public Interest Law, "it is crucial that their major support continue to come from non-governmental sources."

Resolution of 'Minor Disputes'

P ERSONS CONCERNED with improving the quality and broadening the scope of citizen access to legal help have found themselves in the middle of a complex debate over the role of the courts in resolving the conflicts and problems of American society. Among those who argue that the resolution of so-called "minor disputes" should be removed as much as

---

[30] Howard Lesnick, "What Next for Public Interest Law," *Judicature*, May 1977, p. 467.
[31] See Thurgood Marshall, "Financing Public Interest Law Practice: The Role of the Organized Bar," *American Bar Association Journal*, December 1975, p. 1488.
[32] Barbara A. Stein, "Public Interest Law: A Balancing Act," *Trial*, February 1976, p. 14. See also Arthur Penn, "Advocate from Within," *Trial*, February 1976, p. 20.

possible from the traditional legal framework is Chief Justice Warren E. Burger. "The notion that most people want black-robed judges, well-dressed lawyers and fine-paneled courtrooms as the setting to resolve their disputes is not correct," Burger said in a speech May 27. "People with problems, people with pains, want relief, and they want it as quickly and inexpensively as possible." If we do not devise substitutes for the courtroom processes, Burger continued, "we may well be on our way to a society overrun by hordes of lawyers hungry as locusts...."[33]

Burger has long spoken in favor of reducing federal court workloads. Under Burger's direction, the Supreme Court in recent years has handed down a number of decisions that have limited the types of cases that the federal courts may hear.[34] This has been done in some cases simply by stating that federal courts must use great discretion in intervening in state court proceedings. It has been done in other cases either by a stricter interpretation of the standards that a person must meet to get into court or by procedural obstacles to class action suits.

In his campaign to reduce the court's workload and to develop alternatives to litigation, Burger has recently been joined by a powerful ally—Attorney General Griffin B. Bell, a former federal appellate court judge. Bell generally endorses Burger's position that the court system is overcrowded, and he has said that one of his main priorities as Attorney General will be to provide better access to justice without putting an additional strain on the resources of the courts. To help achieve this goal, Bell has set up a new Office for Improvements in the Administration of Justice, headed by a former University of Virginia Law professor, Daniel J. Meador.

Proposed Substitutes for the Judicial Process

The Department of Justice announced recently that it was sponsoring an experimental program to give the public a speedy and inexpensive way to resolve minor disputes through neighborhood justice centers that would serve as alternatives to the courts. Bell said that three experimental centers, all funded with federal money but under local control, would be in operation by the fall. The centers would attempt, through mediation, to settle the sort of disputes—domestic spats, claims by customers against merchants, arguments between landlord and tenants—that clog the dockets of the lower courts in American cities.

---

[33] Burger made his remarks at a conference on the resolution of minor disputes sponsored by the American Bar Association at Columbia University in New York. The conference was a follow-up of an April 1976 conference convened by the Chief Justice in St. Paul, Minn., to commemorate the 70th anniversary of Roscoe Pound's address on "The Causes of Popular Dissatisfaction with the Administration of Justice."

[34] See "Politics and the Federal Courts," *E.R.R.*, 1977 Vol. I, pp. 473-496. See also *CQ Weekly Report*, June 18, 1977, pp. 1229-1234.

Other alternatives to litigation currently being explored include wider use of arbitration, mediation and conciliation; decriminalization of victimless crimes; expansion of the no-fault concept; and promoting the use of ombudsmen and newspaper and radio "action lines." Provisions requiring compulsory arbitration already are in effect in Pennsylvania, Ohio and New York, and in some cases apply to virtually all lawsuits involving claims for damages up to $10,000. Disputes between parties that have a continuing relationship, such as those between landlord and tenants, employer and employees, and certain disagreements over sales of consumer goods, are particularly suitable for resolution by arbitration, according to Junius L. Allison, a professor of law at Vanderbilt University.[35]

There has been much discussion recently of expanding the small claims court system. An ABA task force concluded that "revitalization and expanded use of small claims courts offers substantial promise of assuring the delivery of justice to all citizens in a manner which is both speedy and efficient."[36] Experiments with small claims courts in the United States began about 1913, after Roscoe Pound suggested there was a need to "make adequate provision for petty litigation." In 1924, Reginald Heber Smith, the legal aid pioneer, called for an alternative forum in which the poor litigant could seek relief in matters involving difficulties with landlords, creditors and employers. Early experiments with small claims courts in Oregon, Kansas and Cleveland, Ohio, were based on these suggestions.

The main advantage to the small claims courts, often hailed as "the people's court" or "consumer's forum," is that plaintiffs can file their cases for a small fee, usually about $6, and usually do not have an attorney. The cases are often settled in less than two months. However, even with the relaxed rules, people representing themselves often do not do well in small claims cases. A Virginia judge said recently that most citizens who represent themselves are at a disadvantage because they do not present adequate evidence and testimony. "People just haven't been to law school and they're facing someone who has and they usually end up losing," said Robert M. Hurst, chief judge of the Fairfax County General District Court.[37]

Opposition to Limiting Access to the Courts

The commitment by Burger and Bell to develop alternatives to litigation has provoked much opposition from consumer and

---

[35] Junius L. Allison, "Problems in the Delivery of Legal Services," *American Bar Association Journal,* April 1977, p. 519.

[36] American Bar Association, "Report of Pound Conference Follow-Up Task Force," August 1976, p. 12. The task force was headed by Griffin B. Bell, currently the Attorney General.

[37] Quoted in *The Washington Post,* May 15, 1977.

environmental groups, representatives of the poor and public interest lawyers. They argue that the federal courts ought to remain the principal instruments for resolving many of the disputes under discussion. They also fear that Burger's view of access to the federal courts is in reality an attempt to undermine their cases. Shutting down procedural access to the courts is seen by these individuals and groups as a veiled attack on the substantive rights and remedies that they wish to pursue in the federal courts.

"Obviously, certain matters can and should be resolved in forums that are cheaper, quicker, and more informal than the courts," wrote Charles R. Halpern, executive director of the Center for Public Interest Law. "But the effort to identify these matters and to create these forums should not blind us to the importance of opening the courts to a range of significant cases that are too frequently kept out by doctrinal restrictions and high litigation costs."[38]

Sandy DeMent of the National Resource Center for Consumers of Legal Services questioned Burger's selection of minor disputes as the best cases to be funneled into alternative forums. Why not pick on antitrust cases, contract cases or other large issues, she asked? DeMent told Editorial Research Reports that she is not opposed to developing alternatives to litigation, but she said that it was imperative that their use be kept voluntary. She expressed the fear that people would be coerced into using them, and thus effectively denied their day in court.

Public interest lawyers are particularly concerned about the recent Supreme Court decisions that have limited citizen access to the federal courts. Halpern wrote: "The Supreme Court's decisions on standing, class actions, and awards of attorney's fees reflect a trend toward making legal recourse less accessible to ordinary citizens. Such decisions are likely to increase popular dissatisfaction with the administration of justice. It is essential to reverse that trend."

Numerous bills have been introduced in Congress to overturn many of the restrictive Supreme Court decisions and increase citizen access to the courts. Although the bills differ widely in their focus, the one feature common to all is that they run counter to the Supreme Court's effort to reduce the caseload of the federal courts. President Carter placed himself on record April 6 in his consumers' message as favoring "access to justice" legislation. The issues are complex and the debate is certain to continue for some time to come.

---

[38] Charles R. Halpern, "Should Courts Redress Citizen Grievances?" *Judicature*, November 1976, p. 163.

Selected Bibliography

Books

Buckhorn, Robert F., *Nader: The People's Lawyer*, Prentice-Hall, 1972.
Deitch, Lillian and David Weinstein, *Prepaid Legal Services*, Lexington Books, 1976.
Downie, Leonard Jr., *Justice Denied*, Praeger, 1971.
Levitan, Sar A., *The Great Society's Poor Law: A New Approach to Poverty*, Johns Hopkins Press, 1969.
Marks, F. Raymond, *The Lawyer, The Public, and Professional Responsibility*, American Bar Foundation, 1972.
McCarry, Charles, *Citizen Nader*, Saturday Review Press, 1972.

Articles

Allison, Junius L., "Problems in the Delivery of Legal Services," *American Bar Association Journal*, April 1977.
Carter, Luther J., "Public Interest Lawyers: Carter Brings Them Into the Establishment," *Science*, May 27, 1977.
Hager, Barry M., "Access to Justice," *Congressional Quarterly Weekly Report*, June 18, 1977.
Hall, Carlyle W. Jr., "In the Public Interest," *The Center Magazine*, January-February 1977.
Halpern, Charles R., "Should Courts Redress Citizen Grievances?" *Judicature*, November 1976.
"How to Choose a Lawyer (and what to do then)," *Consumer Reports*, May 1977.
"Lower Fees, Better Service—Changes Coming in Law Practice," *U.S. News & World Report*, Sept. 22, 1975.
Rogovin, Mitchell, "Public Interest Law: The Next Horizon," *American Bar Association Journal*, March 1977.
St. Antoine, Theodore J., "Growth Patterns in Legal Services," *AFL-CIO American Federationist*, March 1976.
"The Chilling Impact of Litigation," *Business Week*, June 6, 1977.
"To Advertise or Not to Advertise," *American Bar Association Journal*, March 1977.
Trial magazine, selected issues.

Reports and Studies

American Bar Association, "A Primer of Prepaid Legal Services," April 1976.
——"Report of the Pound Conference Follow-Up Task Force," August 1976.
——"Report on the National Conference on the Causes of Popular Dissatisfaction with the Administration of Justice," April 1976.
"Causes of Popular Dissatisfaction with the Administration of Justice," Hearings Before the Senate Committee on Constitutional Rights, May 19, 1976.
Editorial Research Reports, "Legal Profession in Transition," 1972 Vol. II, p. 581; "Politics and the Federal Courts," 1977 Vol. I, p. 473.
"Reducing the Costs of Legal Services: Possible Approaches by the Federal Government," A Report prepared for the Senate Subcommittee on Representation of Citizens Interests, Oct. 8, 1974.

Oil Antitrust Action

by

Kennedy P. Maize

**Feb. 10
1978**

OIL ANTITRUST ACTION

A MOVEMENT to break up the major American oil companies has been gaining strength over the last several years and is expected to test its power in Congress again this year. Department of Energy allegations late last year and early this year that the oil companies overcharged[1] consumers during and after the 1973-74 Arab oil embargo helped revive the animosity that many people feel toward the oil companies.

Bills proposing both *vertical divestiture* (breaking up the big companies into separate businesses confined to drilling, transporting, refining or marketing oil, but not all of these operations together) and *horizontal divestiture* (breaking up the companies into businesses that develop only oil, coal, uranium or geothermal energy, but not all of these fuels) have come close to passage in recent sessions of Congress *(See p. 47)*

The close votes obviously have scared the oil companies. Their response has been to mount a well-financed public relations and lobbying campaign directed by the American Petroleum Institute in Washington, D.C. The anti-divestiture campaign is the API's No. 2 priority, second only to its effort to influence the shape of President Carter's national energy plan. The aim of the anti-divestiture campaign is to convince the public and Congress that breaking up "Big Oil," as detractors and sometimes the petroleum industry itself calls the biggest companies, would weaken the American economy and make the energy situation even worse.

The next test of congressional sentiment on divestiture is likely to come soon in the House of Representatives. HR 7816, a bill sponsored by Rep. Morris K. Udall (D Ariz.), chairman of the House Interior and Insular Affairs Committee, would bar the eight largest U.S. petroleum companies—the "majors" *(see box, p. 45)*—from leasing more federal lands for drilling, mining or other forms of energy development. Access to these vast holdings, including underwater tracts offshore, are considered vital to the development of new sources of natural gas, oil, coal and uranium.[2] According to the Western Oil and Gas

---

[1] Overcharge allegations relate to extremely technical aspects of the Energy Act of 1975 governing how oil companies are to treat certain cost items and definitions of "property" in determining the differences between "new" oil (oil that has just been discovered) and "old" oil (oil from wells already in production). "New" oil can be sold for higher prices than "old."

[2] See "Western Land Policy," *E.R.R.*, 1978 Vol. I, pp. 81-100, and "Offshore Oil Search," *E.R.R.*, 1973 Vol. II, pp. 537-556.

Association, "A vote on this type of amendment is likely to be the key test of strength for Udall and the pro-divestiture forces."[3]

The eight largest oil companies are also facing a legal attack from the Federal Trade Commission. The FTC in 1973 charged the majors with violating antitrust laws by trying to drive independent oil refinery and marketing companies out of business. By controlling supply and prices, the agency contends, the vertically integrated majors forced smaller companies to the wall, stifling competition and raising prices to the American consumer.

Antitrust cases often last for years, even decades, and this one is no exception. With stakes amounting to billions of dollars, this case—the "Exxon Case"—will involve years of labor, a blizzard of paper, and battalions of lawyers on both sides. The last big case the federal government brought against the major oil companies, the "Cartel Case," began with a bang of publicity in 1952 and died with a flurry of consent orders in 1968.[4]

In the four years since the current case was filed, the government and the companies have been haggling over procedures. The parties have only recently agreed on the records the government will be permitted to see in pursuit of its contention that the companies illegally restrained trade. The FTC in January agreed to narrow its focus and abandon some lines of attack in order to speed the proceedings. The agency wants to move rapidly in the oil case, according to the director of the FTC Bureau of Competition, Alfred Dougherty Jr., because the proceeding would make public for the first time details about the inner workings of the giant petroleum companies.[5]

Vast Size and Earnings of the 'Majors'

While the courts have held that size alone is not an offense in antitrust matters, there is little doubt that it has made the biggest oil companies exceptionally visible—and hence inviting targets. Sen. John A. Durkin (D N.H.) described his reaction at a Senate antitrust hearing in 1976: "The big oil companies are too big to be controlled by anyone, and they ought to be cut down to size."[6]

The biggest of them are indeed gargantuan. Exxon is the

---

[3] *The Week in Review,* Western Oil and Gas Association newsletter, Nov. 25, 1977.

[4] Consent orders are legally binding agreements that the government will make with an alleged violator in order to settle the matter out of court. Typically, the defendant will agree to stop doing whatever it was that caused the complaint—but without formally acknowledging any wrongdoing.

[5] *The Wall Street Journal,* Jan. 11, 1978.

[6] Testimony before the Senate Judiciary Subcommittee on Antitrust and Monopoly, Feb. 3, 1976.

Oil Industry's Major Companies	1976 SALES (add 000,000)	1976 NET INCOME (add 000,000)
EXXON	$ 48,630	$ 2,640
TEXACO	26,451	869
MOBIL	26,062	942
STANDARD OF CALIFORNIA	19,434	880
GULF	16,451	816
STANDARD (INDIANA)	11,532	892
SHELL	9,229	705
ATLANTIC RICHFIELD	8,462	575

SOURCE: *Fortune*, May 1977

world's largest corporation. Its sales in 1976 exceeded $48 billion, a figure greater than the state tax revenues of California, New York, Pennsylvania and Illinois combined. Together, the income of the eight "majors" ($164 billion) was greater than the tax revenues of all 50 states combined ($101 billion).[7] Five of the eight largest U.S. industrial corporations, and nine of the top twenty, are oil companies, according to *Fortune* magazine's latest annual listing *(see box, p. 49)*

Over the year the oil industry had shown profits somewhat above the average for American manufacturing. Beginning with the Arab oil embargo in October 1973 and subsequent increases in world oil prices, the profits of American oil companies moved even higher. The congressional Joint Economic Committee in 1975 drew up the following comparison of after-tax returns on stockholders' equity among manufacturing companies generally and among the 10 largest oil companies:

	1970	1971	1972	1973	1974
Petroleum	11.2%	11.7%	11.0%	15.4%	18.1%
Manufacturing	9.3	9.7	10.6	12.8	15.0

Oil inventories which the companies had accumulated at the old low prices went to market at the new, higher prices, and the money rolled in. Prices of gasoline at the pumps tripled in some parts of the United States during the winter of 1973-74 before receding somewhat. For the third quarter of 1973, Gulf's profits

---

[7] Corporate data from *Fortune*, May 1977, pp. 364-366; state figures, from Commerce Clearing House News Bureau, Chicago, are for fiscal year 1977.

were 91 per cent higher than a year earlier and Exxon's were 80 per cent higher. Exxon's profits for the entire year 1973 turned out to be $2.5 billion, greater than any corporation, anywhere, had ever achieved.

Shyam Sunder, an accounting professor at the University of Chicago, characterized the results of the record profits as a public relations disaster for the companies: "To many critics of the oil industry little further proof was needed that the oil industry was out to loot the consumer and was being extraordinarily successful."[8] Sunder concluded in his study of oil profits that the situation in 1973 and 1974 was most likely temporary but the political damage had already been done. A Gallup Poll conducted shortly after the companies began announcing their profits indicated that more Americans blamed the oil companies for the energy crisis than blamed the Arab states that imposed the embargo.

Sen. Henry M. Jackson (D Wash.), as chairman of the Senate Permanent Investigations Subcommittee, held hearings in early 1974 into charges that the fuel shortage had been contrived and that the oil industry's profits were excessive. It was in the temper of the times that Jackson called the profits "obscene," creating a wave of publicity and causing consternation among the oil companies. The companies heatedly denied the charges and some of them resorted to full-page newspaper ads to make their views better known. But public opinion appeared to remain hostile. A poll conducted for the API in 1976 reported that 30 per cent of the people who supported divestiture did so because of a feeling that the oil companies were "too big and powerful." Many members of Congress seemed to share those views. And, it appeared, so did the Democratic candidate for President.

Carter's Attack on Oil Industry Lobbying

Jimmy Carter came into office in 1977 pledging to create a comprehensive energy policy to relieve this country's dependence on foreign oil. In April, Carter proposed a legislative package relying on taxes to raise the price of oil so high that consumers would cut back their use of it. The oil companies lobbied diligently against most of the pricing and tax proposals, while the administration lobbied ineffectively for them. By fall, the Carter energy package had passed the House but was tied up in the Senate. It appeared that the administration was not going to get a plan that even remotely resembled the original proposal.

On Oct. 13 the President angrily told a televised news conference that oil company lobbying was transforming his energy

---

[8] Shyam Sunder, *Oil Industry Profits* (1977), p. 66.

package into "the biggest rip-off in history." He said that the issue before Congress was "whether the money should be given partially to the oil companies to encourage production and partially to the American people in a fair way or whether it should all be grabbed by the oil companies at the expense of the American consumer."

The response of the companies was swift and bitter. John E. Swearingen, chairman of Standard Oil (Indiana), said that "the President has made an emotional appeal to defend a tax program that is not defensible." Howard Blauvelt of Continental Oil said, "the effect of his comments was to shed more heat than light."[9] The political effect of the President's attack was further support for the assault on Big Oil. The oil companies' lack of credibility and support in the general public, as indicated by public opinion polls, made them politically vulnerable.

The movement to break up the oil companies through legislative means has grown out of the feeling on Capitol Hill that antitrust suits by the FTC and the Department of Justice are not workable. James F. Flug, director of Energy Action Inc.,[10] a pro-divestiture lobbying group, and a former aide to Sen. Edward M. Kennedy (D Mass.), has said that legislative rather than administrative divestiture would:

> Eliminate the delay, chaos and uncertainty that would result from extended piecemeal antitrust actions; treat all companies evenhandedly rather than having their treatment determined by accidents of timing, location, court, or prosecutory discretion; prevent future harm to national interests instead of waiting to act until serious harm has been inflicted; accelerate programs toward truly competitive energy markets so that we can begin to reduce the need for government regulation.[11]

Close Votes on Recent Anti-Oil Measures

In October 1975, Sen. James Abourezk (D S.D.) put forth an amendment during debate on regulation of natural gas to force vertical divestiture of the largest oil companies. His amendment was defeated 54 to 45, but the closeness of the vote surprised the oil industry. Another vertical divestiture bill came before the Senate in 1976. The Judiciary Committee under the chairmanship of the late Sen. Philip A. Hart (D Mich.), the bill's chief sponsor, sent it to the floor in June but it was set aside in September, chiefly because of the pressure of other legislation

---

[9] Both quoted in *The New York Times*, Oct. 14, 1977.

[10] Energy Action was established in 1975 with the backing of five millionaire liberals to draw attention to economic concentration in America through the example of Big Oil. The initial contributors were Harold Willens of the Factory Equipment Corp., actor Paul Newman, Leopold Wyler of TRE Corp., Miles Rubin of Pioneer Systems, Inc., and economist Stanley Sheinbaum. They gave the organization $500,000 and it operates on a $200,000 annual budget.

[11] Testimony before the House Committee on Interior and Insular Affairs, June 22, 1977.

and the certainty of a veto by President Ford if the bill passed. Since then the momentum of vertical divestiture seems to have lessened, and most observers say this sort of legislation has little chance of passage this year.

Sentiment for horizontal divestiture appears to be growing as the movement for vertical divestiture is lessening. A horizontal divestiture bill sponsored by Kennedy and 11 other senators was voted down 53 to 39 in October 1975. Another Kennedy-backed horizontal divestiture measure, an amendment to the Carter energy package, lost by a vote of 62 to 30 in September 1977.

The loss was attributed largely to poor legislative tactics. The Carter administration opposed the amendment in fear that the divestiture issue would delay passage of the entire energy package. Several senators, including Jackson, were inclined to support Kennedy on the merits of the case but voted against delaying the energy legislation. This year the action shifts to the House, where advocates of horizontal divestiture think they have a good chance of passing a bill.

According to an oil industry official, about one-third of the membership in both the House and the Senate is certain to support any divestiture effort on the basis of a commitment toward basic structural changes in the American economy. About one-third is sure to support the oil industry out of a similar commitment to the status quo. That means the contending forces must concentrate on the uncommitted one-third.

The industry does not think it can convince these legislators on the political rightness of its case. "Nobody likes Big Oil," the official said, "so there isn't really much to be gained from supporting the industry, and a lot to lose." Advocates of divestiture, such as Energy Action, concentrate on the politics of busting up the "oil monopoly." Industry, on the other hand, concentrates on the economics of the divestiture argument, where it believes it has a stronger case.

Horizontal Versus Vertical Divestiture

Advocates of vertical divestiture argue that the majors constitute an oligopoly—a market situation in which a few producers control the demand from a large number of buyers. The late Dr. John Blair, who was chief economist of the Senate Judiciary Subcommittee on Antitrust and Monopoly, made the classic case against oil oligopolies in his book *The Control of Oil.* Blair wrote in 1976:

> Nearly all (93.6%) of the nation's proved reserves of crude oil are held by twenty major companies. The United States can thus secure domestic oil...only to the extent that this small group of companies agrees to its extraction. Any policies on price, taxes,

Top 20 U.S. Industrial Corporations

Company	Rank*	Company	Rank*
Exxon	1.	International	
General Motors	2.	Telephone & Telegraph	11.
Ford Motor	3.	Standard Oil	
Texaco	4.	(Indiana)	12.
Mobil	5.	Shell Oil	13.
Standard Oil		U.S. Steel	14.
of California	6.	Atlantic Richfield	15.
Gulf Oil	7.	E. I. du Pont	
International		de Nemours	16.
Business Machines	8.	Continental Oil	17.
		Western Electric	18.
Geneal Electric	9.	Procter & Gamble	19.
Chrysler	10.	Tenneco	20.

*In terms of sales   Source: *Fortune*, May 1977

etc., with which these companies disagree can result in their oil simply being left in the ground, where its value will appreciate as demand and price levels continue to rise.[12]

Blair argued that higher prices are logical results of oil company policies, and the companies can enforce those prices by manipulating the supply of oil. In short, the free market that Adam Smith described two centuries ago in *The Wealth of Nations* is not permitted to function.

Vertical integration is crucial to this market control, according to those who want to break the oil companies into smaller organizations that perform only one economic task. It is argued that oil companies, by controlling the product from the time it flows from the ground until it goes into the consumer's gas tank, can squeeze out others who want to compete by controlling the competitors' ability to buy raw materials and sell finished products.

Jack Blum, general counsel for the Independent Gasoline Marketers Council, told a House committee in June 1977: "The largest single problem faced by independent marketers is the fact that they compete directly with their suppliers, the integrated oil companies. The company that sells them wholesale supplies has a retail outlet across the way. They find that the more vigorous the retail price competition, the more likely the suppliers are to raise the wholesale price. We are in a classic squeeze."[13]

---

[12] John M. Blair, *The Control of Oil* (1976), p. 129.

[13] Testimony before the House Committee on Interior and Insular Affairs, June 22, 1977.

The oil industry answers that the business is really very competitive. "No oil company accounts for more than 8.5 per cent of U.S. crude production. No one company has more than 11.7 per cent of proved reserves. No one company has more than 8.2 per cent of U.S. domestic refining capacity. No one company has more than 7.9 per cent of gasoline sales." No one company or group of companies, the American Petroleum Institute further argues, can dominate price or production.[14] Thomas E. Kauper, head of the antitrust division in the Department of Justice during the Ford administration, told the Senate Judiciary Committee in June 1976 that "the petroleum industry appears to be one of the least concentrated of our nation's major industries. This data calls into question the property of massive structural reorganization."

Horizontal divestiture has won support among some who oppose legislation mandating vertical divestiture. John H. Shenefield, Kauper's successor at Justice, said at a Senate hearing on the confirmation of his appointment that he supports legislation for horizontal but not vertical divestiture. Shenefield said that current law provides adequate remedies for the abuses of one kind but not the other.

Those who advocate horizontal divestiture argue that it is dangerous to have the large oil companies also dominant in competing fields of energy. In addition to fears that the companies will engage in monopolistic or oligopolistic practices, critics fear that the oil companies will be slow to develop new resources that might compete with oil. Michigan State University economist Walter Adams described those fears at a conference on divestiture held in Washington in January 1977 by the American Enterprise Institute. Adams asked: "Can we really expect these giant firms to undermine their stake in depletable oil and gas resources—the value and profitability of which are enhanced by the progressive scarcity—by investing the huge sums required to promote the rapid development of economically viable substitutes?"[15]

Oil companies are already deeply involved with coal and uranium, the two major competing fuels in electrical generation. According to a study done in 1977 by the Library of Congress for the Senate Subcommittee on Energy Research and Development, 11.8 per cent of the nation's coal reserves are in the hands of the oil companies. The second-largest coal producer, Consolidation Coal Co., is a subsidiary of vertically integrated Continental, the ninth largest oil company. Most of

[14] American Petroleum Institute, *The Need for Energy* (1977), p. 10.
[15] American Enterprise Institute, "Horizontal Divestiture, Highlights of a Conference on Whether Oil Companies Should be Prohibited from Owning Nonpetroleum Energy Resources," Jan. 27, 1977, p. 13.

Gulf Oil and the Uranium Cartel

In 1972 the Canadian government became concerned that the price of uranium might drop on the world market. Uranium is Canada's most important export commodity, and such a drop would have had a bad effect on Canadian balance of payments. The Canadian response was to organize a cartel of international uranium producers, known as the Club.

The Club set up its headquarters in Paris and proceeded to establish rules for fixing prices of world uranium. The cartel also set penalties for members who did not abide by the rules. During the period of its operation—1972 to 1975—the price of "yellowcake" (natural uranium ore) rose from less than $6 per pound to $42 per pound. Whether the cartel was responsible for the price rise is now unknown. The Canadian government says the increase was the result of natural market forces.

One of the companies participating in the cartel was a Canadian subsidiary of Gulf Oil. When the operations of the cartel became known, numerous investigations and lawsuits in this country began to probe the cartel, seeking answers to such questions as whether it pushed up prices, whether Gulf participated voluntarily (the company says it was pushed into the cartel by Canada), and whether Gulf violated any antitrust laws. Answers to any of those questions may be years away.

the top 20 petroleum companies are involved in coal to some extent. In nuclear fuels, oil companies hold 47 per cent of available reserves and 41 per cent of uranium milling capacity. Gulf and Exxon are particularly deeply involved in uranium.[16] Gulf is currently under legal attack for participating in an international cartel in the 1970s that coincided with a fivefold increase in world uranium prices *(see box above).*

Opponents of horizontal divestiture argue that the facts do not support the case for divestiture. A team of economists led by Jesse Markham of Harvard, in a study paid for by the API, concludes: "No single petroleum company controls a large enough share of the petroleum or energy industry...to give that company the power to significantly affect the prices of...oil, gas, coal and uranium...."[17] In examining the coal industry, a report by the General Accounting Office concluded: "A viable state of competition exists in the coal industry and it is unlikely that the industry could be dominated by any firm or group of firms."[18]

---

[16] Library of Congress, "Petroleum Industry Involvement in Alternative Sources of Energy," September 1977, pp. 6-9.

[17] Jesse Markham, Anthony P. Hourihan and Francis L. Sterling, *Horizontal Divestiture and the Petroleum Industry* (1977), pp. 97-98.

[18] General Accounting Office, "The State of Competition in the Coal Industry," Dec. 30, 1977, p. v-1.

Oil's Search for Stability

THE HISTORY of oil is the story of continual fluctuation —from boom to bust, from scarcity to glut. The dominant theme of oil's development is the search for stability—for control of the economic roller coaster that has led to both enormous profits and bitter failure. British journalist Anthony Sampson describes this central trend: "The alternation of shortage and glut; the hectic oscillation of prices; the battles between producers and distributors; the interdependence of oil and transport; and above all the question: Who should control it?"[19] The devices of control—trusts, cartels, joint ventures, and the like—have been a part of oil from the start. And consequently questions of antitrust have been closely associated with oil throughout its history.

In its earliest days, oil showed the classic boom-and-bust pattern. Immediately after the discovery of oil in Pennsylvania in 1859, fortunes soared on prices as high as $20 a barrel, but in a year oil was selling for 10 cents a barrel, cheaper than water. In 1864 a young bookkeeper named John D. Rockefeller entered the oil refining business, determined to bring order out of the free market chaos. By 1888, first through control of railroad transportation, then by control of pipelines, Rockefeller's Standard Oil Corp. monopolized the industry in the United States. Standard had taken control of oil fields and refineries in Pennsylvania, Ohio, Kansas and California. By 1890, the year Congress passed the Sherman Antitrust Act, the company controlled more than 90 per cent of the U.S. market for oil. Moreover it had begun to sell extensively overseas.

Beginning with an attack by Henry Demarest Lloyd in *Atlantic Monthly* in 1881 and reaching a climax 23 years later with Ida Tarbell's book *History of Standard Oil,* muckraking writers turned Rockefeller into a hated and feared man. In 1906 President Theodore Roosevelt's "trust busters," using the Sherman Act, sought to break up Standard Oil. The Supreme Court upheld the government's antitrust case in May 1911 and ordered Standard Oil divided into 38 separate companies. Four of the companies created by the court order—Exxon, Mobil, Standard (Indiana) and Standard of California—are today among the eight oil majors.[20]

---

[19] Anthony Sampson, *The Seven Sisters* (1975), p. 18. The title refers to seven international oil companies: British Petroleum, Royal Dutch Shell, Standard Oil of New Jersey, Mobil, Texaco, Standard Oil of California and Gulf. The origin of the term is unknown but it was popularized by the head of the Italian state oil company, Enrico Mattei, who presented himself as an adversary of Le Sette Sorrell (The Seven Sisters) in the 1950s and 1960s.

[20] For background on the case and the Sherman Antitrust Act, see "Antitrust Action," *E.R.R.,* 1975 Vol. I, pp. 68-71.

In the coming decades, the oil industry was aided by a number of oil-producing states in its continuing attempt to keep prices up through production restraints. These states set up commissions, working in conjunction with the industry, that decreed the number of days each month that the wells could pump oil.[21] Despite these efforts, the specter of instability continued to haunt the industry as enormous new oil fields were discovered outside the United States. This development transformed the oil companies from simple business enterprises into unofficial agents of U.S. policy abroad and complicated questions of antitrust.

Multicompany Agreements in Middle East

The coming of the automobile, combined with wartime demands for oil in 1914-18, had turned the oil glut into an oil shortage. This shortage led the large American companies and two foreign competitors—Shell, a joint Dutch and British venture, and British Petroleum, half-owned by the British government—to embark on exploration projects in the Far East, Latin America and the Middle East. The British already had a significant oil concession in Iran, through BP—which began life as the Anglo-Persian Oil Co.

"The dominant theme of oil's development is the search for stability—for control of the economic roller coaster that has led to both enormous profits and bitter failure."

Short supplies also led to cutthroat competition, particularly between Standard Oil of New Jersey (now known as Exxon) and Shell. Under diplomatic pressure from the U.S. government, American oil companies were included in an international consortium that was formed to explore for oil in the ruins of the Ottoman Empire. Shell, British Petroleum, Texaco and Standard Oil of New Jersey formed the Iraq Petroleum Co., which Anthony Sampson characterized as "both the parent and the prototype for other joint ventures in the Middle East."[22]

---

[21] See Robert Engler's *The Politics of Oil* (1961), pp. 132-150.
[22] Sampson, *op. cit.*, p. 67.

But before those joint ventures could proceed to divide the oil in the Middle East, Shell and Standard had to make peace. A price war that had resulted from a feud between them over access to Russian oil was driving smaller companies out of business and reducing profits of all. The peace-making came about at a series of meetings in 1928 between Shell, Standard and British Petroleum at Achnacarry Castle in Scotland. The resulting "Achnacarry Agreement," kept secret by the companies until the U.S. government forced it into public print in 1952, was never completely implemented, but Sampson concludes that it formed the basis by which the oil companies operated in the international sphere up until the 1960s.

The basic principle behind the agreement was to control production as a means of stabilizing prices—requiring the companies to operate in concert. This cartel arrangement often put the companies into conflict with foreign governments that granted the oil concessions, since the governments usually had a vested interest in high production. They received a royalty on each barrel produced. This conflict sowed the seeds for later problems for the oil companies. But as long as the companies were united and the producing countries were divided, production flowed at the direction of the industry.

OPEC and the Energy Crisis of 1973-74

By the 1960s the balance of power between the oil companies and the oil countries was changing. Saudi Arabia possessed oil reserves so vast that they changed the entire power equation. Just one Saudi field, Ghawar, holds more oil than the proved reserves[23] of the continental United States and Alaska combined, and Ghawar is just one of 37 Saudi fields. The Saudis and several other producing countries became imbued with a growing sense of nationalism in the late 1950s. These countries realized that oil gave them bargaining power in the world economy. They concluded that the private oil cartel was reaping profits at their expense, while assuring a continuous flow of relatively cheap oil to fuel the Western economies. In short, the underdeveloped oil-exporting countries were financing the booming economies of the developed world.

From that realization came, first, the formation of the Organization of Petroleum Exporting Countries[24] in 1960 and, more important, the flexing of its muscles in 1973. The energy crisis was the product of three threads that became woven into the fabric of OPEC policy. First, the Arab governments began in

---

[23] Oil recoverable from known reservoirs under existing economic and operating conditions.

[24] OPEC was formed by Saudi Arabia, Iran, Iraq, Kuwait and Venezuela. Member nations today also include Algeria, Ecuador, Gabon, Indonesia, Libya, Nigeria, Qatar and the United Arab Emirates.

the late 1960s and early 1970s demanding a share of the ownership of the joint ventures that the companies had put together to exploit Arab oil. The oil companies were determined to resist as strongly as they could, making confrontation inevitable.

Second, an oil glut in the early 1960s began turning into an oil shortage in the 1970s. The American oil companies had always relied on the seemingly limitless potential of American fields for their world leverage. But by 1970 American oil production was declining. And worldwide demand was rising, making the oil companies dependent upon their foreign suppliers.

This dependency was made known to the world, forcibly, in October 1973 when war broke out between Israel and its Arab neighbors. The oil-producing Arab states cut production, raised prices and refused to ship oil to countries that aided Israel, including the United States. The embargo was lifted the following spring but world oil prices continued upward, soon quadrupling the pre-October level. The story of oil had been fundamentally changed. The producing countries, by making their price increases stick, were now dominant. In essence, OPEC had forced a partial divestiture of the vertically integrated companies, putting it in a position where it could squeeze Big Oil just as Big Oil was alleged to be squeezing independent refiners and marketers.

From that point on, all discussions of oil policy had to take OPEC into account. The industry's search for stability had been profoundly disturbed, leading Mobil President William Tavoulareas to lament: "In short, international trade in oil badly needs stability. Since the producing country governments are sovereign and not subject to a superior law, it is necessary for the consuming countries to persuade them that their best interests will be served through the maintenance of stable conditions in which commercial commitments can be freely made and relied upon."[25]

Shift to New Forms of Energy

THE LATE E. F. Schumacher, who was for many years chief economist of Britain's Coal Board, argued that the OPEC performed a valuable service, alerting the world to its dependence on oil, a finite resource that was priced so low it en-

---

[25] Testimony before the Senate Foreign Relations Subcommittee on Multinational Corporations, June 6, 1975.

couraged profligacy. Only after the embargo and great rise in prices did the world come to understand that its addiction to oil could be fatal.[26] The Carter energy plan is based on arguments similar to Schumacher's. The crux of the Carter plan is the development of alternatives to Arab oil. American coal is foremost among the alternatives.

America's abundance of coal is on the same scale as Saudi Arabia's oil. Various estimates indicate that the U.S. supply can be expected to last 200 to 300 years at present rates of consumption. But getting that much coal out of the ground is going to be difficult. There are environmental problems associated with both the mining and burning of coal. There are safety problems related to mining. Enormous amounts of capital are required to bring coal fields into production, to develop coal liquefaction and gasification to the point of marketability, and to perform the research and development needed in other, more exotic forms of energy such as geothermal power, solar power, shale oil and nuclear energy.[27] One obvious source of capital is the oil industry, now holding vast amounts of money for investment and eager to diversify into other energy fields.

Predictions of Petroleum Shortages Ahead

Currently the oil industry is in one of its periods of glut. There is too much oil on the global market and the world's slow recovery from the 1975 recession[28] has kept demand down. Arab countries have kept producing at about the usual rates despite the slowing demand. According to Joe T. McMillan, manager of Exxon's supply department, the surplus is on the magnitude of "four million to five million barrels a day of spare crude capacity worldwide."[29] *Dun's Review* concludes that this situation is "something of a mixed blessing. On the positive side, it means that the U.S. balance of trade will benefit. On the negative side, the existence of an oil surplus, however temporary, could make it even more difficult than it has been for the Carter administration to convince the American people that the energy crisis is indeed real."[30]

That the surplus is temporary is accepted as fact by most observers of the oil industry. It is also conventional wisdom that at some point a shortage will come, with devastating results. Political scientist Dankwart A. Rustow, writing in *Foreign Affairs* last spring, speculated that the crunch will come "in the early or mid-1980s." Rustow calculated that the developed

---

[26] Speech at George Washington University, Feb. 20, 1977.
[27] See "New Energy Sources," *E.R.R.*, 1973 Vol. I, pp. 187-204.
[28] See "World's Slow Economic Recovery," *E.R.R.*, 1977 Vol. II, pp. 745-764.
[29] Quoted in *Business Week*, Jan. 9, 1978, p. 50.
[30] "Guess What? We've got an Oil Glut," *Dun's Review*, September 1977, p. 58.

world will need to import at least 35 million barrels a day of oil by 1985, and that OPEC might not be able or willing to export more than 32 million barrels a day. Rustow said his data "portend in the clearest terms a major world oil crisis."[31]

According to this scenario, prices would rise drastically and supplies would fall perilously low. Rustow wrote: "There is serious danger of physical shortages of oil throughout the non-Communist world, of a second price jump comparable in amount to that of 1973-74, and of a series of confrontations not only between the United States and Arab oil exporting countries, but also between the United States and its allies in Western Europe and Japan [over scarce supplies]."

Oil's Role in New Energy Development

The only course of action that can forestall the coming shortage, in Rustow's view, is a reduction in energy consumption in the United States and the development of new energy sources. The divestiture debate is tied to that course of action. Each side in the debate argues that its position is the correct one to advance the national interest through finding new oil, developing coal and other energy sources, and lessening demand for petroleum products. Oilmen say that the Carter energy plan is short on incentives. Establish higher prices for oil and gas, they argue, and their industry will find plenty of new wells. Divestiture, they argue, would result in less exploration. The advocates of divestiture say that the major oil companies have no real stake in increased exploration because new discoveries would devalue existing holdings.

Both sides offer similar arguments to describe the development of coal and other forms of energy. Only oil has the capital necessary to finance the mammoth task of getting the country back on a coal economy, the oil spokesmen say. But the divestiture forces argue that such financing would put Big Oil in control of coal, creating an unhealthy situation economically and politically. The nation's money markets are capable of providing the necessary capital even if the oil companies are broken up. But increasingly, a third line of argument is surfacing: that the best choice for the future is development by the government, which certainly has the capital and, in addition, would protect the national interest in energy. Economist Robert Lekachman, for example, writing in the Dec. 17, 1977, issue of *The Nation*, advanced a scenario for government control through nationalization of the oil companies.

Nationalization has been the trend in the Middle East since

---

[31] Dankwart A. Rustow, "U.S.-Saudi Relations and the Oil Crises of the 1980s," *Foreign Affairs*, April 1977, pp. 509-510.

Russia—The World's Biggest Oil Producer

The leading oil-producing nation in the world is the Soviet Union. It produces 10.5 million barrels a day of oil, and exports substantial amounts, most of it to the West. Oil exports provide cash the Russians use to purchase such things as American grain. Production figures of the five leading oil-producing countries are, according to the Department of Energy:

Soviet Union	10.5 million barrels a day
Saudi Arabia	8.5 million barrels a day
United States	8.1 million barrels a day
Iran	6.0 million barrels a day
Venezuela	2.2 million barrels a day

Russia's oil industry faces trouble in the future, *The New York Times* reported Jan. 24, 1978. The newspaper cited a recently declassified Central Intelligence Agency report that predicts Russia will have to begin importing oil sometime in the 1980s. Part of the Russian problem is the remoteness of the Soviet oil reserves in western Siberia. The U.S.S.R. lacks transportation facilities where the oil is located and the harsh climate makes building them extremely difficult.

before the 1973 embargo. Saudi Arabia now owns 60 per cent of Aramco, the consortium of U.S. oil companies[32] put together in 1948 to exploit the Saudi concession. Eventually, the Saudi government will own the company outright, with Aramco serving as a contractor to perform the day-to-day management of the fields. The OPEC countries are beginning to demand a share of the refining operations, and unless the companies go along willingly, according to OPEC Secretary-General Ali Jaidah of Qatar, "our countries will have no recourse but to adopt collective strategies to achieve their aims."[33]

As OPEC continues to test its power, the Western nations will be driven to consider new ways to protect themselves. This will likely mean an increased involvement of the governments in dealing with the cartel. Sen. Frank Church (D Idaho), a ranking

---

[32] Exxon, Mobil, Standard of California and Texaco.
[33] Quoted in *The New York Times*, Oct. 11, 1977.

member of the Senate Foreign Relations Committee, observed in 1975: "It seems to me that if it is true, as the oil executives themselves have admitted, that their leverage has all but disappeared, then we are facing a new and different situation in which the government might play a constructive role in backing up the oil companies in the hope that we could secure from the Arab and the other oil producing governments more satisfactory agreements upon future prices for crude oil."

Church was issuing a veiled threat, but his remarks also stand as a prediction. Regardless of the economics of the divestiture debate, and they are by no means clear cut, the politics of the situation could compel some form of action. If the shortage predicted for the 1980s occurs, the imperatives of the national interest may well merge with the politics of divestiture to produce a solution that has some of the characteristics of nationalization.

Outright government ownership of American oil companies is unlikely. Britain, through its partial ownership of British Petroleum, provides little evidence that government-owned oil companies behave much differently from American companies. The situation has been similar in France (CFP), Germany (Gelsenberg), Belgium (Petrofina) and Spain (Hispanoil). What is more likely is a solution that falls short of outright government ownership and rigorous federal regulation. All of the possibilities—joint government-industry teams to face OPEC countries, rationing, government-controlled research and development projects, production schedules and the like—are upsetting to oil executives. But the prospect of such alternatives as inflation, worldwide depression or even war might appear far worse to government policymakers.

By the mid-1980s the divestiture question may be solved one way or another. It now appears that legislated vertical divestiture will not come, but that a legislative approach to horizontal divestiture may. In any case, by the 1980s the issues related to oil and its role in the economy will likely have shifted emphasis from matters of divestiture to questions of direct public control.

Books

Blair, John M., *The Control of Oil,* Pantheon Books, 1976.
Coyne, John R. and Patricia S., *The Big Breakup,* Sheed Andrews and McMeel, 1977.
Engler, Robert, *The Politics of Oil,* Phoenix Books, 1961.
Medvin, Norman, *The Energy Cartel,* Vintage Books, 1974.
Mitchell, Edward J., ed., *Vertical Integration in the Oil Industry,* American Enterprise Institute for Public Policy Research, 1976.
Markham, Jesse W., Anthony P. Hourihan and Francis L. Sterling, *Horizontal Divestiture and the Petroleum Industry,* Ballinger, 1977.
Sampson, Anthony, *The Seven Sisters,* The Viking Press, 1975.
Sunder, Shyam, *Oil Industry Profits,* American Enterprise Institute for Public Policy Research, 1977.

Articles

"Carter's Oil War," *Newsweek,* Oct. 24, 1977.
"Guess What? We've Got an 'Oil Glut,' " September, *Dun's Review,* 1977.
Iseman, Peter A., "The Arabian Ethos," *Harper's,* February 1978.
"Energy," *Forbes,* Jan. 9, 1978.
Lekachman, Robert, "On Energy: A Modest Proposal," *The Nation,* Dec. 17, 1977.
Marshall, Eliot, "No Rush," *The New Republic,* Aug. 20 & 27, 1977.
"Oil Industry Under Siege: How it Plans to Meet the Challenge," *U.S. News & World Report,* Oct. 31, 1977.
Rustow, Dankwart A., "U.S.-Saudi Relations and the Oil Crises of the 1980s," *Foreign Affairs,* April 1977.
Sherrill, Robert, "Breaking Up Big Oil," *The New York Times Magazine,* Oct. 3, 1976.
Smith, Adam, "The Arabs, Their Money...and Ours," *Atlantic,* February 1978.
"The Biggest Rip-Off," *Time,* Oct. 24, 1977.
"Unfazed by a Continuing Glut," *Business Week,* Jan. 9, 1979.

Reports and Studies

American Petroleum Institute, "The Need for Energy," August 1977.
Editorial Research Reports, "Antitrust Action," 1975 Vol. I, p. 61; "Arab Oil Money," 1974 Vol. I, p. 365; "International Cartels," 1974 Vol. II, p. 847; "Oil Taxation," 1974 Vol. I, p. 203; "Persian Gulf Oil," 1973 Vol. I, p. 229.
General Accounting Office, "The State of Competition in the Coal Industry," Dec. 30, 1977.
Library of Congress, "Petroleum Industry Involvement in Alternative Sources of Energy," September 1977.

ANTI-SMOKING CAMPAIGN

by

Sandra Stencel

Jan. 21
1 9 7 7

Editor's Note: The anti-smoking campaign won new support early in 1978. The Secretary of Health, Education and Welfare, Joseph A. Califano Jr., announced on Jan. 11 a federal program aimed at curbing smoking in the United States. He asked the Federal Trade Commission to set maximum levels of tar, nicotine and carbon monoxide in cigarettes, and for the Treasury to recommend increases in the federal excise tax on cigarettes with high tar and nicotine content. Califano's program concentrates on "special risk" groups and, as part of that concern, the Food and Drug Administration has imposed a labeling order on oral contraceptives warning that women who smoke "increase dramatically [their] chances of suffering a heart attack or stroke." The order was scheduled to become effective April 3, 1978.

ANTI-SMOKING CAMPAIGN

I N LOS ANGELES, a school district employee quit his job because he was bothered by smoke from co-workers' cigars and cigarettes. The California Unemployment Insurance Appeals Board refused to pay the man unemployment benefits on the ground that he did not have "good cause" for resigning. However, a state court judge overturned the board's decision last July 22 and awarded the man $990 in unemployment benefits.

In Atlantic City, a state court judge ruled last April that an employee of the New Jersey Bell Telephone Co. had a right to work in a smoke-free environment. The employee presented medical documentation of an allergic reaction to cigarette smoke and the judge ordered the company to provide "safe working conditions...by restricting the smoking of employees to non-work areas."

In Chicago, dozens of persons have had to spend the night in jail because they were unable to post a $25 bond after being arrested for smoking on Chicago Transit Authority buses or trains. Since July 1975, hundreds of Chicagoans have been fined up to $300 for violating the city's anti-smoking law.

The battle between smokers and non-smokers is on and will probably get much hotter in 1977, spurred by the increasing activism of anti-smoking groups such as GASP (Group Against Smokers' Pollution) and ASH (Action on Smoking and Health). Buoyed by the success of their four-year-old campaign to ban smoking in public places, militant non-smokers are pressing for more stringent action. "A growing number of smokers now understand that their smoke is annoying to other people," ASH Executive Director John F. Banzhaf has said. "We're finding more and more that they are willing to live with reasonable restrictions."[1]

But according to the tobacco industry, the ultimate goal of the movement is to prohibit the use of tobacco and cripple the industry. To prevent this from happening and to fight the growing number of anti-smoking laws, the Tobacco Institute, the

---

[1] Quoted in *The Christian Science Monitor*, July 7, 1976. Banzhaf is professor of law at George Washington University, Washington, D.C.

lobbying and public relations arm of the industry, has opened a counter campaign aimed at protecting the rights of smokers. Passions run high on both sides. There have been reports of fist-fights and even more serious assaults occurring over demands for smoke-free air. *Washington Post* columnist William Raspberry wrote recently that a column on the no-smoking question had elicited more reader response than to "such presumably weightier matters as capital punishment [and] affirmative action...."[2]

Many of the nation's 53 million[3] smokers claim that laws banning smoking in public places are an infringement of their civil rights. Anti-smoking groups respond by quoting health authorities who say tobacco smoke is hazardous to the health of everyone who breathes it. In fact, according to some findings, smoke from the burning end of a cigarette, cigar or pipe is potentially more dangerous than the smoke inhaled by the smoker. "The time has come when our goal can no longer be simply to protect the smoker from himself," Jesse L. Steinfeld, a former U.S. Surgeon General, told the third World Congress on Smoking and Health in June 1975. "The time has come to protect ourselves from the smoker."[4]

Decrease in Percentage of Adult Smokers

A nationwide survey released last June by the U.S. Public Health Service indicated that the proportion of American adults who smoke cigarettes has decreased in recent years. Of the 12,000 persons surveyed, only one-third smoked cigarettes, as the following figures show:

Cigarette Smokers*	1975	1970	1964
		(in percentages)	
Men	39.2	42.2	52.8
Women	28.9	30.5	31.5
Total	33.5	36.3	42.5

*Ages 21 and older

The survey also provided other evidence that the public's attitude toward smoking had turned increasingly negative *(see table, p. 76)*. However, the picture is not crystal clear. There is evidence of an upsurge in smoking among teenagers *(see box, p. 67)* and, despite the percentage decline in cigarette smoking among adults, the nation's population increase has resulted in record sales of cigarettes year after year. Americans smoked 620 billion cigarettes in 1976, the Department of Agriculture

---

[2] *The Washington Post*, Dec. 13, 1976.
[3] Figure used by U.S. Public Health Service.
[4] The congress, held in New York City, was sponsored jointly by the American Cancer Society and the National Cancer Institute.

reported at the year's end. That was 13 billion more than in 1975 and 84 billion more than in 1970.

Paradoxically, more than half of the smokers interviewed in the Public Health Service survey said they would like to see smoking allowed in fewer places than it is now, and more than one-third of the smokers said it was annoying to be near a person smoking a cigarette. Among non-smokers these feelings were shared by even greater numbers. The nation's smokers are on the defensive, according to Dr. David J. Sencer, director of the U.S. Center for Disease Control. "The American who smokes to-day is finding his world narrowing," Sencer has said. "He is becoming increasingly beleaguered and is usually ambivalent about smoking."[5]

Movement to Ban Smoking in Public Places

Since 1973, at least 30 states[6] and the District of Columbia have enacted laws that ban smoking in certain public places. Moreover, anti-smoking restrictions have been imposed in hundreds of local communities across the nation. These restrictions may in some instances apply only to elevators or public transportation or theaters but, often, also to hospitals, libraries, museums, auditoriums, restaurants and supermarkets.

Arizona in May 1973 became the first state to enact a statewide anti-smoking law. As amended in April 1974, it prohibits smoking in elevators, indoor theaters, libraries, art galleries, museums, concert halls, physicians' waiting rooms and school buildings, and on all buses. Minnesota's anti-smoking law, which took effect Aug. 1, 1975, is considered the toughest in the nation. Known as the Indoor Clean Air Act, it bans smoking in all public places and public meetings except in designated smoking areas. Restaurants must set aside at least 25 per cent of their tables for non-smoking patrons,[7] hospitals must offer wards and offices must provide desks for non-smokers. Violators are subject to fines of up to $100. One of the newest anti-smoking laws in the nation is California's Indoor Clean Air Act, signed by Gov. Edmund G. Brown Jr. on Aug. 30, 1976. It requires that at least half of the space in public meeting rooms be set aside for non-smokers.

Even in states and localities without anti-smoking laws, some businesses ban smoking in their establishments or restrict it to designated areas. At Merle Norman Cosmetics Co. in Los

---

[5] News conference in Washington, D.C., June 15, 1976.

[6] Alaska, Arizona, Arkansas, California, Connecticut, Florida, Georgia, Hawaii, Kansas, Maine, Maryland, Massachusetts, Michigan, Minnesota, Nebraska, Nevada, New Hampshire, New Jersey, New York, North Dakota, Oklahoma, Oregon, Pennsylvania, South Dakota, Texas, Utah, Vermont, Virginia, Washington and Wyoming.

[7] Members of Minnesota's Association for Non-smokers Rights are unhappy about a loophole in the law. Because bars and taverns are exempted from the smoking restrictions, many restaurants in the state now label themselves bars.

Angeles, for example, smoking is forbidden in the offices, rest rooms and production lines. Smokers must wait for their coffee breaks and lunch hour to light up—and then only in a special section of the company cafeteria. Controller Mike Hayes estimates that the company saves about $33,000 a year in reduced housekeeping costs, lower absenteeism and improved productivity. The savings are passed on to the employees.

Some companies offer cash bonuses to non-smoking workers. In Birmingham, Ala., non-smoking employees at a savings bank receive a $20 bonus each month. At the Leslie Manufacturing and Supply Co. in Bloomington, Minn., employees who quit smoking are paid $7 a week. Standard Glass Co. of Phoenix, Ariz., offers its employees $360 if they can kick the habit for a year. The president of Intermatic, a heater manufacturing company in Spring Grove, Ill., permits workers to bet up to $100 that they can quit smoking for a year. If they quit, he pays them the money; if they don't, their bets go to the American Cancer Society.

At the federal level, the Civil Aeronautics Board proposed on Oct. 5 to prohibit pipe and cigar smoking aboard commercial passenger aircraft. In addition, the board solicited public comment on the question of whether all smoking should be banned aboard these planes. A decision is expected early this year. Numerous scientific and medical studies have found that cigar and pipe smoke can be more irritating and harmful than cigarette smoke. "Since pipe and cigar smokers don't inhale as frequently or as deeply as cigarette smokers, they pollute the air with even greater concentrations of toxic substances," said John F. Banzhaf of ASH in a petition asking for the proposed ban. The Tobacco Institute has told the board that the ban is not warranted. Since 1973 the CAB has required separate seating for passengers who want to smoke.

Rep. Robert F. Drinan (D Mass.) sought unsuccessfully in the last Congress to place restrictions on smoking at federal and federally controlled property, including military bases, post offices, courtrooms, federal office buildings, and Congress itself. He wanted to require all federal agencies to separate smokers from non-smokers in work, recreation and eating areas, and to forbid smoking in confined public places.

Evidence of Health Hazard for Non-Smokers

Since 1964, the American public has been bombarded with information concerning the health hazards of smoking. Most of this information pertains to the dangers for the smoker. But in the last five years, public health authorities have grown increasingly concerned about the effects of tobacco smoke on non-smokers. The American Medical Association estimates that at

Increased Smoking by Girls and Young Women

The American Cancer Society is particularly concerned about increases in smoking among teenage girls. A study it released in February 1976 indicated that 27 per cent of the American girls of ages 13 to 17 were smokers—in contrast to 22 per cent in 1969. For boys of the same ages, the figure had remained virtually constant at 30 per cent during that time. Moreover, heavy smoking was increasing among the girls; four of every ten smoked a pack a day or more, whereas in 1969 only one in ten smoked that much.

Young women were also more likely to be smokers than they were a decade earlier, the survey further indicated. Some 36 per cent in the 18-34 age group who were surveyed said they smoked, and of these six of every ten smoked heavily. Comparable figures in 1965 were 34 per cent and five out of ten. Dr. Benjamin F. Byrd Jr., president of the American Cancer Society, called the figures "alarming." The Cancer Society reported that among women the death rate from lung cancer had doubled in the past ten years.

least 34 million Americans are sensitive to cigarette smoke. These include people with emphysema, asthma, bronchitis, sinusitis, hay fever and chronic heart disease. Even the average non-smoker can suffer reactions to tobacco smoke. These reactions include eye irritation, nasal symptoms, headache, cough, wheezing, sore throat, sneezing, nausea, hoarseness and dizziness.

Tobacco smoke is a complex mixture of gases, liquids and particles. There are hundreds of chemical compounds in tobacco and hundreds more are created when tobacco burns. Among the most hazardous compounds are tar, nicotine, carbon monoxide, cadmium, nitrogen dioxide, ammonia, benzene, formaldehyde and hydrogen sulphide. Whenever anyone lights a cigarette, cigar or pipe, tobacco smoke enters the atmosphere from two sources: (1) directly from the burning tobacco (sidestream smoke) and (2) from the smoke the smoker sucks in (mainstream smoke) and then exhales.

According to the American Lung Association, sidestream smoke contains twice as much tar and nicotine, three times as much benzpyrene (suspected of being a cancer-causing agent), five times as much carbon monoxide, and 50 times as much ammonia as mainstream smoke. There also is evidence that there is more cadmium in sidestream smoke.[8] Public health officials are investigating the possibility that cadmium is one of the compounds in cigarette smoke that damages the air sacs of the lungs and causes emphysema.

---

[8] American Lung Association booklet, "Second-Hand Smoke: Take a Look at the Facts," 1974.

Physicians are particularly concerned about the high levels of carbon monoxide in sidestream smoke. "There is no question that non-smokers can develop toxic levels [of carbon monoxide] in smoke-filled rooms," said Dr. Raymond Slavin of St. Louis University and the American Academy of Allergy.[9] When inhaled, carbon monoxide bumps oxygen molecules out of the red blood cells and forms a new compound called carboxyhemoglobin. As the amount of this compound increases in the blood, the cells of the body become starved for oxygen.

The hazards posed by high concentrations of carbon monoxide in sidestream smoke first were reported in the Surgeon General's 1972 annual report to Congress on the health consequences of smoking. The report cited studies showing that carbon monoxide levels in a smoke-filled room or automobile could rise to almost twice the federal occupational safety guideline of 50 parts per million. Individuals exposed to such high levels of carbon monoxide, Public Health Service investigators found, cannot distinguish relative degrees of brightness, lose some ability to judge time intervals, and show impaired performance on other psychomotor tests. Exposure to high levels of carbon monoxide is particularly dangerous for persons suffering from chronic heart and lung diseases.

The contention that tobacco smoke poses a serious health hazard to non-smokers has been questioned by the tobacco industry. "When all of the major evidence is considered, the claim of hazard to non-smokers withstands neither a scientific nor 'common sense' evaluation," the Tobacco Institute said in a paper released in July 1973.[10] A recent publication prepared by the R. J. Reynolds Tobacco Co. cites several studies which support the claim that there is no conclusive evidence that cigarette smoke is harmful to non-smokers.[11]

The publication called attention to the work of Drs. Irwin Schmeltz, Dietrich Hoffmann and Ernest L. Wynder of the American Health Foundation. They reviewed 65 studies concerning tobacco smoke in indoor settings and published their appraisal of these studies in the magazine *Preventive Medicine* in 1975. They concluded: "Little has been done to show whether an individual is adversely affected by exposure to room air contaminated by cigarette smoke. Several authors have considered the problem, but in our view no definite conclusions have been arrived at." They went on to say, "On the basis of available epidemiological evidence, it appears that passive inhalation of tobacco smoke by non-smokers or smokers does not increase

---

[9] Quoted in the *Los Angeles Times,* Aug. 29, 1976.
[10] "Smoking and Non-Smoking: What is the Issue?"
[11] R. J. Reynolds Tobacco Co., "The Facts About Public Smoking," 1976.

their risk for chronic illness such as cancer of the respiratory tract, emphysema, or cardiovascular disease." They also said that they found "no data suggesting that passive inhalation of cigarette smoke increases the risk of developing lung cancer."

The R. J. Reynolds Co. also cited an article by Drs. William C. Hinds and Melvin W. First of the Harvard School of Public Health in the April 17, 1975, issue of the *New England Journal of Medicine.* The authors had measured concentrations of tobacco smoke in public places to evaluate the health implications for non-smokers. They sampled the air in restaurants, cocktail lounges, commuter trains, buses and waiting rooms in the Boston area. They reported that even where they detected the highest concentration of smoke, in a cocktail lounge, a non-smoker would not inhale the equivalent of one filter cigarette even after long exposure.

The federal Occupational Safety and Health Administration last year rejected a proposal from the California Health Department to impose a standard requiring employers either to prohibit smoking or to segregate smokers from non-smokers. "The testimony we received did not conclusively prove what the occupational hazard was to a non-smoker from sidestream smoke," said Mark Ashcraft, staff services analyst for OSHA's health standards board.[12]

Question About Infringement of Civil Rights

The debate over non-smokers' rights goes beyond the question of health. It also has become a civil rights issue. "The idea of legislating an area of personal choice...threatens the very foundation of individual freedom on which this country was built," contends Bill Dwyer of the Tobacco Institute.[13] Similar thoughts were expressed by William D. Hobbs, chairman of the R. J. Reynolds Co. "Of course there are those who are annoyed by cigarette smoke," he said, "just as there are those who object to heavy perfumes, garlic on the breath, barking dogs or any of a thousand other things. But there is no issue between smoker and non-smoker which cannot be solved through mutual common courtesy and respect for the rights of others. If the issues of public smoking cannot be handled in this way, we as a people are opening ourselves to ever-increasing governmental restriction in every area of our lives."

Tobacco industry spokesmen are not the only ones who question the legality, morality and necessity of laws banning smoking in public places. U.S. District Court Judge Jack M. Gordon, in a decision last September dismissing a lawsuit seeking to prohibit smoking and the sale of cigarettes at the New Orleans

---

[12] Quoted in the *Los Angeles Times,* Aug. 29, 1976.
[13] Quoted by Ruth Rosenbaum in *New Times,* Dec. 10, 1976, p. 48.

Superdome, wrote: "For the Constitution to be read to protect non-smokers from inhaling tobacco smoke would be to broaden the rights of the Constitution to limits heretofore unheard of." Defenders of the anti-smoking bans answer with the slogan "Your right to smoke ends where my nose begins." Columnist William Raspberry wrote: "It's well enough to talk about balancing the rights of smokers and non-smokers, but the fact is that non-smoking doesn't hurt anybody. Smoking does, and if the habit is to be an inconvenience to anybody, it ought to be to those who have it."

Some police officials say that they do not have the manpower to enforce the smoking bans. Tobacco Institute President Horace R. Kornegay, in a recent letter to 3,200 police chiefs across the country, said that "it doesn't make sense to enact laws which will divert law-enforcement manpower from the task of apprehending real criminals." But Banzhaf, the ASH director, maintains that "Most people are law-abiding citizens...and they will obey the law if it is properly posted."[14]

History of Anti-Smoking Efforts

S MOKING has been under attack almost continuously since tobacco was introduced to the civilized world over 400 years ago. James I of England, in an essay[15] published in 1604, described smoking as "a custome lothsome to the Eye, hateful to the Nose, harmful to the Braine, dangerous to the Lungs, and, in the black stinking Fume thereof, nearest resembling the horrible Stygian Smoke of the Pit that is bottomless." The monarch threatened to banish doctors who smoked to the "land of the red Indians."

Opposition to smoking in 17th century England was mild compared to measures adopted in other countries. In Turkey, where smoking was thought fit only for the "Christian dog," offenders were led through the streets of Istanbul with pipes thrust through their noses. A Chinese decree of 1638 threatened decapitation to anyone who trafficked in tobacco. Several Popes forbade the use of tobacco on pain of excommunication. In 17th century Russia, where the sale and use of tobacco was banned by Czar Michael, offenders might have their noses cut off.

In the American colonies, the General Court of Massachusetts, beginning in 1629, prohibited the cultivation and use of tobacco both for reasons of morality and practicality;

---

[14] Quoted in *The Washington Star*, Jan. 25, 1976.
[15] "A Counterblaste to Tobacco."

it wanted to prevent fires. An early anti-tobacco tract in America was published in 1798 by a signer of the Declaration of Independence, the Philadelphia physician Benjamin Rush.

The tobacco habit prevailed nonetheless. Official bans on the use of tobacco gradually were supplanted by taxes on the tobacco trade. By the 19th century, the attack on smoking had become largely a matter of crusading by reformist groups. Late in the century it became entwined with the temperance movement. Children were mobilized to sing songs, carry banners, parade and preach sermons to their elders. Clergymen, educators and some businessmen applauded these efforts. Boxing champion John L. Sullivan denounced cigarettes as unmanly. Henry Ford and popular writer Elbert Hubbard spoke against the cigarette. Thomas Edison refused to hire cigarette smokers. A nationwide "Committee to Study the Tobacco Problem" attracted distinguished persons in every field.

Anti-tobacco groups became so influential in the early 20th century that at least 11 states and numerous cities enacted restrictive laws of one sort or another. New Hampshire in 1901 made it illegal for any person, firm or corporation to make, sell or keep for sale any form of cigarette. Under an Illinois statute enacted in 1907, the manufacture, sale or gift of a cigarette was made punishable by a fine of up to $100 or a jail term of up to 30 days. In New York, women and anyone "actually or apparently under 16 years of age" were forbidden to smoke in public. Anti-cigarette laws also were passed in Arkansas, Idaho, Iowa, Kansas, North Dakota, Oklahoma, Tennessee and Utah.

These restrictions did not seem to affect cigarette sales. In 1909, when the last of the state laws was passed, national sales were twice what they had been five years earlier, according to author Susan Wagner.[16] Cigarette consumption increased still further in World War I. The anti-smoking movement enjoyed a brief revival in the 1920s, after the Eighteenth Amendment to the Constitution was adopted outlawing alcoholic beverages. But gradually cigarettes gained general public acceptance. By 1927, all of the state anti-cigarette laws had been repealed. "Spurred by increased advertising, the political emancipation of women, and the widespread use of liquor during Prohibition," Wagner wrote, "the tide turned in favor of smoking."

Controversy Over Health and Cigarettes

Recent controversy over tobacco use has centered on the health consequences of smoking. The contention that smoking causes disease is almost as old as the use of tobacco itself. But it was not until the 1950s that medical evidence of the link between lung cancer and cigarette smoking became so

---

[16] Susan Wagner, *Cigarette Country* (1971), p. 44.

Early Cigarette Promotion

The cigarette industry has been described as a house that advertising built. The chief architect of "hard-sell" cigarette advertising was George Washington Hill, president of American Tobacco from 1925 to 1946. Hill promoted his Lucky Strike brand to sales leadership with such slogans as "It's Toasted" and "Reach For a Lucky Instead of a Sweet."

The latter slogan, Hill openly admitted, was designed to make smoking socially acceptable to women. An alluring series of ads was prepared to point out how much healthier it was to smoke Lucky Strikes than to eat sweets. And figure-conscious women responded by the thousands. By 1931, according to Susan Wagner, in her book *Cigarette Country,* Lucky Strike led all cigarettes in sales and alternated with Camels for the No. 1 spot in brand preference between 1930 and 1950.

During the 1930s and 1940s the cigarette industry was confronted with early intimations of the potential harm of smoking. The industry responded with an ad campaign with a medicinal flavor. Magazine pages and radio air waves were filled with such slogans as "Not a cough in a car load" (Old Gold), "Not one single case of throat irritation due to smoking Camels" and "The throat-tested cigarette" (Philip Morris).

Today cigarette manufacturers insist that advertising's only function is to induce the confirmed smoker to abandon his present brand for a new one, not to recruit new smokers. Early promoters such as Hill were more generous in crediting advertising with profound influence upon the overall consumption of cigarettes. "The impetus of those great advertising campaigns...built the cigarette industry," Hill said.*

* Quoted by Maurine B. Neuberger in *Smoke Screen: Tobacco and the Public Welfare* (1963).

pronounced that health groups spoke out to the public on the health danger. The American Cancer Society resolved on Oct. 22, 1954, to "emphasize to the American people that the...available evidence indicates an association between smoking, particularly cigarette smoking, and lung cancer." Earlier that year the Cancer Society and the British Medical Research Council reported independently, following separate three-year statistical studies, that death rates were higher for cigarette smokers than non-smokers.

In 1962 the Royal College of Physicians of London summarized the evidence on the disease-tobacco relationship and called cigarette smoking a serious health hazard. In a report issued March 7, the society concluded: "The strong statistical association between smoking, especially of cigarettes, and lung cancer is most simply explained on a causal basis." The report went on to say: "The conclusion that smoking is an important cause of lung cancer implies that if the habit ceased, the death rate from lung cancer would eventually fall to a fraction, perhaps to one-fifth, or even, among men, to one-tenth of the present level."

The British government soon instituted an intensive anti-smoking campaign. Pressure for similar efforts in this country by the American Cancer Society and others led President Kennedy to direct the Surgeon General to set up an advisory committee to undertake a comprehensive review of all data on smoking and health.

Publication of the committee's report on Jan. 11, 1964,[17] constituted a turning point in the smoking-health controversy. In his foreword, Surgeon General Luther L. Terry noted: "Few medical questions have stirred such public interest or created more scientific debate than the tobacco-health controversy.... The subject does not lend itself to easy answers. Nevertheless, it has been increasingly apparent that answers must be found."

The central conclusion was that "cigarette smoking is a health hazard of sufficient importance in the United States to warrant appropriate remedial action." The committee based its conclusion on statistical studies which found that "cigarette smoking is causally related to lung cancer in men" and that "the magnitude of the effect of cigarette smoking far outweighs all other factors." Data for women was less extensive but pointed in the same direction.

This report also found that cigarette smoking was associated with coronary artery disease, chronic bronchitis and emphysema. The committee recognized that "no simple cause-and-effect relationship is likely to exist between a complex product like tobacco smoke and a specific disease in the variable human organism." But "the continuing and mounting evidence from many sources" led it to decide that "cigarette smoking contributes substantially to mortality from certain specific diseases and to the overall death rate."

Reaction to 1964 Surgeon General's Report

The American Cancer Society hailed the Surgeon General's report as "a landmark in the history of man's fight against disease." Many Americans were shocked by the report's findings. Cigarette sales dropped sharply. During the first six months of 1964, cigarette sales were 11 billion less than during the same 1963 period, according to the Internal Revenue Service. However, as the shock of the Surgeon General's report wore off, cigarette sales recovered. Approximately 540 billion cigarettes were sold in 1968, about 35 billion more than in 1964.

---

[17] Report of the Advisory Committee to the Surgeon General of the Public Health Service, *Smoking and Health* (1964).

The Federal Cigarette Labeling and Advertising Act went into effect on Jan. 1, 1966, requiring all cigarette packages to carry the statement, "Caution—Cigarette Smoking May Be Hazardous To Your Health." However, the law barred, until July 1, 1969, any requirement of a health warning in cigarette advertising.

On June 2, 1967, the Federal Communications Commission ruled that, under the fairness doctrine, broadcasters were required to make available free air time for anti-smoking messages, since the pro-smoking messages of cigarette commercials were judged a controversial matter of legitimate public importance. As a result of the commission's ruling, thousands of messages warning of the health hazards of smoking appeared on radio and television over the next three and a half years. The anti-smoking spots seemed to have had at least a short-term effect. In 1969 cigarette sales declined by more than 12 billion—a greater drop than immediately after the release of the Surgeon General's report.

Congress, however, on March 19, 1970, approved legislation banning all cigarette commercials on radio and television as of Jan. 2, 1971.[18] Subsequently the Federal Communications Commission ruled that broadcasters need not continue running anti-smoking messages. "As a result, the anti-smoking campaign on television shriveled to a relative handful of 'public service' messages."[19] Cigarette sales have increased substantially each year since 1971, reaching a new peak of 620 billion in 1976.

Faced with the possibility of regulation by the Federal Trade Commission, U.S. tobacco companies agreed in February 1971 to disclose the tar and nicotine content of the cigarettes they advertised in print. The following November, the Interstate Commerce Commission imposed a rule restricting smoking to the rear five rows of seats on interstate buses and strengthening ICC regulations regarding non-smoking areas on trains. In making the rule, the commission declared "second-hand" smoke to be an "extreme irritant to humans, particularly with respect to its effect upon eyes and breathing" and judged it "capable of adversely affecting the adequacy and availability" of interstate passenger carrier service. Based on similar reasoning, the CAB in July 1973 required all commercial airlines to provide separate non-smoking sections.

---

[18] The law also changed the health warning on cigarette packages to read "Warning: The Surgeon General Has Determined That Cigarette Smoking Is Dangerous To Your Health." But at the same time it prohibited the Federal Trade Commission from requiring any health warning on printed cigarette advertising before July 1, 1971.
[19] "New Medium For The Message," *Consumer Reports*, May 1976, p. 278.

Pressures on the Cigarette Industry

A FTER CIGARETTE commercials were removed from radio and television in 1971, relatively little attention was given to the issue of cigarette advertising. "Ads in magazines and newspapers simply do not generate the same kind of outrage that TV commercials engendered," Sen. Frank E. Moss (D Utah, 1959-76) said last year.[20] However, pressure to place further restrictions on cigarette advertising has been building. The American Cancer Society, in opening a new five-year campaign against cigarette smoking last October, called on Congress to ban cigarette advertising within five years except for brands with a tar and nicotine content at least 50 per cent below averages for the previous year.

A total ban on tobacco advertising and promotion, including the sponsorship of sporting and other public events, was recommended by the World Conference on Smoking and Health in June 1975. The consumer-products testing group Consumers Union has come out strongly in favor of a total ban on cigarette advertising. "It is uncertain whether an advertising ban would by itself, without an extensive anti-cigarette campaign, significantly reduce the number of new recruits to cigarette smoking," the testing group said in the May 1976 issue of *Consumer Reports*. "But the main argument is an ethical one: It is immoral to permit the advertising of an addictive product that causes lung cancer and contributes to heart disease, emphysema, bronchitis and vascular disease." The Public Health Service survey of adult smoking habits found that a majority of adults it polled (56 per cent), including 42 per cent of the smokers, wanted to stop all cigarette advertising *(see p. 76)*

Many anti-smoking advocates contend that magazines and newspapers should be encouraged to turn down cigarette advertising. Author James Fallows, who advocates such a policy, concedes that "a few publications rely so heavily on cigarette ads that they might not survive a boycott." But, he goes on to say, "For the majority of the publications, this is hardly a question of economic survival.... For most of them taking cigarette ads is not a matter of making a profit, but only of maximizing it."[21] Among the publications that already refuse cigarette ads are *Reader's Digest, National Geographic, Good Housekeeping, The New Yorker* and *The Christian Science Monitor*.

---

[20] Quoted in *Consumer Reports*, May 1976, p. 279.
[21] James Fallows, "The Cigarette Scandal," *The Washington Monthly*, February 1976, p. 13.

Public Attitudes Toward Cigarette Smoking

	Smokers Agree		Non-Smokers Agree	
	1970	1975	1970	1975
Smoking should be allowed in fewer places than it is now.	41.6%	51.0%	65.6%	80.1%
Smoking is enough of a health hazard for something to be done.	79.1	71.8	90.0	90.0
Cigarette advertising should be stopped completely.	49.9	42.6	66.6	62.5
The public knows all it needs to know about the effects of smoking.	49.0	43.4	40.1	38.2
Teachers should set an example by not smoking.	58.1	62.3	79.0	84.1
It is annoying to be near a person smoking cigarettes.	34.1	34.8	72.5	77.0

SOURCE: U.S. Public Health Service, "Adult Use of Tobacco, 1975," June 1976

Katharine Graham, publisher of *The Washington Post,* defended her newspaper's policy of accepting cigarette advertising. "Once a product is admitted to public sale in this country, I see no reason its producers should not be permitted to advertise in the *Post* or elsewhere," she said. Similar thoughts were expressed by John J. McCabe, senior vice president of *The New York Times:* "It seems to us, particularly in this tendentious time, that the advertising columns of *The New York Times* should be available for any legitimate message that our advertisers wish to deliver. This does not mean that we abrogate our responsibility for good taste or fairness. It does mean, however, that we accept advertising [which] may be in conflict with the editorial opinion of the paper."[22]

Inquiry Into Charges of Unfair Advertising

The Federal Trade Commission on July 28, 1976, accused the six major cigarette companies—R.J. Reynolds, Philip Morris, Lorillard, Liggett & Myers, Brown & Williamson, and American Brands—of not living up to a 1972 agreement to make health warnings on cigarette ads "clear and conspicuous." In new amendments to a lawsuit originally filed in U.S. District Court in New York City in October 1975, the commission said the manufacturers had failed to place easily readable health warnings on cigarette ads ranging from billboards to transit posters. The original suit alleged a failure to include proper warnings in

---

[22] Letters to the editor by Graham and McCabe, *The Washington Monthly,* April 1976, p. 3.

newspaper and magazine advertisements and in promotional displays for vending machines and store counter racks.

Two months earlier, on May 17, 1976, the FTC announced that it would investigate whether the tobacco industry was using deceptive or unfair advertising that would overly influence young people to start smoking. The commission said it would pay special attention to the various promotional activities of the tobacco companies. After cigarette commercials were removed from radio and television, the companies redirected large chunks of their promotion budgets to the sponsorship of such public affairs as music festivals and sports events. Cigarette manufacturers insist that they are not trying to induce non-smokers to start, but merely are competing with one another for larger shares of a market that already exists.

The outcome of the investigation "is likely to bring a series of new recommendations for laws to regulate the advertising of cigarettes," *Business Week* magazine reported July 5, 1976. In requesting the investigation, the anti-smoking group Action on Smoking and Health had asked the commission to:

> Limit illustrations in cigarette advertising to the product and package themselves, thus eliminating photos that imply smoking is a healthy habit engaged in by handsome, vigorous people.
>
> Prohibit misrepresentations that cigarettes with comparatively lower tar and nicotine contents are not dangerous to the smoker.
>
> Require that every ad discloses the specific tar and nicotine contents of the product in milligram multiples of the lowest ranked brands.
>
> Require full disclosure of the amount of carbon monoxide generated by a cigarette of that brand.
>
> Prohibit the promotional use of any merchandise, premiums, coupons, discounts, contests or other programs designed to induce the purchase and consumption of cigarettes.
>
> Prohibit billboard advertising of cigarettes.
>
> Require that every ad carry this message as prominently as the current warning: "NOTICE: Many people find it very difficult, if not impossible, to quit smoking once they start."
>
> Require that every ad also carry this prominent warning: "NOTICE: Your cigarette smoke may bother, discomfort, and endanger the health of those around you."

Popularity of Brands Low in Tar, Nicotine

Some members of Congress have been pushing the idea of limiting tar and nicotine content in cigarettes. Sens. Gary Hart (D Colo.) and Edward M. Kennedy (D Mass.) say they plan to reintroduce a bill to tax cigarettes on the basis of their tar and nicotine content—the higher the content, the heavier the tax. The bill did not come to a vote in the Senate during the last

Congress. Hart and Kennedy call their bill a reasonable response to persistent evidence linking cigarette smoking to cancer and heart disease. "On the one hand, we want to preserve the option and freedom of individuals to select whatever brand of cigarette they want," Kennedy said. "But we also want to provide an important incentive to the industry itself to come up with lower tar and nicotine cigarettes."[23]

Opponents of the bill contend that it singles out cigarettes unfairly for punitive tax treatment, threatens economic hardship for tobacco-producing areas and ignores the tobacco industry's voluntary shift to the production of cigarettes with less tar and nicotine. The National Cancer Institute noted last year that the average tar content of American cigarettes had dropped to 18 milligrams from 43 milligrams in 1955. During the same period, the average nicotine content dropped to 1.2 milligrams from 2.8 milligrams. Tests conducted by the Federal Trade Commission, announced Dec. 11, 1976, gave the best rating to Carlton 70s, an unusually short, filter cigarette not widely sold, with 0.5 milligrams of tar and .05 milligrams of nicotine. Next were the more popular Carlton king-size cigarettes and a new brand called Now, both with 1.0 milligram of tar and 0.1 milligram of nicotine. At the opposite end of the scale was Players, a brand made by Philip Morris for the American market, with 64 times more tar and 44 times more nicotine than Carlton 70s.

James C. Bowling, vice president of Philip Morris, the second-largest cigarette manufacturer in the United States, contends that there is no medical evidence that links tar and nicotine with disease. "It is all supposition," he said.[24] A study published in September 1976 by Dr. E. Cuyler Hammond, chief of epidemiology and statistics for the American Cancer Society, contradicts that view. The study reported the death rate among smokers of cigarettes high in tar and nicotine was 16 per cent higher than among comparable smokers of cigarettes with low levels of those substances. According to the study, the mortality from lung cancer was 26 per cent lower among the low-tar-and-nicotine smokers than among those who smoked stronger brands. For heart disease, the mortality rate was 14 per cent lower.

On the basis of his findings, Hammond suggested that high-tar-and-nicotine cigarettes should be taken off the market. He also warned that new brands of low-tar-and-nicotine cigarettes that contain additives to enhance flavor should be fully tested to make sure that the chemicals themselves do not pose a cancer risk.

---

[23] Quoted in *Congressional Quarterly Weekly Report*, April 10, 1976, p. 845.

[24] Quoted in *Business Week*, July 5, 1976, p. 51.

Anti-Smoking Campaign

Any hope of turning the United States into a non-smoking society in the near future is unrealistic, according to Dr. Gio B. Gori, deputy director of the National Cancer Institute's Division of Cancer Cause and Prevention. Therefore, he insists, more attention should be paid to the development and use of less-hazardous cigarettes. "It is important that we protect those people who continue to smoke despite all warnings," Dr. Gori said. "Leaving them to their fate is neither humane nor economical...."[25]

Issue of Abstinence Vs. Safer Cigarettes

"It may be possible to remove toxic smoke components selectively and thus reduce specific hazards," he said, adding that evidence indicates that there may be "critical" amounts of such hazardous components of smoke as tar, nicotine and carbon monoxide. These amounts could be calculated, Gordi said, and cigarettes could be designed to stay below these critical levels. Gordi also said that the incidence of cigarette-related disease would be lowered if the smoke yield of cigarettes was reduced.

There are others who say that encouraging smokers to quit is the only answer to the smoking problem. Jesse Steinfeld, the former Surgeon General, told the World Congress on Smoking and Health: "Until research can provide a cigarette which is truly harmless and from which the toxic components are removed, society's goal must remain the cessation of smoking...." The Public Health Service's survey of adult smoking habits showed that 61 per cent of the smokers interviewed had made at least one serious effort to quit. Nine out of 10 smokers said they probably would stop smoking if there was an easy way to quit. However, 57 per cent said they expected to be smoking five years from now.

There are all kinds of drugs and devices on the market to help smokers quit. Some smokers turn to commercial clinics such as Smokenders, Smoke Watchers and the Schick Corporation Clinics. Others try methods offered by non-profit organizations such as the American Cancer Society, the American Lung Association or the Seventh Day Adventist Church. "At this time it is virtually impossible to say that one approach is better than another," according to Dr. Donald T. Frederickson, associate professor of public health at New York University School of Medicine.[26] Some smokers may not want to kick the habit. But if the non-smokers' rights movement has its way, they may eventually have to restrict their smoking to the privacy of their homes and a few specifically designated public places.

[25] Gio B. Gordi, "Low-Risk Cigarettes: A Prescription," *Science,* Dec. 17, 1976, p. 1243.
[26] Quoted in *Medical World News,* Nov. 1, 1976, p. 53.

Selected Bibliography
Books

Neuberger, Maurine B., *Smoke Screen: Tobacco and the Public Welfare*, Prentice-Hall, 1963.
Trop, Jack Dunn, *Please Don't Smoke in Our House*, Natural Hygiene Press, 1976.
Wagner, Susan, *Cigarette Country: Tobacco in American History and Politics*, Praeger, 1971.

Articles

Action on Smoking and Health (ASH) Newsletter, selected issues.
Banzhaf, John, "Please Put Your Cigarette Out; the Smoke is Killing Me!" *Today's Health*, April 1972.
Dampier, William, "Smoke If You Must—But Not Here!" *Maclean's*, June 28, 1976.
Demarest, Michael, "Smoking: Fighting Fire With Ire," *Time*, Jan. 12, 1976.
Fallows, James, "The Cigarette Scandal," *The Washington Monthly*, February 1976.
"Giving Up Smoking: How the Various Programs Work," *Medical World News*, Nov. 1, 1976.
Gori, Gio B., "Low-Risk Cigarettes: A Prescription," *Science*, Dec. 17, 1976.
Hay, D.R., "Smokers—A Gloomy Prospect for the Neglected Addicts," *Modern Medicine*, Nov. 15, 1976.
"Less Tar, Less Nicotine: Is That Good?" *Consumer Reports*, May 1976.
"New Medium For The Message," *Consumer Reports*, May 1976.
"No Smoking—Some States Mean It," *U.S. News & World Report*, Oct. 20, 1975.
Rosenbaum, Ruth, "Skirmish Over Smokers' Rights," *New Times*, Dec. 10, 1976.
The Tobacco Observer, selected issues.

Reports and Studies

Action on Smoking and Health, "Digest of Non-smokers' Rights Legislation," Nov. 3, 1976.
American Cancer Society, "Report to the Board of Directors from the Task Force on Tobacco and Cancer," 1976.
Hammond, E. Cuyler, "Some Recent Findings Concerning Cigarette Smoking," American Cancer Society, September 1976.
Editorial Research Reports, "Advertising in A Consumer Society," 1969 Vol. I, p. 371; "Regulation of the Cigarette Industry," 1967 Vol. II, p. 863; "Smoking and Health," 1962 Vol. II, p. 813.
R.J. Reynolds Co., "The Facts About Public Smoking," 1976.
Tobacco Institute, "Smoking and Non-Smokers: What Is The Issue?" July 1973.
U.S. Public Health Service, "Adult Use of Tobacco, 1975," June 1976.
—"State Legislation on Smoking and Health, 1975," December 1975.
—"The Health Consequences of Smoking, 1975," June 1975.

MEDIA REFORMERS

by

William V. Thomas

Dec. 23
1 9 7 7

Editor's Note: A new development since the original publication of this report was the Federal Trade Commission's vote on Feb. 22, 1978, to consider restrictions on television advertising aimed at children. The commission stopped short of proposing an outright ban on certain commercials as recommended by an FTC staff report. The proposal under consideration would prohibit any type of TV commercial directed at audiences containing "a significant proportion" of children "too young to understand" the purpose of the ad. The proposed rule would also prohibit commercials for sugared products seen by older children. Such ads, according to the media reform group Action for Children's Television (ACT), pose serious health risks to youngsters *(see p. 87)*.

MEDIA REFORMERS

L IKE MANY AMERICAN institutions in the last decade, the press and broadcast media have come under increasing criticism. The old debate over their rights and responsibilities has been marked recently by the appearance of hundreds of citizen-organized reform groups. Representing a broad cross-section of political and religious leanings, they are drawn together by the common goal of gaining a greater voice in setting media standards. As the number of so-called "watchdog" organizations has grown, so, it seems, has their determination. Network executives and newspaper editors "may not know it yet," said a spokesman for a religious group, "but they're about to be hit by a revolution."[1]

The charge most frequently made by reform groups is that the press and commercial television networks are more concerned with profits than principles of accuracy and fairness. Particular complaints cover a wide range of alleged faults from biased news coverage in daily papers to a distorted depiction of life on television. Yet underlying nearly every aspect of the current protest is a belief that the First Amendment's guarantee of freedom of the press also implies the right of readers and viewers to help in determining how that freedom should be used.[2]

A general dissatisfaction with news ethics, prompted partly by Nixon administration attacks on the press,[3] has been credited with encouraging the appearance of journalistic self-criticism in many of the nation's papers as well as an increase in space allotted to letters to the editor. Under viewer pressure, a few television advertisers have even said they would withdraw their support from shows that depict violence. But, according to Charles B. Seib, ombudsman for *The Washington Post*, media owners "have not faced up to...the fundamental issues" being raised by angry consumers.[4]

Reed Irvine, chairman of Accuracy in Media (AIM), an organization that monitors press and television news reporting, takes the position that the big media corporations have used

---

[1] Carl Richardson of the Church of God, quoted in *TV Guide*, Oct. 1, 1977. The Church of God, which claims 457,000 members, organized a TV boycott the week of April 10-16, 1977, to protest "televised violence and sex."
[2] See "Access to the Media," *E.R.R.*, 1974 Vol. I, pp. 447-470.
[3] See "First Amendment and Mass Media," *E.R.R.*, 1970 Vol. I, pp. 41-60.
[4] Charles B. Seib, *The Washington Post*, Nov. 5, 1976.

their power in a biased and therefore potentially dangerous fashion. AIM calls itself a watchdog group devoted to promoting "fairness in reporting on critical issues," which it feels are often shaded by the media's liberal perspective. Others, however, have accused AIM of allowing a politically conservative bias of its own to color much of its activity. Speaking last year to a meeting of journalists, Irvine expressed AIM's basic philosophy this way: "No society is truly free without a free press, but the existence of a free press does not necessarily guarantee a free society. Unfortunately, history indicates that a free press may contribute to its own destruction and to the destruction of all other freedoms.... There is some reason to question whether or not we have gone too far for our own good, perhaps creating a monster which may [destroy] many of the freedoms we cherish, including freedom of the press."[5]

While many reform groups agree on the general goal of increasing access to the media, most of them seek to further their own particular interests. Some have been mobilized to challenge a single news story or broadcast, as was the case when various pro-gun groups joined together in 1975 to protest a CBS-TV program, "The Guns of Autumn," that was critical of hunting. Among business corporations, General Motors and the Mobil Oil Co., monitor the media and run aggressive "opinion advertising" to correct what they consider erroneous news coverage of matters relating to their operations.

Campaign Against Violence on Television

The one issue that seems to unite the often disparate factions of the media reform movement is television violence, which, it is claimed, gives young watchers a warped conception of human behavior. That theory received considerable national attention in October when 15-year-old Ronald Zamora of Miami was tried and convicted of murdering an elderly woman. The defense attorney contended that Zamora was innocent of willful homicide because "he was suffering from and acted under the influence of prolonged, intense, involuntary, subliminal television intoxication.... The tube became [the boy's] parents, his school and church." Zamora, he added, had been so conditioned to kill by watching "endless hours" of televised violence that murder itself was no more than the "acting out of a television script."

A Dade County (Fla.) jury found Zamora guilty and sentenced him to 25 years to life in prison. But the trial, which incidentally was televised in Florida as part of a special experiment allowing cameras in court, raised a number of questions about the effects of watching dramatized mayhem on television. A University of Pennsylvania study in 1976 revealed

---

[5] Speech to the Missouri Press Convention in St. Louis, Oct. 22, 1976.

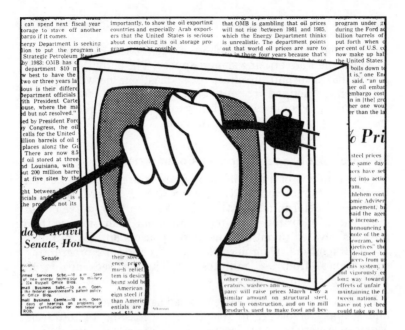

that the index of television violence that year had increased sharply over the previous year—despite a network policy of setting aside a two-hour "family viewing" period free of violence each weekday evening. The most violent shows, the survey found, were those broadcast on Saturday morning and aimed exclusively at children. The study concluded "that while all viewers absorb TV 'lessons' of fear, suspicion and mistrust, children are the most affected by the 'mean world syndrome' of television programing."[6]

Figures cited in July by the National Parent-Teachers Association, which last year began a vigorous campaign against violence on television, indicated that the average child now watches 6 to 6½ hours of television a day, while preschool children view 25 hours of television a week. "We don't think [children] can watch...rape and murder night after night, week after week without being affected by it," said William M. Young, project director of the PTA's current boycott of products that sponsor violent shows. Although some critics of television violence believe that protests should be directed at the networks instead of program sponsors, reform groups have been successful in forcing changes in some programs through the threat of product boycotts.

Media Watch, a monthly newsletter published by the National Citizens Committee for Broadcasting, a Washington-based reform organization, reported in February that a number of companies are concerned about demonstrations of buyer un-

6 *Violence Profile, No. 8,* 1976.

rest and have revised their policies to define the kinds of shows in which their advertising should appear. The activity of reform groups has also had an effect on at least one network, NBC, which has pledged to cut back its support for violent programing. "People have said they want another direction, and that's what we're going to give them," said NBC President Robert T. Howard.[7]

Pressures to Change Offending Commercials

"The function of a television program is to make commercial breaks available," author Les Brown wrote.[8] According to the latest FCC determination, those breaks fill 9½ minutes out of every hour of prime time on commercial television, with 6 minutes devoted to national network sponsors and 3½ minutes to local sponsors. Commercial time in children's programing runs higher—from 9½ minutes per hour on weekends to 12 minutes per hour on weekdays.[9]

Numerous protests have been voiced against the use of ethnic and sexual stereotypes in television advertising. In 1967, the Mexican-American Anti-Defamation Committee launched a campaign against the "Frito Bandito," a Mexican cartoon character used in television ads for Frito-Lay corn chips. After four years of controversy, during which time protest groups picketed supermarkets and TV stations in the Southwest, the Frito-Lay Co. finally agreed to discontinue "Frito Bandito" commercials.

The National Organization for Women, whose media task force monitors television commercials, has managed to have some ads "offensive to women" changed or canceled. But a recent NOW survey of 1,241 TV commercials concluded that most product advertisers continue to portray women in a bad light, "as dependent, unintelligent, submissive creatures who are the adjuncts of men."[10]

A U.S. Civil Rights Commission study on women in the media reported that women are misrepresented not only in television advertising but also in most network comedy shows where they frequently are seen in demeaning roles. "The women in situation comedies still tend to be subordinate to the men in their lives," the study said. "Mary [in the "Mary Tyler Moore Show"] calls her boss 'Mr. Grant' even though everyone else calls him 'Lou.' Edith [in "All in the Family"] scoots into the kitchen to fetch Archie a beer and rarely fails to have dinner on

---

[7] Quoted in *Media Watch,* January-February 1977.
[8] Les Brown, *Television: The Business Behind the Box* (1971), p. 65.
[9] Federal Communications Commission, "Report and Policy Statement on Children's Television Programs," *Federal Register,* 1974, p. 39400.
[10] NOW survey cited in the U.S. Civil Rights Commission study "Window Dressing on the Set," August 1977, p. 12.

Rating Television Violence

The following rankings were compiled by the National Citizens Committee for Broadcasting over a two-week period during the spring 1977 television season. They were based on the number and length of violent incidents per show compared to the total time and incidents of violence in all prime time programing. NCCB defines violence as "an overt expression of physical force (with or without weapon) against oneself or other.... An action to be considered violent must be plausible and credible and must include human or human-like characters. It may be an intentional or accidental action, humorous or serious or a combination of both...."

10 Least Violent Shows		10 Most Violent Shows	
Program	Network	Program	Network
Alice	CBS	Starsky and Hutch	ABC
All in the Family	CBS	Wonder Woman	ABC
Bob Newhart	CBS	Baa Baa Black Sheep	NBC
Phyllis	CBS	Baretta	ABC
Maude	CBS	Walt Disney	NBC
Good Times	CBS	Rockford Files	NBC
Welcome Back Kotter	ABC	Quincy	NBC
Fish	ABC	Charlie's Angels	ABC
Happy Days	ABC	Police Woman	NBC
M.A.S.H.	CBS	Kojak	CBS

the table by 6 p.m."[11] The commission's appraisal of television programing itself became a target of criticism in the press. Its recommendations for policing the networks were greeted as an exercise in bureaucratic overkill.

The current focus of the campaign to reform television commercials is on advertising directed toward children. Action for Children's Television (ACT), a public-interest group with the goal of improving children's programing, asked the FCC in 1970 to eliminate all advertising from children's shows and to require every television station to broadcast at least 14 hours of commercial-free children's programs a week. In response to the ACT petition and other expressions of citizen concern, the FCC in 1974 created a special unit to study problems related to children's television. Since that time, the commission's policy has been to rely on the sponsors and producers of children's shows to adopt their own standards of self-regulation, governing commercials and program content. Advertising revenue pays for the programs, the FCC reasoned, and banning all ads on children's television "could have a very damaging effect on the amount and quality of the shows."[12]

---

[11] *Ibid.*, p. 23.
[12] "Report and Policy Statement on Children's Television Programs," *op. cit.*, p. 39399.

The commission's approach has not pleased the critics, who say it has tended to place the interests of broadcasters above the public interest. "In view of the FCC's reluctance to force producers to limit advertising," said Maureen Harmonay of ACT, "we have requested permission to air counter-commercials that inform parents and children about the hazards of certain foods and other products advertised on TV." In November, the U.S. Court of Appeals for the District of Columbia upheld an FCC rule exempting most product commercials from the obligations of the "fairness doctrine" *(see p. 91)*, which requires stations to broadcast opposing opinions. However, the appeals court ordered the commission to consider requiring stations to set aside one hour a week for the presentation of messages and lengthier programing by members of local communities and public-interest spokesmen.

News Council's Forum for Grievances

Since its founding in 1973, the National News Council has proven to be one of the most respected news monitoring organizations in the country. Set up under the auspices of the Twentieth Century Fund, the independent council, composed of 18 voluntary members, has two main goals: "to examine and report on complaints concerning the accuracy and fairness of news reporting in the United States [and] to initiate studies and report on issues involving freedom of the press."

In judging the alleged misdeeds of the news media, however, it has no legal authority to enforce its decisions. Like the 24-year-old British Press Council, on which it is modeled, its power is derived solely from its ability to influence public opinion. Yet that power, wrote Executive Director William B. Arthur, "is totally dependent on the judgment of editors to publish the council's findings."[13]

Although some major news organizations, including *The New York Times* and the Associated Press, opposed its creation in fear that it would breed an atmosphere of regulation, the National News Council has received considerable praise from many leaders in journalism for its professional standards. But its work remains largely unknown to the public. In its 1975 report on ethics, the American Society of Newspaper Editors said the council's "integrity...is without question.... It has established a record that deserves more attention than either editors or the public have so far given it."

In January 1977, CBS became the first major broadcast network to pledge its cooperation with the council. CBS Chair-

---

[13] William B. Arthur, "The News Council Lives!" *The Bulletin of the American Society of Newspaper Editors,* November-December 1973, p. 6.

Major National Media Reform Groups

Accuracy in Media (AIM), Washington	Corrects alleged errors or omissions in news reporting
Action for Children's Television (ACT), Newtonville, Mass.	Works for improvement of children's television programing
Alternate Media Center, (AMC), New York	Studies the uses of cable television and ways in which citizens can gain access to the medium
Aspen Institute Program on Communication and Society, Washington	Studies communications policy issues and publishes books and research papers
Cable Television Information Center, Washington	Monitors legal developments affecting cable television and assists local governments in establishing cable TV operations
Citizens Communications Center, Washington	A nonprofit public interest law firm specializing in communications cases before FCC and courts
National Association for Better Broadcasting (NABB), Los Angeles	The first national consumer group to promote the public interest in broadcasting, it evaluates network programing and participates in hearings before Congress and FCC
National Black Media Coalition (NBMC), Washington	A coalition of over 70 black media reform groups promoting minority needs in national broadcasting
National Citizens Committee for Broadcasting (NCCB), Washington	Seeks to make broadcasting responsive to public interest
National Federation of Community Broadcasters (NFCB), Washington	Represents the interests of community radio stations before the FCC and other federal agencies
National News Council, New York	Examines complaints of inaccuracy and unethical conduct by news-gathering organizations
National Organization for Women, Media Task Force, Washington	Promotes the positive image of women in the media and monitors the FCC
Office of Communication of the United Church of Christ, New York	Provides assistance in negotiating public grievances with local broadcasting stations
Public Advertising Council, Los Angeles	Produces public service announcements for public interest groups
Reporters Committee for Freedom of the Press, Washington	Offers legal defense and research services for journalists

man William Paley said the council "has furnished an impartial and expert group to which aggrieved parties can appeal for review in the interest of fair treatment by the news media."[14] Paley added that CBS News will report any council findings adverse to the network. In a further effort to publicize the council's proceedings, the *Columbia Journalism Review*, a bimonthly media magazine, recently began carrying reports of its decisions.[15]

More than 450 complaints have been ruled on by the National News Council in its four years of existence. In November, for example, it decided that an NBC News documentary entitled "Danger! Radioactive Waste" was "seriously flawed" in reporting two instances of possible radioactive harm to persons and animals. The council said it could not find evidence for a portion of the program which suggested radioactive waste material caused medical problems for one family and some cattle.

NBC responded that it stands by the facts presented in the show, but promised it would carefully look into the complaints. Among allegations currently under investigation are: (1) charges by the Teamsters Union against *Time* magazine for its reporting last July of mismanagement of a union pension fund; and (2) a grievance filed against WBBM-TV, a CBS affiliate in Chicago, for its broadcast of a news series in March that allegedly gave the impression the drug Laetrile "was effective in combating cancer."

In an attempt to bridge the gap between the public and the press, a small number of regional news councils have been started in this country and Canada. According to the National News Council, there are at present five regional media review organizations in the United States: the Minnesota Newspaper Association, the Iowa Freedom of Information Council, the Delaware News Council, the Honolulu Community-Media Council, and the Riverside, Calif., Press Council. The Ontario Press Council, the only such group in Canada, was created in 1972 when eight Ontario dailies[16] agreed to establish a "self-governing council...to control and discipline the press and other news media."[17]

---

[14] Quoted in an Associated Press interview, Jan. 25, 1977.

[15] The *Columbia Journalism Review* began its coverage of National News Council activity in its March-April 1977 issue.

[16] *The Brantford Expositor, The Kitchener-Waterloo Record, The London Free Press, The Hamilton Spectator, The Ottawa Citizen, The Owen Sound Sun-Times, The Toronto Star* and *The Windsor Star.*

[17] From a 1968 report of the Royal Commission on civil rights in Ontario, quoted in *The Bulletin of the American Society of Newspaper Editors*, January 1974, p. 13.

Matters of Federal Regulation

T RADITIONALLY, the First Amendment rights to freedom of speech and of the press have been invoked by broadcasters and publishers to defend their operations from government interference. But increasingly, public-interest groups have begun to cite those same rights to justify their demands for access to the media. Pointing to the growing number of communications companies that control newspapers as well as radio and television outlets,[18] reformers contend that today's giant media monopolies pose a dangerous threat to individual freedom of expression.

"Freedom of the press must be something more than a guarantee of the property rights of media owners," wrote law professor Jerome A. Barron, a leading advocate of greater public access to mass communication.[19] Barron argued this theory before the Supreme Court in 1974 in a case in which an unsuccessful candidate for state office in Florida, Pat L. Tornillo, was denied the right to reply to a critical editorial in *The Miami Herald.* Arguing that the concentration of news media ownership was a potential abridgement of rights assured by the First Amendment, Barron maintained the establishment of a federal right-to-reply law was needed to offset the Supreme Court's 1964 decision in *New York Times v. Sullivan.* In the 1964 case, the Supreme Court ruled that in order to win a libel judgment, a public figure or other newsworthy person must prove he was the victim of a deliberate, false accusation published with "actual malice" in mind.

The court decided unanimously against Tornillo's right-to-reply petition, emphasizing that the First Amendment gave editors final authority over what should be published in their papers. However, since then the court has retreated somewhat from its 1964 position on libel. In at least two cases, the court has limited the broad protection of news organizations by drawing a narrow definition of "public figures."[20] In the 1974 case of *Gertz v. Robert Welsh,* the court ruled that Elmer Gertz, a civil-rights activist and author, was not a public figure. In a similar ruling in 1976, *Time* magazine had to pay damages for inaccurately reporting information about a prominent Florida socialite, Mary Alice Firestone, whom the court determined was not a "public figure" because she played no major role "in the affairs of society."

[18] See "News Media Ownership," *E.R.R.*, 1977 Vol. I, pp. 183-202.
[19] Jerome A. Barron, *Freedom of the Press for Whom?* (1973), p. iv.
[20] See "The Demise of the Public Figure Doctrine," by John J. Watkins, in *Journal of Communications,* summer 1977.

Unlike the press, broadcasting is already subject to right-to-reply laws. In 1959, the FCC set forth its "fairness doctrine," requiring radio and television stations to air opposing points of view on public issues. The doctrine was extended in 1967 to require broadcasters to notify persons or groups when they were the subject of criticism in on-the-air discussions of controversial issues and to give them an appropriate opportunity for rebuttal.

The Supreme Court upheld the constitutionality of the fairness doctrine in the 1969 *Red Lion Broadcasting* decision,[21] in which the court decided that a radio station that had broadcast a "personal attack" had to provide reply time free of charge. The court declared that the fairness doctrine was necessary "in view of the...scarcity of broadcast frequencies, the government's role in allocating those frequencies, and the legitimate claims of those unable without government assistance to gain access to those frequencies for the expression of their views...."

The need for federal regulation of broadcasting became evident shortly after the invention of radio. While the medium was still in its infancy, Congress passed the Radio Act of 1912, which gave the Department of Commerce the authority to distribute operating licenses. But by the early 1920s, there were so many stations on the air, some of them using the same frequencies, that listeners often had trouble receiving clear, consistent reception. With radio station owners clamoring for the enforcement of power and frequency assignments, Congress created the Federal Radio Commission in 1927, designating the public interest as the most important criterion by which it should regulate the radio industry.

The Federal Communications Commission, established by the Communications Act of 1934, replaced the FRC. Its jurisdiction was expanded to cover both wire and wireless interstate transmissions. Through its license renewal authority, the FCC was empowered to hold local broadcasters accountable for the way in which they used the public airwaves. The Supreme Court affirmed the FCC's charter in a 1940 ruling in which it decided that:

> ...[N]o person is to have anything in the nature of a property right as a result of the granting of a license. Licenses are limited to a maximum of three years' duration, may be revoked, and need not be renewed. Thus the channels presently occupied remain free for a new assignment to another licensee in the interest of the listening public. Plainly it is not the purpose of the FCC to protect the licensee against competition, but to protect the public.[22]

---

[21] *Red Lion Broadcasting v. Federal Communications Commission,* 395 U.S. 369.
[22] *Federal Communications Commission v. Sanders Brothers Radio Station,* 309 U.S. 470, 475.

The coming of television not only increased the number of broadcast stations nationwide but made it necessary for the FCC to adopt regulations suitable to the new medium. In an effort to bring television to as many communities as possible, the commission generally awarded large cities three VHF (very high frequency) channels. By 1945, it had assigned or reserved all available VHF channels, even though channels in some sparsely populated regions went unused for years. As the demand for television grew in the 1950s and 1960s, the FCC opened the UHF (ultra high frequency) range of channels (14 through 83) for use by both commercial and public broadcasting.

Through the years, the stated aim of FCC policy has been to promote local ownership of broadcast outlets. But in the so-called "prime market" cities—cities with the biggest potential audiences—"absentee" media corporations, including the networks, control many of the radio and television stations. Critics of the FCC contend that it has never actively enforced its local ownership policy in a way that would discourage the networks from purchasing choice local stations.

FCC Action on Licensing and Programing

Newton N. Minow, upon being named FCC chairman by President Kennedy in 1961, quickly identified himself as an outspoken critic of commercial television, describing its fare as a "wasteland." He told the National Association of Broadcasters: "...[W]hen television is bad, nothing is worse. I invite you to sit down in front of your television set when [a] station goes on the air...and keep your eyes glued to that set until the station signs off. I can assure you that you will observe a vast wasteland. You will see a procession of game shows, audience participation shows, formula comedies about totally unbelievable families...violence, sadism, murder...private eyes, gangsters, more violence, and cartoons. And endless, commercials—many screaming, cajoling and offending...."[23]

Minow warned that the FCC would use its license renewal power to force broadcasters to upgrade their offerings. "Renewal will not be *pro forma* in the future," he said. "There is nothing permanent or sacred about a broadcast license." His warnings marked the beginning of a period of increased commission activity, particularly in educational or "public" television, which it encouraged as an alternative to commercial TV. The first important backing came in 1962 when Congress authorized the federal government to make grants for the construction of noncommercial television stations. An amendment to the Communications Act of 1952 prohibited the FCC from interfering with the actual purchase of a broadcast facility.

---

[23] Speech to the National Association of Broadcasters, Washington, D.C., May 9, 1961.

However, Minow, who was determined to increase the number of educational television channels, held up FCC approval of the sale of a New York station to a commercial group until non-commercial buyers could be found. His action, in 1962, drew heated criticism from network officials, who complained to the White House that the commission had overstepped its bounds. But President Kennedy gave Minow his full support. "You keep this up!" the President told him.[24]

Later, Minow virtually assured the future of public television when he persuaded Congress to pass a law requiring all television sets sold in the United States after January 1963 to be equipped with VHF as well as UHF channels. Previously, according to television historian Erik Barnouw, "set manufacturers, many of whom had VHF stations, had been in no hurry to spread the competition."[25]

There was no mistaking the government's anti-monopoly attitude toward the television networks in the Kennedy administration. In 1963, under Minow's leadership, the FCC banned the "option clause" in contracts between commercial networks and their local affiliates. The clauses gave the networks control over large blocs of time on affiliate stations. The elimination of the "option clause," however, had only a minimal effect on commercial programing, since most stations continued to fill their schedules with network shows.

Facilitating Access to the Media

THE FOUNDING FATHERS believed that the free flow of information and ideas was necessary to the function of democracy in America. But that ideal, some observers suggest, is being threatened by mergers and acquisitions in the communications industry. The concern is that the concentration of ownership reduces journalistic competition and, it is feared, the sense of responsibility to the public. As Congress prepares to rewrite the Federal Communications Act fully for the first time since 1934, these matters seem certain to receive legislative attention. The House Interstate and Foreign Commerce Subcommittee on Communications hopes to begin a draft revision of the act in January.

According to the author of a study on "cross-ownership," 60 million Americans live "in areas where at least one newspaper

[24] Quoted in Erik Barnouw, *Tube of Plenty: The Evolution of American Television* (1975), p. 303.

[25] *Ibid.*, p. 303.

Campaign Against Cigarette Advertising

The 1964 Surgeon General's report linking smoking and cancer marked the beginning of a vigorous campaign by anti-smoking groups to have cigarette commercials banned from radio and television. Under pressure from the American Cancer Society and other health and consumer organizations, the Federal Communications Commission ruled in 1967 that broadcasters were required under the fairness doctrine to make air time available for anti-smoking messages, since the pro-smoking messages contained in cigarette ads were judged a controversial matter of legitimate public interest.

As a result, the commission's order opened the way for thousands of messages warning of the dangers of smoking. By 1969, cigarette sales had dropped by more than 12 billion from the 540 billion cigarettes sold the previous year.

In 1970, Congress passed legislation that prohibited all cigarette commercials from radio and television. Subsequently, the FCC ruled broadcasters were no longer required to carry anti-smoking messages, and the spots all but disappeared. The following year, cigarette sales began to increase steadily, reaching a new peak of 620 billion in 1976.

Cigarette ads in newspapers and magazines were unaffected by the ban. They simply did not "generate the same kind of outrage that TV commercials engendered," former Sen. Frank E. Moss (D Utah, 1959-1976) said. However, the tobacco industry agreed in 1971 to disclose the tar and nicotin content of the cigarettes they advertised in print.

and one television station have the same owner."[26] While many owners maintain that joint newspaper-broadcast operations afford customers superior service, media reform groups across the country are almost unanimous in viewing them as a threat to public access and independent news coverage. In January, the Supreme Court is expected to hear arguments on the constitutionality of the cross-ownership question. Over 200 media combinations in 44 states could be affected by the outcome.

At issue in the case, *American Newspaper Publishers Association v. National Citizens Committee for Broadcasting,* is whether newspaper owners may be prohibited from acquiring radio and television stations in the same city in which their papers are published, and whether the FCC or the courts are empowered to order divestiture where newspaper and broadcast facilities are co-owned in a single "market" area. The Department of Justice has long contended that cross-ownership is an

[26] William T. Gormley Jr., "How Cross-Ownership Affects News-Gathering," *Columbia Journalism Review,* May-June 1977, p. 38. Gormley is the author of "The Effects of Newspaper-Television Cross-Ownership on News Homogeneity," a study published in 1975, funded by the John and Mary R. Markle Foundation.

antitrust violation in that it virtually eliminates competition for advertising revenue.

An FCC ruling in 1975 prohibited common control of newspapers and radio and television stations but allowed joint operations to continue in localities having only one daily newspaper and one broadcast outlet. However, the U.S. Court of Appeals for the District of Columbia ordered the commission to apply the rule to all media combinations so long as the public interest is not harmed.

The American Newspaper Publishers Association has contended that the appeals court went beyond its authority in the review of FCC decisions. The publishers association argued that in the licensing of broadcasters—many of whom also happened to own newspapers—the commission had declared they were serving the public interest. In a brief to the Supreme Court, ANPA said: "The prospective rules promulgated by the FCC and the retrospective divestiture required by the court of appeals seriously impair the constitutionally protected right to publish a newspaper.... Moreover, these rules will prevent broadcasters—often the only persons in a community who can combine journalistic expertise with adequate capital—from starting a new daily newspaper or acquiring an existing newspaper which otherwise might cease publication."

Should the appeals court ruling stand, cross-ownership in dozens of cities would be broken up. In early December, *The Washington Post* and *The Detroit News* announced plans to trade company-owned television stations in the two cities. The exchange, which will not become final until it gains FCC approval, is seen as a response to the divestiture decision by the court of appeals.

Udall's Bill to Aid Independent Newspapers

In a related effort aimed at helping independent newspapers survive, Rep. Morris K. Udall (D Ariz.) in October introduced a bill to create a trust fund to finance estate tax liabilities incurred by small weekly or daily papers. The fund would be supported by contributions from individual newspapers that stand to benefit from it and would be open only to papers not owned by a chain[27] or a public corporation. The American Newspaper Publishers Association reports that 1,762 daily newspapers were published in the United States in 1976 and, according to newspaper analyst John Morton, six of every ten were under group—chain—control.[28]

Media critic Ben H. Bagdikian, a professor of journalism at

---

[27] Udall's bill defines a chain as a company owning two or more newspapers.
[28] Morton is with the Washington office of the New York-based brokerage firm of Colin, Hochstin Co. He issues the *John Morton Newspaper Research* newsletter.

the University of California at Berkeley, said the bill "is a good idea for the remaining papers, mostly small, that are family held...and for people who start up a paper and build it up so it has a great deal of value.... It's medicine applied late, but better late than never."[29] The ANPA, which opposes divestiture, said it supports Udall's bill "as an important first step" in correcting present tax inequities that fall the hardest on small independent newspapers.

Many who favor the dismantling of the giant media corporations contend that diversity is not necessarily synonymous with size. Concentrations of ownership, they add, more often tend to foster a uniformity of judgment rather than a free traffic of varying opinion. Typical of this thought is a comment by Jim Hoge, editor-in-chief of the Chicago *Sun-Times* and *Daily News:* "All the good will in the world by conglomerates...is just not the same as a number of different voices owned by different groups."[30]

The current upsurge in media "empire building" began in the 1960s and is now marked by acquisitions as diverse as film production companies, book publishing enterprises and cable television systems. In contrast to those who look upon this development with misgivings, CBS President John D. Backe argues that only big communication corporations are strong enough to oppose the excesses of big government. "This is an age," he said recently, "when public opinion is the target of every special interest and special pleader. So it is very important that our journalistic and communications institutions be strong enough and diverse enough to resist those who want to foist their particular ideology on the public."[31]

Community Programing on Cable Television

Another "access" issue centers on cable television. The Federal Communications Commission ruled in 1976 that all U.S. cable television systems must provide community access to their facilities. But nurturing public use of cable TV, which transmits video signals by wire rather than over the airwaves, has not been easy. According to David Hoke of the National Federation of Local Cable Programers, "most communities are not aware that public access exists." A National Cable Television Association survey in 1976 reported that only 52 per cent of the operators responding had broadcast community-produced programs.

The idea of participatory television is relatively new. "Community people have long been oriented to the passive role of

---

[29] Quoted in *The Washington Post,* Oct. 7, 1977.

[30] Quoted in *U.S. News & World Report,* Aug. 15, 1977.

[31] Quoted in *The Washington Post,* Dec. 2, 1977.

broadcast television viewing," Hoke said. "Users do not generally break down the doors of access centers or operator-provided production facilities just because they are available."[32] Communities need to be educated about cable television and the opportunities provided by access, he added.

At present, there are 3,700 cable television systems operating in the United States, serving nearly 12 million households. The industry estimates that the number of subscribers will grow to 20 million by 1980. Under FCC regulations, local governments are responsible for awarding cable franchise privileges, while cable operators themselves have the obligation of alloting time to community groups. But a common complaint, access advocates say, is that many cable owners who hold an unfavorable view of public access rights tend to give little or no assistance to local users. It is further argued that operators who charge exorbitant rental fees for playback and studio facilities are not meeting the FCC goal of providing low-cost community television.

Current federal guidelines permit individual cable systems to carry up to three "distant signal" stations. However, the recent development of so-called "super signal" stations that combine cable television and domestic communications satellites may necessitate a reassessment of FCC policy. Satellites enable a local broadcast outlet to become, in effect, a national station by beaming its signal far greater distances than do conventional broadcast towers. The use of such techniques has been a source of concern to proponents of community access who fear "super signal" cable broadcasts may preclude community-centered programing. One "super signal" station, WTCG in Atlanta, is already in operation. Plans are under way for similar stations in Chicago, San Francisco and Los Angeles.

Carter's Proposals for Public Broadcasting

The Carter administration has underscored its determination to expand community participation in public broadcasting. In October it sent recommendations to Congress that are intended to increase the level of federal subsidy for public radio and television and to encourage more local programing. The White House recommendations, written into the proposed Public Broadcasting Financing Act of 1978, address such problems as public accountability by individual stations, editorializing and minority ownership.

The bill, now before the House Subcommittee on Communications, awaiting action in 1978, proposes raising the funding authorization for public broadcasting from the present

---

[32] David Hoke, "Cable Access: Myth or Reality?" *Access*, November 1977, pp. 1-4. *Access* is a monthly publication of the National Citizens Committee for Broadcasting.

level of $121-million in fiscal year 1978 to $200-million by 1981. In addition, the amount that stations must raise themselves in order to receive federal money would be lowered slightly. The current ratio is 250 to 100; 225 to 100 is the proposed ratio. Some media reformers have wondered if that ratio will be adequate, but a spokesman for the White House Office of Telecommunications Policy said the figure is not final and could be revised if circumstances warrant. The Carter legislation would also require public broadcast stations to open their meetings and their financial records to public scrutiny. The bill further proposes:

1. Earmarking 25 per cent of the money appropriated to the federal Corporation for Public Broadcasting to be used for program development, including local access programing.

2. Setting aside $30-million annually in grants to aid women and minorities who want to start public stations.

3. Lifting the current ban on editorializing from all stations not licensed to local or state governments. Under the terms of the bill, the ban would still apply, for example, to stations operated by community or state-supported colleges.

The prohibition against editorializing has been in effect since 1967 when Congress established the CPB.[33] But media reform groups as well as Carter administration officials now believe it should be removed so as to allow stations to air editorial comment on issues of public importance. "We cannot see why simply because a station bases its revenues on the sale of commercial products...it has a greater right or takes a greater risk in editorializing than one whose funds are a mixture of individual, foundation and corporate donations, and federal funds," said Frank Lloyd of the Office of Telecommunications.[34]

Media reform groups generally view the new proposals as a boost for public broadcasting. "What's most heartwarming about the Carter action," said Nicholas Johnson, chairman of the National Citizens Committee for Broadcasting, "is that it demonstrates that [the President] has taken the time and interest to grasp the potential and purpose and needs of this alternative broadcast system. It is the first time in 10 years, since President Johnson proposed the Corporation for Public Broadcasting, we could say that about a President...."[35] Yet while the government's change in attitude may be significant, it addresses only a part of the problem of public access to the media. The public demand is for a greater role in shaping broadcast and newspaper policies and practices.

[33] See "Financing of Educational Television," *E.R.R.*, 1967 Vol. I, pp. 161-180, and "Public Broadcasting in Britain and America," 1972 Vol. II, pp. 805-824.

[34] Testimony at hearings before the House Subcommittee on Communications, Oct. 19, 1977.

[35] Nicholas Johnson, "Carter Looks at Public Broadcasting," *Access*, November 1977, p. 8. Johnson served as chairman of the FCC from 1966 to 1973.

Selected Bibliography

Books

Barnouw, Erik, *Tube of Plenty: The Evolution of American Television,* Oxford, 1975.

Lazarus, Simon, *The Genteel Populists,* Holt, Rinehart and Winston, 1974.

Paletz, Donald L., Roberta E. Pearson and Donald L. Willis, *Politics in Public Service Advertising on Television,* Praeger, 1977.

Price, Monroe and John Wicklein, *Cable Television: A Guide for Citizen Action,* United Church, 1972.

Schorr, Daniel, *Clearing The Air,* Houghton Mifflin, 1977.

Schwartz, Barry N., ed., *Human Connection in the New Media,* Prentice Hall, 1973.

Smith, Ralph Lee, *The Wired Nation: Cable TV the Electronic Communications Highway,* Harper & Row, 1970.

Winn, Marie, *The Plug-In Drug: Television, Children and the Family,* Viking, 1977.

Articles

"America's Press: Too Much Power for Too Few?" *U.S. News & World Report,* Aug. 15, 1977.

Bagdikian, Ben H., "Woodstein U.: Notes on the Mass Production and Questionable Education of Journalists," *The Atlantic,* March 1977.

——"First Amendment Revisionism," *Columbia Journalism Review,* May-June 1974.

Broadcasting, selected issues.

Columbia Journalism Review, selected issues.

Epstein, Edward J., "Journalism and Truth," *Commentary,* April 1974.

Hamilton, John Maxwell, "Ombudsmen for the Press," *The Nation,* March 16, 1974.

"In-House Press Critics: A Selection of Recent Work by Newspaper Ombudsmen," *Columbia Journalism Review,* July-August 1977.

Mallette, M. F., "Should These News Pictures Have Been Printed?" *Popular Photography,* March 1976.

Mencher, Melvin, "The Arizona Project: An Appraisal," *Columbia Journalism Review,* November-December 1977.

[MORE], selected issues.

Powers, Thomas, "Right-to-Reply Laws," *Commonweal,* May 17, 1974,

Reports and Studies

Davis, Pamela, ed., "Citizens Media Directory," National Citizens Committee for Broadcasting, April 1977.

Editorial Research Reports, "Access to the Media," 1974 Vol. I, p. 447; "News Media Ownership," 1977 Vol. I, p. 183; "First Amendment and Mass Media," 1970 Vol. I, p. 41.

National Cable Television Association, "Guidelines for Access," August 1972.

U.S. Commission on Civil Rights, "Window Dressing on the Set: Women and Minorities in Television," August 1977.

CONTROLLING HEALTH COSTS

by

Suzanne de Lesseps

**Jan. 28
1 9 7 7**

Editor's Note: Since this report was first published the Carter administration has taken its first steps toward controlling national health care costs. Joseph A. Califano Jr., Secretary of Health, Education and Welfare, announced March 8, 1977, the creation of a Health Care Financing Administration to consolidate health funding within his department, including Medicare and Medicaid.

President Carter, in a message to Congress on April 25, 1977, singled out hospital costs as his first target in controlling health costs. He proposed to limit cost increases for most hospitals to 9 per cent in the fiscal year beginning the following Oct. 1, and his fiscal 1979 health budget was premised on the compulsory ceiling being in effect by July 1, 1978.

In congressional action so far in 1978, a compromise version of Carter's plan was approved by a House Ways and Means subcommittee, giving hospitals about a year to trim their spending voluntarily before a mandatory federal limit on revenue increases would be imposed. Meanwhile, Sen. Edward M. Kennedy (D-Mass.) has said he is "committed to bringing a hospital cost containment bill to the floor of the Senate this year."

CONTROLLING HEALTH COSTS

L AST NOVEMBER a woman checked into New York University Medical Center to have a portion of her stomach removed. Three weeks later, while still recuperating in the hospital, she received a bill for hospital charges up to that time. The bill totaled $10,000. The surgeon's fee "for services rendered" came to $3,000. The anesthesiologist's bill was $700. Luckily, the woman was covered by Medicare insurance, for without it, her life savings could have been wiped out.

Stories like this are not uncommon in the United States any longer. For the cost of health care is spiraling. One night in a hospital can cost $200. Intensive care can cost over $300 a day. The cost of health care in the United States has risen far faster than prices in general (see p. 105). It has increased tenfold during the last 25 years, tripled during the last 10 years and almost doubled since 1970. The nation's medical spending bill approached $140-billion during fiscal year 1976 and is expected to exceed $150-billion in fiscal 1977. By 1980, it is projected to reach $223-billion.

The increased cost of medical care is portrayed in still other terms. The U.S. Bureau of Labor Statistics, in compiling the nation's monthly Consumer Price Index, keeps tab on the cost of medical care items. According to its findings, the amount of medical care that $100 would have purchased in 1967 was costing $184.70 last year. That figure represents an overall average for doctor and dental fees, hospitalization, drugs and eye exams and eyeglasses. Hospital costs showed the biggest increase of all in that period; a semi-private room was nearly three times costlier than in 1967. And physicians' fees had nearly doubled (see table, p. 107).

Many Americans, both government officials and private citizens, are concerned about this nation's continued ability to provide needed health services for everyone if costs are not brought under control. "We are coming close to a situation where we are going to have to decide who to treat and who not to treat," the American Society of Internal Medicine was told last May. "The concept of cost-effective medicine is getting nearer," said the speaker, Duncan Heuhauser, an assistant professor of health services administration at the Harvard School of Public Health.[1]

Causes of Continued Rise in Medical Prices

Why have health care costs been rising so drastically? The answers are numerous and complex. Some of the reasons have to do with the growth of private health insurance, which has enabled many families to make fuller use of health services by shifting medical costs to a third party. Besides increasing demand, health insurance has also removed the patient from the direct-payment process and isolated him or her from the reality of rising costs.

"With public spending acounting for some 40 per cent of all health expenditures and something like two-thirds of private costs being met through health insurance, the typical consumer seldom comes face to face with his share of the national health bill," Charles C. Edwards, a former commissioner of the U.S. Food and Drug Administration, wrote last May. "Yet for a family of four that share is approaching $2,500 a year. For most Americans that would be catastrophic if it came in the form of doctor or hospital bills they had to pay out of current income or savings."[2] According to public opinion polls, most Americans do not identify the cost or quality of health care as a top national concern.

Another cause of higher health costs has to do with advances in medical technology that entail expensive equipment and highly trained personnel. Three years ago, for example, Massachusetts General Hospital purchased a newly developed X-ray device called a Computerized Axial Tomography (CAT) scanner for $385,000. Today the machine sells for $575,000. According to some accounts, competition among hospitals for status and prestige has created widespread duplication of expensive new equipment in the same city or community. "The virtual explosion in medical technology is both a function of increased demand and, in turn, a cause of it," Andrew H. Nighswander, commissioner of the Massachusetts Rate Setting Commission, explained to the Council on Wage and Price Stability last year.

"The so-called CAT scanner is only the most recent example of chaotic, unplanned and frequently badly used technology, expensive to purchase and equally expensive to operate," Nighswander added. "Increasing numbers of hospitals now believe that their technological armamentarium is incomplete

---

[1] Quoted in *American Medical News,* May 17, 1976.
[2] Charles C. Edwards, "Our Ailing Health Care System," *The Denver Post,* May 2, 1976.

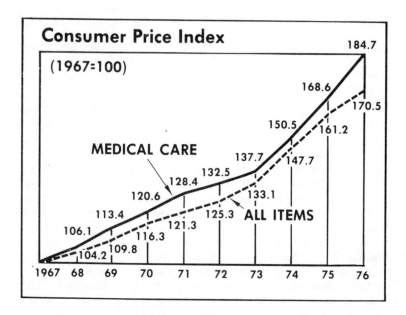

Consumer Price Index

(1967=100)

184.7

168.6

170.5

150.5

161.2

MEDICAL CARE

137.7

147.7

132.5

128.4

120.6

133.1

113.4

125.3 **ALL ITEMS**

106.1

121.3

116.3

104.2 109.8

1967 68 69 70 71 72 73 74 75 76

without it." Several other persons also told the council that many hospitals, particularly those in urban areas, have expanded unnecessarily. "It has been estimated that on any given day 200,000 hospital beds in this country are empty," said Roger C. Sonneman, chairman of the U.S. Chamber of Commerce Special Committee on the Nation's Health Care Needs. "If only one half of this excess capacity were eliminated, the savings could amount to about $1-billion annually."

Even in the best of circumstances, hospital expenses have shot up. A stainless steel bedpan today costs $20 and, according to E. Kash Rose of the Hospital Financial Management Association, a simple IV (intravenous) pole sells for $105. And after decades of low pay, nurses and other hospital attendants in recent years have pressed—and sometimes have even gone on strike—for more money. All of these factors have combined to make hospital costs rise faster than any other element of health care.

Critics of the present health-care system complain that health insurance, which repays doctors and hospitals after costs have been incurred, offers them no incentive to control expenses. Another complaint is that health insurance places too much emphasis on costly hospital care and too little on preventive care. Still another cause of inflation in the medical field has been the flood of malpractice lawsuits against hospitals and doctors—and a tendency among juries to make high awards.

The malpractice problem creates higher costs for the patient in two ways. It has prompted a rise in the cost of malpractice insurance—an extra cost that has been passed on to the consumer. And the increase in lawsuits has caused many doctors to overtreat their patients in an effort to protect themselves from possible legal action.

A survey taken by the Texas Medical Association in 1976, for example, showed that 67 per cent of the Texas physicians surveyed were ordering more X-rays now than they were before the malpractice crisis erupted. Sixty-six per cent said they were ordering more lab tests, 65 per cent were advising their patients to obtain second medical opinions from other physicians, 51 per cent were setting limits on the procedures they were willing to perform, 50 per cent were delegating less responsibility for their patient's care to others and 48 per cent were hospitalizing their patients more.[3] According to estimates by Blue Shield of California, the practice of "defensive medicine" plus the cost of malpractice insurance adds as much as $20-billion a year to the nation's health bill. The American Medical Association (AMA) has estimated that patients paid an extra $1.25 per visit for physician malpractice insurance in 1975.[4]

Inflation in Medicare and Medicaid Programs

Medicare and Medicaid, two government-funded health programs enacted in 1965, have also been charged with inflating health costs by boosting demand and allowing doctors and hospitals to charge too much for their services. Opponents of a comprehensive national health insurance program argue that its potential inflationary effect would far exceed what Medicaid and Medicare have experienced. Of the $40-billion the federal government spent on health care in fiscal 1976, $26-billion billion went to Medicare and Medicaid—a $16.5-billion increase since 1970. Moreover, it is estimated the federal government will spend $32-billion on the two programs in fiscal 1977, a 40 per cent jump in two years.[5] A large part of the increases in recent years has been traced to general inflation and overuse of health services. But another part is attributed to inefficiency, fraud and abuse within the health programs.

Evidence of inefficient administration in the Medicare and Medicaid programs was documented as far back as 1970.[6] More recent examples of fraud and abuse were revealed last summer when the General Accounting Office (GAO) reported the existence of widespread price-gouging by physicians on medical laboratory tests. The agency reported to Congress that some

---

[3] Results reported in *American Medical News,* Oct. 25, 1976.

[4] For background, see "Malpractice Insurance Crunch," *E.R.R.,* 1975 Vol. II, pp. 925-944.

[5] The $32-billion estimate for fiscal 1977, ending Sept. 30, was made in the federal budget for fiscal 1978 that President Ford sent to Congress on Jan. 17, three days before he left office.

[6] See Report of the staff to the Senate Committee on Finance, "Medicare and Medicaid: Problems, Issues, and Alternatives," Feb. 9, 1970.

Consumer Price Index for Medical Care Items

Year	Physicians' Fees	Dentists' Fees	Optometric Exams and Eyeglasses	Semi-private Hospital Rooms	Prescriptions and Drugs
1967	100.0	100.0	100.0	100.0	100.0
1968	105.6	105.5	103.2	113.6	100.2
1969	112.9	112.9	107.6	128.8	101.3
1970	121.4	119.4	113.5	145.4	103.6
1971	129.8	127.0	120.3	163.1	105.4
1972	133.8	132.3	124.9	173.9	105.6
1973	138.2	136.4	129.5	182.1	105.9
1974	150.9	146.8	138.6	201.5	109.6
1975	169.4	161.9	149.6	236.1	118.8
1976	188.5	172.2	158.9	282.6	126.0

SOURCE: U.S. Bureau of Labor Statistics

doctors were overcharging Medicare and Medicaid by 100 to 400 per cent for lab tests ordered from outside laboratories.[7]

In testimony before the Senate Finance Subcommittee on Health last July, Sen. Frank E. Moss (D Utah, 1959-76), estimated that Medicare fraud on the part of doctors, nursing home operators and others cost the taxpayers $1.5-billion in fiscal 1975. Moss said that physicians alone were responsible for $300-million in fraudulent claims. During the same hearings, Gov. George Busbee of Georgia reported that dentists in his state had billed Georgia for more than $200,000 in Medicaid payments for work that was not done. "We discovered nursing homes billing the state for a water ski boat, trips to Hawaii and purchases at a large Atlanta department store for which there was no accounting," Busbee testified. States pay between 22 and 50 per cent of Medicaid costs.[8]

Partly as a result of these hearings, Congress established an Office of Inspector General in the Department of Health, Education and Welfare (HEW) to investigate fraud and abuse in all departmental programs and specifically required the inspector general to set up a separate staff within his office to investigate abuses in federal health programs. Eliminating fraud and cutting costs in the Medicare and Medicaid programs are issues expected to receive high priority in Congress this year. Sen. Herman E. Talmadge (D Ga.) has reintroduced his proposal to tighten penalties for fraud and abuse, and hearings on the measure may begin as early as February. Another Talmadge bill, the Medicare and Medicaid Administrative and

[7] General Accounting Office, "Tighter Controls Needed Over Payments for Laboratory Services Under Medicare and Medicaid," Aug. 4, 1976.

[8] For an explanation of how Medicare and Medicaid work, see "Medicare and Medicaid After Ten Years," E.R.R., 1975 Vol. II, pp. 527.

Reimbursement Reform Act, is being redrafted with help from the new Carter administration.

A key section promotes the concept of "prospective reimbursement"—compensation for services rendered at rates that have been previously established. The prevailing method is to pay hospitals on the basis of their "after the fact" charges. Third-party payers—the insurance companies—virtually always pay the amount submitted. Talmadge wants to tie routine hospital operating expenses to a formula based on average routine expenses incurred by similar hospitals. After a phase-in period, a hospital would be eligible for a bonus if its actual costs fell below the established rates. Costs up to 20 per cent above the rates would be paid, but any beyond 20 per cent would have to be absorbed by the hospital. President Carter has endorsed the "prospective reimbursement" concept.

State Attempts to Regulate Hospital Costs

In an attempt to gain tighter control over health spending, several states have created public regulatory agencies to set repayment limits on hospital costs before they are incurred. The leader in this movement has been Maryland, which began operating its Health Services Cost Review Commission in 1974. Although the commission does not have the power to disapprove hospital budgets, it can regulate specific rates and fees. In this way, it functions in a manner similar to a public utility commission. "We look at each department in a hospital and compare that hospital with all other similar hospitals," Alvin M. Powers, chairman of the commission, has explained. "If their costs are among the top 20 per cent and they can't tell us why, we hold public hearings to look for the reasons."[9]

In testimony before the Council on Wage and Price Stability last year, an official of the Maryland Health Services Cost Review Commission, John S. Cook, estimated that daily expenses incurred by Maryland hospitals during 1975 increased 11.3 per cent, under the national average of 14.7 per cent. Cook predicted that the rate of increase would be 4 or 5 per cent below the national average in fiscal 1977 and "at that point the accumulated savings to the public will be on the order of $100-million per annum." Connecticut, California, Massachusetts, New Jersey, New York, Oregon, Rhode Island, Washington and Wisconsin also have created public rate-setting agencies to hold down health costs. Although the regulatory structures in these states differ from one another, they all operate under the same philosophy: that it is cheaper in the long run to compensate a hospital at rates that have been set before, and not after, the health care has been delivered.

---

[9] Quoted by Robert P. Bombay in *The National Observer*, June 19, 1976.

The federal government has been experimenting with prospective rate-setting. Under authority granted by the National Health Planning and Resources Act of 1974 *(see p. 114),* the Social Security Administration has agreed to pay Medicare bills in South Carolina, Rhode Island and some in western Pennsylvania at predetermined rates. In addition, the agency is planning payment experiments with state rate-setting offices in Maryland, Washington, New Jersey, Massachusetts, Connecticut and California.

It has awarded a contract to the Blue Cross Association to test and develop a "prospective reimbursement" system in Rochester, N.Y. The Rochester program is unique in that it will be based on the needs of all hospitals in one community rather than the individual needs of each institution. "...[H]ospitals will need to innovate and maintain sound management practices as well as join forces to stay within the limits of the community budget," Blue Cross President Walter J. McNerney said when the contract was awarded last November. "If this means the sharing of more services between hospitals, this will be done in order to make for a more efficient and economical operation..."

Health Insurance and Public Policy

NOT EVERYONE believes the federal government, given its record with Medicare and Medicaid, is capable of controlling health care costs. The private sector is being urged to take a more active role in this effort. William Lilley, acting director of the Council on Wage and Price Stability, believes that corporations and labor unions in particular are motivated to work at holding down health costs for their members and employees because it is in their economic self-interest to do so. "We have seen, in every phase of our investigation into this problem, that cost-control incentives proposed by the private sector...promise to be more effective than those imposed by the multitude of government agencies which have attempted to tackle the problem," Lilley wrote in his introduction to a recent council study on rising health costs.[10]

One section of the study identified 119 cost-control projects that have been undertaken by a variety of large employers and unions. The United Federation of Teachers in New York City, for example, is currently saving approximately $1-million a year

---

[10] "The Complex Puzzle of Rising Health Care Costs," December 1976, p. iii.

in dental claims through a program that determines whether cases of proposed dental treatment are truly necessary. Other projects described in the study included an insurance-claims-review program sponsored by Rockwell International Corp., and contracts between retail pharmacies and two labor unions that allow members to pay the wholesale price of prescription drugs.

According to a survey by *Business Week* magazine,[11] health insurance costs for some companies have doubled or tripled in five years. As an illustration of this trend, General Motors announced in March 1976 that it spent more money on health insurance for its employees than it did on steel. Several companies, including such giants as Commonwealth Edison and Goodyear Tire & Rubber, provide their own health-care insurance. Rather than buy the insurance and pay premiums, they pay claims directly to doctors and hospitals. Such a system not only eliminates some administrative costs but allows the company to monitor claims directly. "Once we discover inappropriate levels of utilization or pricing, we exert whatever leverage we can," said Richard M. Martin, manager of health services at Goodyear.[12]

"General Motors...spent more money on health insurance for its employees than it did on steel."

Hospital administrators told the Council on Wage and Price Stability last year that their institutions had achieved significant savings by sharing equipment with other hospitals, purchasing insurance through group plans and by rearranging staffing patterns. O. Ray Hurst, president of the Texas Hospital Association, estimated that member hospitals had saved up to $20-million in this way. In Boston, Massachusetts General joined with nine other hospitals to form a reinsurance company and reported savings of $1.7-million in 1976 on its malpractice insurance premiums. The hospital also created a panel of staff members to review requests for new services and equipment. Since its inception in 1974, the panel has disapproved about half of these requests.

One cost-control idea that has gained in popularity among labor unions, businesses and Blue Cross groups is that of pre-

---

[11] Issue dated May 17, 1976.
[12] Quoted in *Forbes*, Sept. 1, 1976, p. 80.

surgical review. Persons whose doctors recommend surgery are encouraged or required to get a diagnosis from another physician. The patient does not have to accept the opinion of the second doctor, and the cost of the second visit is covered by the employee's health insurance plan. The purpose of presurgical review is to eliminate costly and "unnecessary" surgery, thereby reducing claims and lowering insurance costs.

A study conducted by Dr. Eugene G. McCarthy at Cornell University Medical College suggested that between 11 and 13 per cent of the patients who are advised by their physicians to undergo surgery probably do not need it. When extrapolated nationally, these figures indicate that two million or more operations performed annually in the United States could be avoided. "The findings more than justify the wide adoption of second-opinion programs for elective surgery for appreciable improvement in the quality of care and effective cost utilization," McCarthy said.[13] He had organized two pre-surgical review programs for labor unions in New York City in 1972.

Many physicians have questioned estimates of "unnecessary" surgery, arguing that it is difficult to arrive at a definition of "necessary" in any discussion of medicine. Just because two doctors disagree over a medical matter does not make either of them wrong, it is argued. Nevertheless, many experts believe that a good deal of surgery could be avoided.[14]

Background of the Government's Involvement

Commercial health insurance owes its beginning to the development of accident insurance during the mid-19th century when traveling businessmen began to suffer from frequent railroad and steamboat accidents. Before long, coverage was offered for accidents of all descriptions. Generally, policyholders were reimbursed for pay lost due to disability. Likewise, the early health insurance policies offered protection against the loss of income as a result of a number of diseases, including typhus, scarlet fever, smallpox and diphtheria. At the end of the 19th century a handful of casualty companies began to offer very limited coverage of hospital expenses in conjunction with the income-loss disability policies.

"Modern health insurance was born," the Health Insurance Institute reports, "in the Great Depression of the 1930s as a means of helping people cope with the costs of health care, and of bringing financial relief to hospitals faced with empty beds and declining revenues."[15] Just as the American Hospital

---

[13] Quoted by Jane E. Brody in *The New York Times,* May 3, 1976.

[14] For a summary of the debate, see "How Much Unnecessary Surgery?" *Medical World News,* May 3, 1976.

[15] "Source Book of Health Insurance Data 1975-76," p. 11.

Association had encouraged the development of Blue Cross for the payment of hospital fees, Blue Shield programs received a boost in 1938 when the AMA approved the concept of voluntary health insurance—largely to ward off the threat of "socialized medicine." Blue Shield reimbursed surgeons and physicians for specified services either directly or through the patients.

Besides providing impetus for the growth of private health insurance, the depression also stimulated interest in a national health insurance program sponsored by the government. This was the threat of "socialized medicine" that was so feared by the medical association. In 1934, President Roosevelt's Committee on Economic Security endorsed the principle of compulsory national health insurance. But a health insurance program was not included in the Social Security Act of 1935 for fear it would endanger passage of the act as a whole. The act did, however, provide for a broad range of social insurance and public assistance programs.[16]

From 1935 on, compulsory health insurance bills were introduced in Congress annually. After Roosevelt's death in 1945, the new President, Harry S Truman, proposed a comprehensive medical insurance plan for all persons, to be financed through an increase in the payroll tax that finances Social Security. The Truman plan and various other proposals were defeated, however, in a lobbying war that pitted labor unions and liberal organizations against the AMA, private health insurers and conservative business groups.

In 1965 Congress amended the Social Security Act to establish Medicare and Medicaid programs. Medicare provided persons 65 and older with insurance to cover most medical costs and was financed by the Social Security trust fund to which employers and employees are required to contribute. The Medicaid section provided federal matching grants to states that chose to make medical services available to welfare recipients and the medically indigent.

Recent Federal Steps to Lower Health Costs

Congress quickly began to recognize that health costs were rising faster than it had expected. Yet federal efforts to control these costs were spotty and weak. In 1967, as part of the Social Security amendments approved that year, the lawmakers authorized the Department of Health, Education and Welfare to experiment with new Medicare payment methods to achieve efficiency and economy. Although this authority was broadened in 1972 and 1974, it was not until 1976 that HEW began par-

---

[16] For background on the Social Security Act, see "Retirement Security," *E.R.R.*, 1974 Vol. II, pp. 974-977.

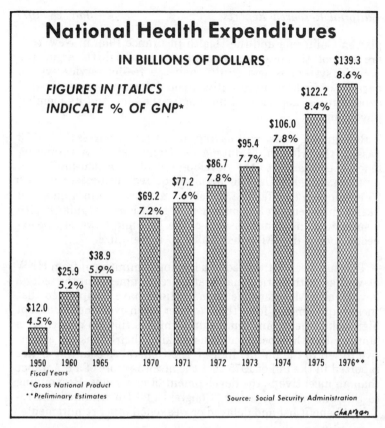

National Health Expenditures

IN BILLIONS OF DOLLARS

FIGURES IN ITALICS
INDICATE % OF GNP*

$139.3
8.6%

$122.2
8.4%

$106.0
7.8%

$95.4
7.7%

$86.7
7.8%

$77.2
7.6%

$69.2
7.2%

$38.9
5.9%

$25.9
5.2%

$12.0
4.5%

| 1950 | 1960 | 1965 | 1970 | 1971 | 1972 | 1973 | 1974 | 1975 | 1976** |

Fiscal Years
*Gross National Product
**Preliminary Estimates

Source: Social Security Administration

ticipating in actual trial projects with state rate-setting agencies *(see p. 109)*.

Besides broadening the department's power to experiment with Medicare reimbursement methods, the Social Security Amendments of 1972 also attempted to curb health costs by giving Medicare and Medicaid patients the option of joining a health maintenance organization (HMO) and by establishing professional standards review organizations (PSROs). The latter are panels of physicians who review the work of their colleagues to prevent unnecessary or substandard health care. They periodically review, for example, the length of time that Medicare or Medicaid patients are hospitalized. If the stay is deemed too long, the patient is told that the government will no longer pay the bill.

HMOs, on the other hand, are organized systems of health care that typically provide comprehensive services for enrolled members on a pre-paid basis.[17] For a fixed sum paid at regular intervals, enrollees are entitled to any of the benefits offered without having to pay anything extra. The Kaiser-Permanente

[17] See "Health Maintenance Organizations," *E.R.R.*, 1974 Vol. II, pp. 603-619.

plan in California and the Health Insurance Plan in New York are two of the best known. Advocates of HMOs argue the prepaid system is less costly than the fee-for-service system because of its built-in incentive to hold down expenses. Wasted expenditures mean loss of income for the plan and its member physicians.

Recognizing this cost-saving potential, Congress in 1973 passed the Health Maintenance Organization Act offering federal assistance to the development of both non-profit and profit-making HMOs. The law also required businesses with over 25 employees to offer the option of membership in a qualified health maintenance organization in addition to regular health insurance plans. Since passage of the 1973 act, however, the expected boom in HMOs has failed to materialize.

This has been attributed to a lagging commitment from HEW as well as to the strict qualification requirements in the federal law. Health Maintenance Organizations have complained that these requirements force them to offer extensive benefits, accept high-risk patients and charge uniform fees that do not reflect a family's health experience, thus making their plans too expensive to sell to the public. Indeed, the General Accounting Office reported in the fall of 1975 that the law was more of a hindrance than an incentive to the development of new plans. Responding to this and other criticism, Congress in 1976 trimmed the required benefit list and delayed or weakened other requirements.

Creation of U.S. Health Planning Agencies

Congress made another attempt to hold down medical costs by authorizing the creation of a network of health system agencies (HSAs) to review all proposed health projects and to recommend that HEW withhold funds from those that are not needed. The legislation, the National Health Planning and Resources Development Act of 1974, also sharply restricted federal assistance for construction of new hospitals. Although the health planning program has suffered from personnel problems and legal challenges, 196 HSAs have been designated. They are now taking steps to carry out their congressional mandate. The Health Planning and Resources Development Act is likely to be extended, with few changes, beyond its mid-1977 expiration date. However, there may be pressure to give the HSAs stronger regulatory powers.

A regulatory approach has been advocated before. Charles C. Edwards, the former FDA commissioner, argues that the health care system should be defined as a public utility because there is no competition and because it is heavily supported by public funds. "Managed as a public utility," Edwards has said, "the health care system would be subject to public regulation to make sure that its day-to-day activities and its long-range plans were consistent with a realistic and on-going assessment of public needs." Edwards proposed that a "national health authority" be created by Congress and given broad powers to regulate the health industry.[18]

Action Toward National Insurance

CRITICS OF the current health care system in the United States contend that a major restructuring job is clearly in order. Many see national health insurance as the best way of controlling costs and guaranteeing everyone the same coverage. But national health insurance is an idea that has been stalemated in Congress for decades. Prospects for passage seemed bright for a while in 1974 when Sen. Edward M. Kennedy (D Mass.) and Rep. Wilbur D. Mills (D Ark., 1939-76), then chairman of the Ways and Means Committee, drafted a long-awaited compromise plan. But the measure went nowhere and may have stirred up more controversy than it dispelled.[19]

President Ford, refusing to advocate any new social programs in order to save money, declined in 1975 to resubmit the Nixon administration's health insurance plan. In his State of the Union address the following year, Ford hardened his position: "We cannot realistically afford federally dictated national health insurance coverage for all 215 million Americans. The experience of other countries raises questions about the quality as well as the cost of such plans." Jimmy Carter, in contrast, called national health insurance a "must" during the 1976 election campaign. But Joseph A. Califano, during congressional hearings into his nomination as Secretary of HEW, told the Senate Finance Committee Jan. 14 that Carter would not submit a national health plan to Congress until at least 1978.

It is in discussing the specific design of a national program that supporters of national health insurance often part ways. One divisive issue is the role of the federal government. Organized labor, which backs the most liberal and far-reaching proposal *(see box)*, would like the federal government, instead of private insurance companies, to run the program. The plan it supports would use new payroll taxes matched by federal

---

[18] Writing in *The Denver Post*, May 2, 1976. For another public control approach to health care, see "A Revolutionary Answer to Medical Costs" by Charles Peters in *The Washington Monthly*, October 1976.

[19] See 1974 *Congressional Quarterly Almanac*, p. 386.

revenues from the general treasury to finance a mandatory program. This draws the opposition of hospitals, doctors and private health insurers who sense a threat of federal control. They would like the private insurance industry to run a program of standardized health benefits for all who want to participate.

Argument Over Cost-Control and Financing

Proponents of various health insurance proposals also continue to argue about the most realistic methods of controlling costs. Basically, there are three general methods of financing that, according to research and experience, have the potential for containing health-care inflation. The first relies on tight public controls and the second on a restructuring of the private medical system to provide doctors, hospitals and other health-care providers with incentives to hold down costs. The second method would mean, for example, encouraging the development of HMOs and other pre-paid delivery systems. "Prospective reimbursement" would also be part of this cost-control approach, although it overlaps with the first approach since it would have to be compulsory to be successful.

The third approach focuses on cost-sharing—that is, the amount of a medical bill that the patient is required to pay out of pocket. Supporters of cost-sharing say that under the current insurance system of third-party payment, the patient has little incentive not to overuse the health services. They maintain that a national health insurance program should require the patient to pay something to avoid overuse and make him or her aware of the costs involved. This could be done through "deductibles" or "coinsurance."[20]

Of the six major proposals for national health insurance that form the basis for congressional debate—all have been or are expected to be reintroduced in the new 95th Congress—five contain cost-sharing provisions. The only one that does not is the Health Security Act, a bill with organized labor's backing that Sen. Edward M. Kennedy (D Mass.) and Rep. James C. Corman (D Calif.) offered in the last Congress. It relies instead on stringent federal controls to prevent runaway costs. The plan would provide the entire population with a broad range of health services in place of the present dual system of private insurance and public programs for the poor and elderly. It would restrict the national health budget to a fixed amount to be derived from a combination of payroll taxes and general revenues.

The most vocal objections to the Health Security Act can be expected to come from the private health insurers. For if health insurance is reorganized into a federal system, the health in-

---

[20] A deductible is the amount a patient must pay before insurance coverage begins. Under coinsurance, a patient pays a fixed percentage of the bill.

Major Health Insurance Plans

Plan	Support	Estimated* Cost by 1980 (in billions)
National Health Care Services Reorganization and Financing Act	Rep. Al Ullman (D Ore.), American Hospital Association	$25.1
Health Security Act	Sen. Edward M. Kennedy (D Mass.), Rep. James C. Corman (D Calif.), AFL-CIO, Committee for National Health Insurance	24.8
Comprehensive Health Care Insurance Act	Rep. Tim Lee Carter (R Ky.), Sen. Clifford P. Hansen (R Wyo.), American Medical Association	20.3
Comprehensive Health Insurance Plan	Rep. Tim Lee Carter (R Ky.) supported modified version of Chip in 94th Congress	11.3
National Health Care Act	Sen. Thomas J. McIntyre (D N.H.), Rep. Omar Burleson (D Texas), Health Insurance Association of America	11.0
Catastrophic Health Insurance and Medical Assistance Reform Act	Sen. Abraham Ribicoff (D Conn.), Sen. Russell B. Long (D La.)	9.8

* By the Department of Health, Education and Welfare

surance companies would be legislated out of existence. "Health security is too risky," Susan Irving, a health economist on the staff of Sen. Abraham Ribicoff (D Conn.), said recently. "You can't simply dismantle the insurance industry and expect no consequences. Besides, who said that HEW could run the program efficiently? Its record with Medicare suggests the opposite."[21]

Proposals for Mixed Public-Private Approach

Four of the six major proposals offer a combination of private and public control. One is sponsored by the Health Insurance Association, another by the American Hospital Association and still another by the AMA. The fourth, the "Comprehensive Health Insurance Plan" (Chip), is closely patterned after a proposal that President Nixon sent to Congress in 1973. As ex-

---

[21] Quoted by Richard J. Margolis in "National Health Insurance—the Dream Whose Time Has Come?" *The New York Times Magazine,* Jan. 9, 1977.

plained by Saul Waldman, an economist with the Social Security Administration, all four of these plans would:

1. Require or encourage employers to offer private health insurance to their employees.

2. Establish a plan for low-income persons that would be administered and financed by the federal or state governments.

3. Continue the Medicare program or provide for other special coverage of the elderly.[22]

All four plans contain deductibles or forms of coinsurance. Under the AHA, AMA and HIA plans, hospital rates would be set "prospectively" by the states, while reimbursement rates under Chip would be set by the states in accordance with federal regulations.

The AMA House of Delegates, the medical association's governing body, voted Dec. 7, 1976, to reindorse its health insurance proposal as a means of assuring doctors some voice in the drafting of new legislation. Some delegates wanted the association to oppose any national health insurance program at all. But the leaders argued that this course would cause the AMA to lose the opportunity to counteract support for the Kennedy-Corman plan. "We cannot face the issue by turning our backs to it," AMA President Richard Palmer told the delegates. "If we are to offer nothing in the way of [national health insurance] legislation, we run the terrible risk of getting clobbered with everything. 'Everything' would be the Kennedy-Corman bill, all at once or blow by blow."

Carter's Position on National Health Care

During the presidential campaign last year, Jimmy Carter endorsed key aspects of the Kennedy-Corman plan. He voiced support of a mandatory program that would provide comprehensive benefits. Carter also favored the financing of such a program through payroll taxes and general revenues, although he offered no cost estimates. He said he would like to emphasize preventive care and impose quality and cost controls. Echoing these thoughts, Carter's chief domestic policy adviser, Stuart Eizenstat, told a group of news reporters at a luncheon in Washington, D.C., on Jan. 10 that "cost containment" would be emphasized in the new administration's approach to health care.

Beyond this framework, Carter has offered few specifics. He has not, for example, said what role private insurers would have. Nor has he stated how much of the costs would be financed by payroll taxes and how much by general revenues. And while he has proposed predetermined rates of payment for doctors and

---

[22] Saul Waldman, "A Comparison of the Costs of Major National Health Insurance Proposals," executive summary for HEW, September 1976.

National Health Insurance in Canada

Canada has had a national insurance plan for hospital care since the late 1950s and for medical care since the late 1960s. In 1972 the two plans were combined into one system. This health care insurance is administered by the 10 provincial governments, which are repaid for about half of their costs by the federal government in Ottawa under an involved cost-sharing arrangement. Canadian doctors bill the appropriate government agency, rather than the patient, for their services.

The labor-backed Kennedy-Corman plan appears closer to the Canadian system than any of the other under consideration in the United States. Indeed, the Canadian system has been studied by Kennedy's staff, especially as it operates in Ontario, Canada's most populous and industrialized province.

A member of *The Wall Street Journal's* Toronto bureau, Amanda Bennett, wrote recently that the system is "amazingly hassle-free"—"the long waits and indifferent service that many complain about in England don't exist here." But, she added, "medical costs appear to have risen faster in the years after adoption of national health insurance than before—or than in the U.S. during the same period."*

Since 1972 the federal contribution has risen about 15 per cent annually and Ontario's spending for health insurance has gone up even faster, having doubled in that time. To help it meet the rising costs, the provincial government has had to charge individuals of families an annual premium based on their income.

* *The Wall Street Journal,* Dec. 13, 1976.

hospitals, he has not said whether the federal government or the states should set these rates.

One aspect that Carter has been certain about is that it will be phased in, in stages. "As President, I would want to give our people the most rapid improvement in individual health care the nation can afford, accommodating first those who need it most, with the understanding that it will be a comprehensive program in the end," Carter said last April 16. "...National priorities of need and feasibility should determine the stages of implementation." House Speaker Thomas P. O'Neill Jr. (D Mass.) has said the Carter program might be phased in over a period as long as 12 years. The first stage, O'Neill said, would probably come in the form of catastrophic health insurance.

In deciding to give welfare reform and employment priority over health insurance, Carter has given himself another year in which to define the specifics of his plan. In the meantime, medical costs will no doubt continue to mount, absorbing an increasingly larger share of the nation's resources and putting more pressure on the government to act.

Selected Bibliography

Books

Davis, Karen, *National Health Insurance: Benefits, Costs, and Consequences,* The Brookings Institution, 1975.

Ehrlich, David Alan, ed., *The Health Care Cost Explosion,* Hans Huber Publishers, 1975.

Fuchs, Victor R., *Who Shall Live?,* Basic Books Inc., 1974.

Harris, Richard, *A Sacred Trust,* The New American Library, 1966.

Kennedy, Edward M., *In Critical Condition,* Simon & Schuster, 1972.

Ribicoff, Abraham, *The American Medical Machine,* Saturday Review Press, 1972.

Articles

Edwards, Charles C., "How President Carter Can Get Federal Health Care Planning Off Dead Center," *Modern Medicine,* Jan. 1, 1977.

Frederick, Larry, "How Much Unnecessary Surgery?" *Medical World News,*" May 3, 1976.

Iglehart, John K., "Government Searching for a More Cost-Efficient Way to Pay Hospitals," *National Journal,* Dec. 25, 1976.

Klarman, Herbert E., "The Financing of Health Care," *Daedalus,* winter 1977.

Margolis, Richard J., "National Health Insurance—The Dream Whose Time Has Come?" *The New York Times Magazine,* Jan. 9, 1977.

Mitchell, Bridger M. and William B. Schwartz, "The Financing of National Health Insurance," *Science,* May 14, 1976.

Peters, Charles, "A Revolutionary Answer to Medical Costs," *The Washington Monthly,* October 1976.

Roberts, Marc J. and Ted Bogue, "The American Health Care System: Where Have All the Dollars Gone?" *Harvard Journal on Legislation,* June 1976.

"The Skyrocketing Costs of Health Care," *Business Week,*" May 17, 1976.

Studies and Reports

Congressional Budget Office, "Budget Options for Fiscal Year 1977," March 15, 1976.

Council on Wage and Price Stability, "The Complex Puzzle of Rising Health Care Costs," December 1976.

Department of Health, Education and Welfare, Office of Planning and Evaluation, "A Comparison of the Costs of Major National Health Insurance Proposals," executive summary, September 1976.

Editorial Research Reports, "Malpractice Insurance Crunch," 1975 Vol. II, p. 925; "Medicare and Medicaid After Ten Years," 1975 Vol. II, p. 523; "Health Maintenance Organizations," 1974 Vol. II, p. 603; "Health Care in Britain and America," 1973 Vol. I, p. 439.

Health Insurance Institute, "Source Book of Health Insurance Data 1975-76."

COLLEGE TUITION COSTS

by

William V. Thomas

**Feb. 24
1 9 7 8**

Editor's Note: A U.S. Census Bureau report released in mid-March contradicted the federal government's contention that rising tuition costs are keeping students from middle-income families out of college. The study, "School Enrollment: Social and Economic Characteristics of Students," found that "the trend of declining enrollment among middle-income students had reversed and returned to higher levels." Between 1967 and 1974, it stated the percentage of students from families with incomes in the $10,000-$15,000 range dropped from 51.9 to 41.4. But this pattern reversed in 1975 and the percentage rose in 1976 to 47.5 per cent.

In another development expected to further cloud the tuition relief issue, a recent study by the College Entrance Examination Board found that the more money parents earn, the less they are inclined to contribute to their children's higher education. The board concluded that there are "substantial and significant differences between ability and willingness" to pay college costs. The findings, in the study "The Willingness of Parents to Contribute to Post-Secondary Educational Expenses," were drawn from income information on student applications for federal aid.

COLLEGE TUITION COSTS

THE AMERICAN MIDDLE-CLASS got some bad news last year. The shock came in the form of a study published by the Population Reference Bureau, a private statistical information organization. It calculated that the average family will spend $64,215 to rear a child from birth to age 21. That amount represents an increase of nearly 50 per cent over a 1969 forecast of child-rearing costs, according to economist Thomas J. Espenshade, who wrote the study.[1]

College tuition still is the biggest single expense parents have to meet. Average four-year costs—including room and board—at a state university amount to $10,000; four years at a private college average $25,000. Current college fees are up 4 per cent over the 1976-77 school year. By 1995, when today's babies are old enough to be freshmen, it is estimated that the cost will have risen to $47,330 at a public university and to $82,830 at a private one.[2]

Between 1969 and 1976, according to the Congressional Budget Office,[3] college enrollment of students from families earning $15,000 or more dropped by 5.5 per cent; enrollment of students from families with incomes between $10,000 and $15,000 fell by 6.4 per cent. The decline in middle-class college enrollment, some observers believe, is an indication that a growing number of families cannot afford to support their children's postsecondary education.

This belief has produced what Rep. Al Ullman (D Ore.), chairman of the House Ways and Means Committee, called "one of the hottest political issues" of the current Congress—tuition relief. So far, 87 bills have been introduced in the House and Senate to provide some form of tax credit or tax deduction[4] for families sending children to college. "Tuition

---

[1] Thomas J. Espanshade, "The Value and Cost of Children," Population Reference Bureau, April 1977, p. 25.

[2] Estimates by the Oakland Financial Group, Inc. of Charlottesville, Va., an independent financial consulting organization. Projected costs are based on a yearly inflation rate of 6 per cent.

[3] See "Report on Hearings before the Task Force on Tax Expenditures, Government Organization and Regulation on College Tuition Tax Credits," House Budget Committee, April 28 and May 12, 1977, p. 16.

[4] A tax deduction lowers the income base on which tax is paid; a tax credit lowers the amount of the tax itself.

relief is an idea whose time has come," said Sen. William V. Roth Jr. (R Del.), author of a measure that would allow heads of families a yearly tax credit of up to $500 for each family member attending college full-time. Roth's proposal has passed the Senate three times in the last three years, but each time House leaders have prevented it from reaching the floor for a vote.

Critics of tax-related tuition relief complain that it constitutes an outright subsidy to the middle class. But according to Roth, such support is necessary. "There are millions of families today who are neither affluent enough to afford the high cost of college nor considered poor enough to qualify for the government assistance programs which their taxes make possible," Roth said. "We are rapidly approaching a situation in this country where only the very rich and the very poor will be able to attend college, and I am convinced that action must be taken to ease the financial plight of middle-income families."[5]

Despite broad support in Congress for tax-related tuition relief, the Carter administration has opposed the concept, calling it too expensive. A $500 tax credit, for example, could cost the federal government as much as $5 billion annually in lost revenue. In an effort to head off congressional action, the administration has proposed to increase the education assistance budget for fiscal 1979 by some $1.5 billion and at the same time expand scholarship grants and loans to students from middle-income families. Nevertheless, Congress in this election year appears determined to put its stamp of approval on legislation to reduce taxes for families with children in college. The question is how much the U.S. Treasury can afford to lose for the sake of cutting the cost of higher education and how far any of the proposed measures will go to cover ever-rising college fees.

Debate Over Packwood-Moynihan Bill

The most comprehensive tuition relief plan now before Congress is the Packwood-Moynihan bill, introduced jointly by Sens. Robert Packwood (R Ore.) and Daniel P. Moynihan (D N.Y.). The bill, which has 47 Senate co-sponsors, would provide a tax credit of up to $500 not only for parents with children in college but also for those paying tuition at private elementary or secondary schools. In addition, the bill would authorize comparable payments to lower-income families with children in non-public schools but who have little or no income tax to pay. This provision "guarantees that benefits will be evenly distributed among the various economic classes," said a spokesman for Packwood.

Private education groups generally favor the Packwood-Moynihan proposal. During three days of hearings before the

---

[5] *Congressional Record*, Dec. 15, 1977, p. 19847.

Family Income and College Enrollment
(families with at least one dependent in college)

Per cent of households

Family income	UNDER $5,000	$5,000 To $9,999	$10,000 To $14,999	$15,000 To $19,999	$20,000 To $24,999	ABOVE $25,000
	17.2	26.7	34.1	44.8	46.5	63.7

SOURCE: U.S. Bureau of the Census, 1975 figures.

Senate Finance Committee in January, witnesses argued that a tax credit would promote diversity in education and help both low- and moderate-income families meet the cost of private schooling. It was pointed out that parents who send their children to non-public schools must pay twice for a single education—once through their taxes for public schools and again in tuition for the private ones. John E. Tirell, vice president for governmental affairs of the American Association of Community and Junior Colleges, also voiced support for tuition tax credits, saying that they would open educational opportunities to many students who could not otherwise afford to attend college. A $500 tax credit would pay nearly the entire cost at many two-year colleges and thus attract more students to those institutions.

Some educators believe tax credits will draw students away from public education by making private schools more affordable. But Victor Solomon, director of educational affairs for the Congress of Racial Equality (CORE), told the Senate Finance Committee Jan. 19 that a tax write-off was needed to increase the "educational choices" of poor parents by enabling them to send their children "to better, non-public schools when the public schools have failed them." He added that "perhaps tax credits will even provide a competitive stimulus to the public schools to improve."

One of the most controversial aspects of the Packwood-Moynihan bill is that it would give direct financial aid to parents with children in parochial schools. During the 1976 presidential campaign, candidate Jimmy Carter declared his commitment to finding "a constitutionally acceptable method"[6] of providing such aid. However, because of the administration's strong opposition to tuition tax credits, Sen. Moynihan charged the President with "reneging"[7] on his campaign promise and predicted that Carter's stand will cost Democrats votes in this year's congressional elections. "I have invited the administration to devise other means of assisting parents of parochial school children, if it disagrees with our bill. But nothing of this sort is being done, or, as I understand, is even under consideration," Moynihan said.

Opponents of an education tax break concede that support for the idea is substantial. Nevertheless, they vow to fight it because of what they consider the serious constitutional implications of using the tax system as a vehicle to aid non-public schools. Andrew L. Gunn, president of Americans United for the Separation of Church and State, a group opposed to federal assistance to religious education, said the Packwood-Moynihan bill clearly violates the Constitution's principle of church-state separation. At recent hearings, Gunn told the Senate Finance Committee Jan. 19 that the measure was "an effort to get public funding for parochial schools to teach religion."

In other testimony, Leo Pfeffer, professor of constitutional law at Long Island University in New York, said "as the proposed law relates to tuition at elementary and secondary schools, it is irremediably unconstitutional." But Pfeffer noted that the Supreme Court has made a distinction between federal aid to parochial elementary and secondary schools and aid to colleges which, though church-related, perform essentially secular educational functions *(see box p. 127)*.

Economic Opposition to Tax Credit Plan

Although college costs have risen sharply in the last decade, in many cases the increases have been offset by the upward trend in gross family incomes.[8] From 1967 to 1975, average family earnings rose by 72.9 per cent compared to an increase in

---

[6] In a letter to the Rev. Russell M. Bleich, president of the Chief Administrators of Catholic Education, Oct. 19, 1976.
[7] Quoted in *The Washington Post,* Jan. 20, 1978.
[8] See Congressional Budget Office, "Tax Allowances for Post-Secondary Education Expenses," July 1977, pp. 14-15.

college costs of about 65 per cent. "Because of this growth in family income," the Senate Budget Committee concluded, college costs in 1975 actually made up a "significantly smaller portion of income than in 1967."[9] Student charges at public institutions decreased from 13.4 to 12.7 per cent of median family income, while student charges at private institutions fell from 27.8 per cent of median family income to 26.7 per cent. Increases in college fees also have been met by increases in federal aid to students, which, according to the committee, grew by 281 per cent between 1967 and 1975.

Armed with these statistics, some have expressed doubts about the argument that middle-class families need a special education tax break. Appearing before the House Budget Committee last May, Laurence N. Woodworth, a former Assistant Treasury Secretary, and Mary F. Berry, Assistant Secretary of Health, Education and Welfare, both questioned the advisability of universal tax relief that would extend tuition aid to families that don't need it along with those that do. Woodworth predicted that if the proposed tax credit plan were to take effect

[9] Senate Budget Committee, "The College Tuition Tax Credit: An Analysis and Possible Alternatives," Dec. 19, 1977, p. 9.

there would be immediate consumer pressure to raise it. "When your bill is $4,000," he reasoned, "$500 isn't much."[10] Once a system of credits was adopted, Woodworth added, nothing would prevent colleges from raising their fees, thus eliminating the advantage of a tax adjustment.

Instead of tax credits or deductions, the Carter administration wants to expand access to existing tuition subsidy programs by readjusting family income requirements so as to make more middle-income students eligible to receive educational aid funds. Current federal policy provides financial assistance to students based on family need. Families with annual incomes above $16,000 do not qualify for basic education grants, except in cases where they have more than one child in college.

Carter Program for Student Assistance

Earlier this month, President Carter asked Congress to raise the 1979 student assistance budget from $3.8 billion to a record $5.25 billion. Included in the plan is a $1.5 billion expansion of existing scholarship and loan programs that would make some 60 per cent of the nation's college students eligible for federal aid. Carter said that he intends "to work" for passage of the proposal and would use his veto powers, if necessary, to prevent enactment of a tax credit bill.[11] He added that the country cannot afford both increased student scholarships and loans and a tax reduction.

The Carter plan for student aid contains the following major elements:

1. The basic educational opportunity grant program (BEOG), which provides tuition scholarships to students based on family income and the cost of college attendance, would be increased by $1 billion over the $2.1 billion appropriated in 1978. By the administration's calculations, this would make basic grants available to 3.1 million additional students, raising the total from 2.2 to 5.3 million.

2. College students from families with incomes in the $16,000 to $25,000 range, previously not eligible for the BEOG program, would receive annual grants of $250. Grants for students from families that earn $8,000 to $16,000 would be raised from the present $850 to $1,050, while maximum awards for students whose families earn under $8,000 would increase from $1,600 to $1,800.

3. The college work-study program, which provides 80 per cent of the salary payments for student campus employment, would receive an added $165 million over the current $435 million allotment. That amount, according to the administration, will open part-time work opportunities to as many as 380,000 new

---

[10] Quoted in *The National Observer*, May 5, 1977.
[11] Speaking at a White House press conference, Feb. 8, 1978.

Federal Student Assistance Programs

Basic educational opportunity grants (BEOG) provide tuition aid to needy students. The size of an individual grant—up to $1,600 in 1977—is determined on the basis of family and student contribution. Last year, awards to deserving students averaged $847.

Supplemental educational opportunity grants offer additional aid for exceptionally needy students. In 1977, grants ranged from $200 to $1,500; they averaged $525 per recipient.

Direct student loan program supplies funds to colleges and universities for low-interest, long-term loans to needy students. The average loan last year was $690.

Guaranteed student loan program enables students to borrow up to $2,500 per year from private lending institutions. Loans are guaranteed either by state or federal agencies, and borrowers have up to 10 years to repay them. The average loan in 1977 was $1,245.

Work-study program provides part-time campus employment to students. Last year, nearly 800,000 earned an average of $545.

students from families making over $16,000.

4. The guaranteed student loan program, which assures repayment of low-interest student loans, would get an additional $327 million over the $540 million appropriated in fiscal year 1978. This change, it is anticipated, would support 260,000 new loans to students from families with incomes above $16,000. In fiscal 1978, about 1 million students will receive federally guaranteed loans.

Should Congress go along with these proposals, the White House predicts that the number of awards in federal student assistance programs will more than double from approximately 3.2 million in 1978 to more than 7 million in fiscal 1979. "Because some students receive awards under more than one program," a spokesman for the Department of Health, Education and Welfare said, "we estimate that more than 5 million college students nationwide will receive financial assistance from the federal government in fiscal 1979, an increase of 2 million students over last year."

Rep. Ullman has indicated that he favors the President's package. In the past, Ullman has repeatedly blocked House action on Senate-approved education tax credit bills. The Ways and Means Committee, however, was almost evenly divided on the issue the last time it came up for a vote in 1977. Advocates of the credit have said they hope to line up enough support this year to bring the measure through the committee. Sen. Roth, a leader of this group, labeled Carter's proposal "just an effort to derail" the credit legislation.[12] Spokesmen for organizations seeking "parochiaid" also said they would continue the fight for a tax break. They oppose Carter's plan because it includes no provisions to give financial assistance to parents of children in non-public elementary and secondary schools.

Federal Aid for Higher Education

THOMAS JEFFERSON believed that an educated electorate was the best assurance of the survival of democracy in America. For this reason, Jefferson and other Founding Fathers advocated the establishment of free public schooling. Public school systems were set up in most states in the early part of the 19th century. The movement to promote public colleges and universities did not gain headway until the Civil War period. The Land-Grant College Act of 1862, also known as the Morrill Act, was the federal government's first, and perhaps its most significant, investment in higher education. Under the terms of the act, over 11 million acres of public land were transferred to the states for the endowment of agricultural and mechanical colleges.

The Morrill Act was intended "to promote the liberal and practical education of the industrial classes in the general pursuits and professions of life." But it did not require the institutions that benefited from it to be state-run. Private schools such as Cornell University and the Massachusetts Institute of Technology have received funds under the original legislation and its subsequent amendments. While the Morrill Act originally emphasized agriculture and science, its provisions were flexible enough to allow for expansion into many fields.

In this century, federal support for higher education grew as colleges and universities increasingly came to be viewed as tools for solving national problems. The government subsidized "research, specialized services, and—through student aid—instruction," wrote Earl F. Cheit, dean of the School of Business at the University of California at Berkeley. "But unlike governments in some countries and unlike other supporters of education in this country..., the federal government showed little inclination to control the colleges...its investments helped to fund."[13]

Unlike federal grants to colleges and universities, government aid to students was largely a post-World War II development. During the 1930s, a federally supported student work program

---

[12] Quoted in *The Washington Post*, Feb. 9, 1978.
[13] Earl F. Cheit, "Benefits and Burdens of Federal Financial Assistance to Higher Education," *The College Board Review*, spring 1977, p. 14.

was provided as an emergency relief measure, and during World War II students in disciplines where manpower was scarce received loans to help them complete their training.

Tuition Assistance for U.S. Veterans

The Servicemen's Readjustment Act of 1944, the famous "GI Bill," opened a new era of federal support for higher education. Under the measure, the federal government provided veterans enrolled as full-time students with a monthly living allowance and made direct payments of up to $500 per year to institutions for tuition, fees and other school costs. The educational provisions of the original act have been revised several times to increase the benefits and broaden the types of training covered. One study, completed in the early 1950s, reached the conclusion that 20 to 25 per cent of the World War II veterans who took advantage of the GI Bill would not have attended college without it.[14]

The Korean War (1950-1953) made far less of an impact on college enrollment than World War II did since full-time students in good standing generally were able to get military deferments. Vietnam veterans, like Korean War vets before them, receive a fixed stipend, from which they must pay all their college expenses, including books and tuition. The current basic monthly education benefit paid by the Veterans Administration is $311. However, the rapidly rising cost of higher education in recent years has made it difficult for many Vietnam-era veterans to meet college expenses.[15]

There are wide disparities in tuition charges in different regions of the country. Tuitions generally are lower in the southern and western states than in the eastern and midwestern states. Since all veterans, regardless of where they attend school or how much tuition they must pay, receive the standard education allotment, those in the East and Midwest often find it harder to cover their college expenses. For instance, a veteran choosing to attend Long Beach State College in California, where resident fees are $200 a year,[16] would use only 7 per cent of his $2,799 nine-month education allotment to pay tuition. A veteran at Indiana University, a state-run institution costing residents $722 a year, would spend 25.8 per cent of his benefits on tuition. At Dartmouth, a private college costing $4,230, a veteran would need to supplement his VA payments by $1,431 in order to meet tuition charges alone.

---

[14] Norman Fredricks and W. B. Schraeder, *Adjustment to College: A Study of 10,000 Veteran and Non-Veteran Students in Sixteen American Colleges* (1951), p. 34.

[15] See "Vietnam Veterans: Continuing Readjustment," *E.R.R.*, 1977 Vol. II, pp. 785-804.

[16] Costs for 1976-77, excluding room and board, according to the Life Insurance Marketing and Research Association, an independent actuarial organization.

The education provisions in the G.I. Bill Improvement Act of 1977, passed last November, may help to eliminate some of the problems veterans have faced in the past. It called for:

1. Increasing educational benefits by 6.6 per cent.

2. Increasing the maximum annual amount of VA direct education loans from $1,500 to $2,500.

3. Removing the requirement that a veteran must first be turned down by a private lender before he can apply for a VA loan.

4. Setting up joint federal-state programs to provide special funds to assist veterans in paying off VA loans for tuition at more expensive schools.

The latest VA figures show that some 8.7 million Vietnam-era veterans have taken advantage of GI Bill education benefits—64.7 per cent of those eligible. That compares to a 50.5 per cent participation rate by World War II veterans and 43.4 per cent by Korean War vets.

Government Aid to Colleges Since 1950s

The launching of the Russian satellite Sputnik I in late 1957 provided impetus for a new wave of financial support for higher education. Reacting to charges that America was falling behind the Soviets in scientific know-how, Congress passed the National Defense Education Act of 1958. This law provided scholarships, loans and grants to improve teaching in science and foreign languages. It was followed in 1965 by the Higher Education Act which featured extensive aid for needy students.

As federal assistance to education increased, many educators began to worry that government aid would bring greater federal control over recipient institutions. Earl F. Cheit wrote: "Federal money has always carried with it regulations to assure that program purposes were followed, and that money was legally used. As a basis for regulation, both concepts have been extended to include nondiscrimination and affirmative action. The concept of program purpose has been enlarged to mean that federal financial assistance to one program...subjects any other...to regulation."[17]

Because of the fear of federal control, a few private institutions—Brigham Young University in Utah, Hillside College in Michigan and Wabash College in Indiana—have refused to accept federal aid, including student assistance. Other schools receiving government support have expressed the need to be free of what they consider the excessive federal "red tape" that goes along with it. According to John Gardner, Secretary of Health, Education and Welfare in the Johnson administration, most

---

[17] Earl F. Cheit, *op. cit.,* p. 15.

College Costs—1976-77

Private Colleges	Tuition and Fees	Room and Board	Total
Boston Univ.	$3,640	$1,850	$5,490
Brown	4,322	1,975	6,065
Bryn Mawr	4,190	1,875	5,490
Cornell	4,110	1,900	6,010
Univ. of Chicago	3,510	2,075	5,585
Dartmouth	4,230	2,025	6,255
Duke	3,250	1,420	4,670
Harvard	4,100	2,330	6,430
Notre Dame	3,030	1,260	4,290
Princeton	4,300	1,830	6,130

Public Colleges	Tuition and Fees*	Room and Board	Total
Univ. of California, at Los Angeles	$ 630	$1,500	$2,130
Univ. of Colorado	710	1,500	2,210
Grambling Univ.	414	910	1,324
Univ. of Houston	328	1,260	1,588
Indiana Univ.	722	1,229	1,951
Univ. of Massachu- setts, Amherst	596	1,481	2,077
Michigan State Univ.	838	1,335	2,173
Univ. of Missouri	584	1,220	1,804
Ohio State Univ.	810	1,400	2,210
Purdue	750	1,390	2,140
San Francisco State Univ.	192	1,134	1,326
Texas Tech.	351	1,030	1,381

* Fees higher for non-state residents.

Source: Life Insurance Marketing and Research Association's 1976/1977 list of college costs, latest available figures.

college presidents prefer the "leave it on the stump" method of support—funding with no strings attached.

To increase or maintain enrollment without having to depend on government programs, many schools have adopted tuition deferral arrangements. Yale put such a plan into effect in 1971. First suggested by economist Milton Friedman in 1955, tuition deferral amounts to a long-term student loan. After graduating, the student-borrower has the option of extending loan repayment over a long period of time. At Yale, this method involves the graduate's paying the school four-tenths of one per cent of his or her yearly taxable income for each $1,000 borrowed. The obligation lasts until participants have either repaid their loans, which Yale expects to take about 27 years, or until 35 years have elapsed. Anyone can "buy out" of the plan at any time by paying Yale 150 per cent of the outstanding loan and interest. Although the deferred tuition concept has been praised by many economy-minded educators, some observers have criticized it as a way of masking tuition increases by raising the interest rates on loans.

Past Action on Tuition Relief Proposals

Congress has been debating the issue of college tuition assistance since the early 1950s. Most of the proposed plans have included some form of tax deduction or personal exemption to cover the costs of higher education. While every Congress since 1964 has considered tuition credit bills, none of them has managed to pass both houses. In 1965, lawmakers approved legislation creating the guaranteed student loan program. The measure was aimed at families with moderate incomes and was regarded at the time as an acceptable substitute for tax relief. A recent congressional study concluded: "Given the dual assumption that (1) there were substantial future income benefits to be derived from higher education and (2) that middle-income families suffered not from a deficiency in wealth but from a cash flow problem in paying the costs of higher education, a loan program was enacted as the most effective and least costly means to aid middle-income families."[18]

In 1967, Sen. Abraham Ribicoff (D Conn.) introduced the first Senate-passed tuition relief plan. That measure and subsequent ones like it offered in 1969, 1971 and 1973, went down to defeat in the House of Representatives after passing in the Senate. Senator Roth in 1976 submitted a tax credit proposal that differed from the previous bills in that it sought to award to low-, middle- and high-income families a fixed credit—$500 by 1980—not limited to a percentage of college expenses. Last December, Roth's plan, which has won Senate approval three times, was attached to the Social Security bill until House-Senate conferees voted to drop it when it threatened to hold up passage of that legislation.

New Approaches to Cost-Control

D URING the 1976 presidential campaign Jimmy Carter promised to improve the effectiveness of government by reorganizing the management and budgeting of more than 2,000

---

[18] "The College Tuition Tax Credit," *op. cit.,* p. 6.

federal agencies.[19] As part of his overall effort to restructure the bureaucracy, Carter has asked Congress to approve the establishment of a Cabinet-level Department of Education. At present, most federal education policies are implemented by the Office of Education in the Department of Health, Education and Welfare. In February 1976, Carter wrote that he supported the creation of an Education Department in order to "consolidate grant programs, job training...and other functions currently scattered throughout the government."[20] He reiterated this argument in his January State of the Union address.

Sentiment favoring creation of a Cabinet-level education post has been building in Congress, although not as rapidly or as enthusiastically as the administration might have wished. The Senate Government Operations Committee has scheduled three days of hearings in mid-March on a bill authorizing a Department of Education. Sen. Abraham Ribicoff (D Conn.), who introduced the measure, has predicted swift action in both houses of Congress and probable passage before the end of the year. But pockets of opposition to the bill could delay or even defeat it.

"There are millions of families today who are neither affluent enough to afford the high cost of college nor considered poor enough to qualify for the government assistance programs which their taxes make possible."
Sen. William V. Roth (R Del.)

A number of educators have voiced misgivings about creating a separate department. According to *The Chronicle of Higher Education,* many are particularly concerned that education programs "would be more vulnerable to congressional attack if their appropriations were not part of a larger HEW package."[21] *The New York Times* editorialized that the establishment of an Education Department would "cheapen the Cabinet." "Even if the administration is willing to spend political capital generously," the Times concluded, "the legislative bargaining process is quite likely to erode the scope of a broad new department, leaving it no more than a new label for the old Office of Education."[22]

---

[19] See "Federal Reorganization and Budget Reform," *E.R.R.,* 1977 Vol. II, pp. 661-680.
[20] Jimmy Carter, "If I Am Elected," *Change,* February 1976, p. 11.
[21] *The Chronicle of Higher Education,* Dec. 12, 1977.
[22] *The New York Times,* Jan. 16, 1978.

The federal government spends some $30 billion annually on education programs. About half of them are in HEW; the rest are spread throughout other bureaus and departments. That situation, Education Department proponents maintain, has led to costly rivalry among various agencies and needless work duplication. HEW Secretary Joseph A. Califano Jr. is on record opposing a Cabinet-level education office. Creation of a new agency could eliminate an estimated $15 billion from the HEW budget.[23] In place of a Department of Education, Califano, in a memo to President Carter last November, proposed creating three separately funded sub-agencies within HEW for health, education and welfare (modeled after the operation of the Department of Defense) with a Cabinet Secretary to coordinate their activities.

High Rate of Default on Student Loans

Since passage of The National Defense Education Act nearly 20 years ago, the government has dispensed about $17 billion in educational loans to some 15 million students. The Department of Health, Education and Welfare, which is responsible for overseeing most federal student aid programs, estimates that as many as 14 per cent of the loans have not been repaid. HEW officials say the high rate of default is the result of inefficient collection methods, sloppy bookkeeping and, in some cases, fraud on the part of recipients. In a separate educational loan program conducted by the Veterans Administration, records show that since 1975 ex-GIs have failed to repay 2,267 loans. In December, *The Chronicle of Higher Education* reported that between June and September in 1977 veterans defaulted on 1,005 loans.[24]

Leo Kornfeld, deputy commissioner of education, admitted that HEW bears a large part of the blame for the high rate of default. "The major point, as far as collections [are concerned], is the fact that students, for much longer than a year, even as many as four and five and six years, have not received a letter from the federal government telling them that they owe money," Kornfeld acknowledged on a recent CBS News broadcast.[25] An HEW survey taken last year found 205,000 errors in one master list of 50,000 student loans.

The Office of Education and the Veterans Administration have promised to crack down on defaulters and, they hope, recover close to $1 billion in outstanding debts. HEW Secretary Califano recently announced that his agency's "get-tough"

---

[23] The HEW budget in fiscal 1978 was $162 billion—the highest of any Cabinet department.

[24] See *The Chronicle of Higher Education,* Dec. 12, 1977.

[25] CBS Evening News, Feb. 7, 1978.

policy would include reorganizing computer files, bringing in more workers to handle the job of keeping track of student borrowers and contracting with an outside company to collect overdue payments. Meanwhile, the VA has put GI defaulters on notice that the names of veterans who refuse to pay their debts will be turned over to the Justice Department for prosecution.

If missing borrowers are located, HEW may have some legal difficulty in securing repayment. According to federal bank regulators, many of the original loan applications signed by students did not contain required truth-in-lending information, thus making them invalid. Critics of the federal student loan program argue that the government is responsible for most of the repayment problems. Consumer specialist Jean Carper wrote: "The uncontrolled release of federal funds for private vocational schools, starting in the late 1960s, created an atmosphere of deception and fraud, entrapping many students whom the Office of Education now wants to pay up. OE officials generally did little or nothing to protect students—they depended on self-serving accrediting agencies to approve the schools—and in many cases even collaborated in their entrapment."[26]

Maury Tansey, OE's debt collection chief, has said that students who have a valid defense may be excused from paying their loans. But according to Jean Carper "there is no firm policy [within the Office of Education] about how students can prove" their reasons for not repaying the loans are valid, and "no effort has been made by OE to identify or notify such students who may be paying unnecessarily."

Carter vs. Congress on Education Policy

It seems almost certain that a tuition relief bill will become law before the year is out. What is uncertain is whether relief will take the form of a tax credit allowance, which numerous members of Congress now are demanding, or an increase in existing scholarship and student loan programs, as proposed by President Carter. The ensuing legislative battle could provide a telling indication of the President's influence over Congress and, depending on the kind of measure finally adopted, a prediction of the administration's chances of achieving a balanced budget, as promised, by 1981.

Normally, a President's opposition to a tax reduction measure would be a formidable obstacle to passage, but feeling in Congress seems to be running strongly in favor of challenging the White House on this issue. "The voters are angry about rising education costs, and the pressure reached Capitol Hill

[26] Jean Carper, writing in *The Washington Post*, January 15, 1978.

Alternatives to College

"When the college gates start to close, nothing less is at stake than the future of an open, upwardly mobile, democratic society." This comment from a recent *New York Times* editorial reflects the traditional American faith in the value of a college education. But lately, it appears that a growing number of students—and their parents—are beginning to ask whether the time and money spent earning a college degree could be put to better use.

"However good or bad it might be for the individual students," wrote social critic Caroline Bird, "college is a place where young adults are set apart because they are superfluous people who are of no immediate use to the economy." In her book, *The Case Against College* (1975), Bird theorizes that college is not for everybody and cites estimates by teachers and administrators that only about 25 per cent of a given student body is interested in school. "For the other 75 per cent," she suggested, "college is at best a social center, a youth ghetto, an aging vat...or even a prison." Besides often failing to instill students with higher values, institutions of higher learning, Bird said, ultimately fail to provide most students with a degree that is worth anything in the job market.

Despite a slight improvement in job prospects for graduates, some college students are dropping out of school before graduation to pursue careers not requiring a degree. Others have taken to "stopping-out," leaving school for a period of time to work. Education specialist Gordon F. Sander has speculated that as many as two million college undergraduates—about 20 per cent of the national total—left school in 1976 "to spend some time in the outside world, or to try some other form of education" before returning to finish their degrees.

Educators still contend that college is the best preparation for a wide variety of later career possibilities. Nevertheless, many now encourage stopping-out. Stanford University has even established a stop-out counseling center to advise students on the educational and financial advantages of taking a leave of absence from school. "Our experience with stopping out has been a positive one," said Alean Clark, who works with the Stanford program. "We find that most students who stop out come back with a better perspective on things."

Americans over age 25—many far above—are filling what would otherwise be vacant seats in some college classrooms. Without the older students, enrollments would have sagged badly in recent years. Students 25 and older numbered 1.7 million and accounted for 22 per cent of the campus population in 1970. By 1975, these figures had jumped to 34 per cent and 3.7 million and, according to a Census Bureau estimate, four of every ten collegians may be 25 or older by 1985 if current enrollment rates by age continue at the prevailing pace.

before it reached the White House," said one congressional aide. "The people want the government to do something about two major expenses that have gotten far too high: hospitalization and college tuition."

If hospital care is a practical necessity, a college education is something sacred to most Americans, who regard the attainment of a degree as one way up the social and economic ladder. Speaking in Washington recently, the Rev. Ernest Bartell, director of the Fund for the Improvement of Postsecondary Education, said: "After losing its reputation as a healer of all social ills and faced with financial pressures to sustain enrollments, higher education will probably continue to find its principal entrée to the public purse strings through programs of financial assistance to students and institutions that link [it] to social goals of equality of opportunity. Access to educational opportunities endurses as a principal vehicle, if not for guaranteed career success, at least for removing barriers to social and economic mobility."[27]

Although the job market value of a liberal arts degree recently has been called into question by some educators and economists, few disagree that rising tuition rates threaten to price many aspiring students out of a higher education. "One way or another," said Sen. Roth "the country will have to pay when children stop going to college." What Congress must decide is which of the many proposals now before it offers the best hope for holding down soaring college costs.

[27] Speech to the 64th annual meeting of the Association of American Colleges, Feb. 8, 1978, Washington, D.C.

Books

Bird, Caroline, *The Case Against College,* David McKay, 1975.

Brubacher, John S. and Willis Rudy, *Higher Education in Transition,* Harper & Row, revised edition, 1976.

Eidenberg, Eugene and Roy D. Morey, *An Act of Congress: The Legislative Process and the Making of Education Policy,* Norton, 1969.

Smith, Bardell L., et al., *The Tenure Debate,* Jossey-Bass Publishers, 1973.

Suchar, Elizabeth, et al., *Student Expenses at Postsecondary Institutions, 1977-78,* College Entrance Exam Board, 1977.

_____ *Guide to Financial Aid for Students and Parents,* Simon & Schuster, 1975.

Articles

AAUP (American Association of University Professors) *Bulletin,* selected issues.

Cheit, Earl F., "Benefits and Burdens of Federal Financial Assistance to Higher Education," *The College Board Review,* spring 1977.

Carter, Alan M., "Faculty Needs and Resources in American Higher Education," *Annals of the American Academy of Political and Social Science,* November 1972.

Evans, M. Stanton, "The Tuition War," *National Review,* Jan. 20, 1978.

Gross, Theodore, "How to Kill a College: The Private Papers of a Campus Dean," *Saturday Review,* Feb. 4, 1978.

Gunn, Andrew L., "1978: Year of Crisis for Religious Liberty," *Church & State,* January 1978.

Higher Education Daily, selected issues.

Hoyt, Robert G., "Learning a Lesson from the Catholic Schools," *Saturday Review,* Sept. 12, 1977.

Leary, Mary Ellen, "Caught in the Purse Strings," *The Nation,* Jan. 28, 1978.

"Middle-Class Protest against College Costs," *U.S. News & World Report,* Jan. 30, 1978.

The Chronicle of Higher Education, selected issues.

Reports and Studies

Editorial Research Reports, "Future of Private Colleges," 1976 Vol. I, p. 305; "College Recruiting," 1974 Vol. II, p. 661; "Academic Tenure," 1974 Vol. I, p. 161.

Espenshade, Thomas J., "The Value and Cost of Children," Population Reference Bureau, April 1977.

The Carnegie Council on Policy Studies in Higher Education, "Low or No Tuition," Jossey-Bass Publishers, 1975.

Twentieth Century Fund Task Force on College and University Endowment Policy, "Funds for the Future," McGraw-Hill, 1975.

U.S. Senate, "Description of Bills Relating to Tuition Credits and Deductions Listed for Hearing by the Subcommittee on Taxation and Debt Management of the Committee on Finance," Jan. 17, 1978.

C ASUALTY INSURANCE: TROUBLED INDUSTRY

by

Marc Leepson

**Feb. 11
1 9 7 7**

Editor's Note: After four consecutive years of underwriting losses, the casualty insurance industry rebounded in 1977. According to preliminary figures compiled by A.M. Best Co., casualty insurers experienced underwriting gains of some $1.1 billion in 1977—the first year since 1972 that premium income exceeded claims paid, expenses and dividends. Best estimated that the total premiums written in 1977 amounted to $72.7 billion, up some $12.3 billion from 1976.

CASUALTY INSURANCE: TROUBLED INDUSTRY

A JURY in Brooklyn, N.Y., awarded singer Connie Francis $2.5-million as compensation for being raped in a Howard Johnson's motel room. In Alaska, a jury awarded $2-million to a man who had been shot in the ankle by a defectively designed revolver. In California, a jury awarded $4-million in punitive damages for a company's failure to pay a disputed auto liability insurance claim. A 19-year-old boy in California won $3-million after being paralyzed following a dive off a railroad trestle—a jury found the railroad company liable for not posting a "no diving" sign.

Those cases made headlines in 1976. They reflect a phenomenon that insurance companies call "social inflation," the tendency of judges and juries to make larger monetary awards in civil suits and for a greater number of causes. Social inflation has hit the property-casualty insurers—firms that insure automobiles, homes and businesses against accidental losses—especially hard. It contributed heavily to the companies' underwriting deficit of some $2.6-billion in 1974. The next year's losses totaled $4.2-billion, making 1975 the "worst year in the industry's 225-year history," according to William A. Pollard, president of Reliance Insurance Co.[1] A. M. Best Co., which compiles the industry's statistics, reported that in 1976 casualty insurers sustained underwriting losses of some $2.3-billion.[2] Best said the industry last year paid out nearly $103 in claims and expenses for every $100 it earned in premiums. For the five-year period of 1972-1976, underwriting losses amounted to $8.17-billion (see box, p. 145)

Industry observers cite economic inflation as another basic reason for the loss figures. Automobile insurers were particularly hurt. Best reported that expenses resulting from automobile bodily injuries doubled from 1967 to 1976 and that costs of physical damage to cars tripled. From mid-1973 to mid-1975, prices on grilles, radiators, water pumps, trunk lids, bumpers and other parts most often damaged rose by more than 47 per cent. In the same two-year period, the Consumer Price Index for all items increased by 20.7 per cent and new-car prices by 14 per cent.

[1] Quoted in *Business Week*, Sept. 6, 1976, p. 46.
[2] *Best's Insurance Digest*, Jan. 3, 1977.

Medical care costs were also rising during the period.[3] According to the Department of Health, Education and Welfare, medical care prices rose an unprecedented 12.5 per cent in fiscal 1975 and then 10.2 per cent in fiscal 1976. The highest annual increase prior to 1975 was 6.9 per cent in 1971. Still another reason cited by property-casualty industry observers for its large underwriting losses is the manner in which the industry is regulated. There is general agreement that state regulatory commissions are unwieldy and lack the power to control the industry or its problems.

Finally, the industry itself shares the blame for the losses. Starting in the early 1970s, many companies cut rates by around 15 per cent in an effort to attract more premium income. The idea was to invest heavily in the stock market and to reap greater profits from investments rather than from premiums. But the stock market turned sour and inflation soared. The insurance companies were forced to deplete their cash reserves to pay the growing claims of policyholders. One large automobile insurer, Government Employees Insurance Co. (Geico), came perilously close to financial collapse in 1976. Only a bail-out by the nation's other major property-casualty insurers and a transfusion of cash from stockholders saved the company from insolvency *(see p. 154)*

Problems With Product Liability Coverage

Liability insurance, a form of casualty insurance, protects the insured person against claims resulting from injuries or damage caused by (1) ownership of property, (2) manufacturing or contracting operations, (3) the sale or distribution of products, or (4) the rendering of professional services. Medical malpractice and "no-fault" automobile insurance have come to public attention in recent years but, of all the types of liability insurance, the industry's No. 1 problem currently is product liability. It offers a manufacturer, merchant or distributor protection from financial losses arising out of claims that the product user suffered bodily harm or property damage.

The manufacturers of industrial machinery have been affected the most. But makers of sporting goods, drugs, chemicals, aircraft parts and power lawn mowers also have been sued. As the monetary value of legal judgments against manufacturers climbs, so does the cost of product liability insurance. Some manufacturers are finding it impossible to buy product liability insurance.

The Select Senate Committee on Small Business, in hearings last September, heard manufacturers tell of experiencing large

---

[3] See "Controlling Health Care Costs," *E.R.R.*, 1977 Vol. I, pp. 61-80.

Property-Casualty Insurance Balance Sheet

Year	Premium Income	Total Claims Paid, Expenses, Dividends	Gain or Loss
		(in thousands of dollars)	
1972	38,888,700	37,815,390	1,073,310
1973	42,018,993	42,026,396	−7,403
1974	44,630,964	47,279,916	−2,648,952
1975	49,476,366	53,730,719	−4,254,353
1976*	59,540,000	61,868,950	−2,328,950
Totals	234,555,023	242,721,371	−8,166,348

*Estimated. Final figures are not released until fall 1977

SOURCE: *Best's Insurance News Digest,* Jan. 3, 1977

cost increases or cancellations of their product liability insurance—even though some said no claims had been filed against them. Several said the costs had forced them to drop their coverage and face the danger it entails. The loss of one or more lawsuits might spell insolvency.

The Havir Manufacturing Co. of St. Paul, Minn., a manufacturer of small-punch presses, was hit by a series of lawsuits filed by machinists from all over the country who said they had injured themselves while using Havir's products. The cost of Havir's product liability insurance rose from $2,000 in 1970 to $10,000 in 1975 and then was canceled. When Havir learned that to buy a policy from another insurer would cost $200,000, equal to 10 per cent of annual sales, it decided to go out of business.[4]

A long list of companies with similar problems was presented to the Senate committee. The American Dryer Corp. of Fall River, Mass., said its policy was abrutly canceled in March 1976 although no claims had been filed against the company in eight years. The insurer subsequently agreed to provide the same coverage as before for an annual premium of $12,000—up from $1,000—for $300,000 worth of coverage. The owner of the business decided to operate without insurance.

Manufacturers faced with the higher cost of insurance protection attempt to recoup the added expense by raising their prices. "The cost of liability insurance has become a major part of business-operating expenses," Myron Du Bain, chairman and president of the Fireman's Fund American Companies, has said. "Today it accounts for as much as 10 per cent of the costs of some products."[5]

---

[4] See *The Wall Street Journal,* June 3, 1976.
[5] "Insurance Costs: Burgeoning Headache for Businessmen," *U.S. News & World Report,* July 5, 1976, p. 100.

Two federal government units, the Bureau of Domestic Commerce and a special Interagency Task Force on Product Liability, undertook studies on product liability problems last year. The bureau's staff study found the causes of the problems complex and it listed, but did not recommend, specific remedies. The staff study also called for extensive further study. The special task force has yet to finish its study, but said in a briefing that the probable causes of the product liability insurance industry's troubles were: state rate-making procedures, the tort system, manufacturing problems, inflation, and increased consumer awareness. Bills have been introduced in Congress this year to help small firms obtain coverage at affordable prices. One would authorize the Small Business Administration to provide reinsurance; another would establish a National Product Liability Administration.

Tort System and No-Fault Auto Insurance

One complaint is that the tort system—wherein civil cases are decided—encourages lawyers and plaintiffs to ask for large amounts of money in compensation for damages. A lawyer may—and often does—set his or her fee as a percentage of the client's award, collecting no payment if the case is lost. If the plaintiff wins, the lawyer typically receives from 30 to 50 per cent of the settlement. Some plaintiffs' attorneys are encouraged to push for astronomically high settlements. The overwhelming majority of the nation's courts put no limit on the amount of monetary awards. Trial lawyers respond that it is not they but the insurance companies and the manufacturers who are responsible for high awards.

Louis N. Massery II, a member of the Massachusetts bar, recently offered this argument in *Trial,* the magazine of the Association of Trial Lawyers of America. He said the reasons for the increase in the number and amount of product liability judgments are: (1) the insurance industry's inability to "collect essential rate-making data," (2) "defective products" of the manufacturers, (3) "consumerism" and (4) economic inflation.[6]

The tort system remains under attack and, in the case of "no-fault" automobile insurance,[7] has been modified in some states. Massachusetts led the way when, under a law that became effective Jan. 1, 1971, it abandoned the time-honored "adversary system" of determining who was at fault in automobile accidents and making the guilty party's insurer pay damages. *State Legislatures* magazine reported last year that 16 states[8]

[6] Louis N. Massery II, *Trial,* May 1976, p. 31.
[7] See "Auto Insurance Reform," *E.R.R.,* 1971 Vol. I, pp. 25-44.
[8] Colorado, Connecticut, Florida, Georgia, Hawaii, Kentucky, Kansas, Massachusetts, Michigan, Minnesota, Nevada, New Jersey, New York, North Dakota, Pennsylvania and Utah.

Liability Insurance and Swine Flu Vaccine

An example of the wide effect of the problems of liability insurance came in the summer of 1976 when insurance companies balked at providing coverage to the manufacturers of the swine-flu vaccine. Insurers' fears of lawsuits arising from possible harmful side effects of the vaccine resulted in weeks of wrangling among insurers, manufacturers, legislators and federal health officials. Finally, on Aug. 10, Congress approved a bill freeing the four vaccine makers—Parke, Davis and Co.; Merck, Sharpe & Dohme Co.; Wyeth Laboratories; and Merrell-National Co.—from liability in any malpractice suits. The legislation provided that all claims must be filed against the federal government.

Thus far, the insurance companies' fears of large suits appear to be justified. The federal swine-flu program was halted Dec. 16 followed repeated incidences of a paralysis known as Guillain-Barre syndrome among those recently inoculated. In spite of the curtailment, 61 claims for damages in connection with swine-flu vaccinations, including three suits involving deaths, are pending against the Justice Department. The suits ask for a total of $19-million.

had enacted no-fault laws, enabling insured motorists to collect on personal injury claims that did not exceed specified limits without establishing who was at fault. The limits—called "thresholds" in the industry—range from $200 to $2,000, depending on the state. Larger claims may still be subject to litigation.

Congress has debated instituting a national system of no-fault automobile insurance since 1970, but has yet to enact legislation. The latest congressional attempt to pass a no-fault bill was voted down 49-45 in the Senate on March 31, 1976. Allied in opposition to the measure were the American Trial Lawyers Association, the Ford administration and several major insurance companies including Allstate, the nation's second largest. The AFL-CIO, some other unions, consumer groups and some insurance companies including State Farm Mutual, the nation's largest, lobbied for the federal no-fault bill.

State Legislatures reported that while its survey of the no-fault states found "most of them very satisfied with the system," there were some flaws.[9] One complaint was that although small claims were being settled out of court, several of the no-fault states experienced no reduction in the number of cases involving large claims. And insurance rates had continued to rise in most states—although some fell initially—despite expectations to the contrary. Lower rates were a major aim of

[9] "A Look at the No-Fault States," *State Legislatures*, March-April 1976. The magazine is a publication of the National Conference of State Legislatures, Denver, Colo.

no-fault laws. But in regard to another major aim—faster payment to the accident victim—most of the no-fault states reported they were well pleased.

Automobile insurance is the No. 1 source of liability claims, far outstripping any other branch of liability insurance. The number and amount of claims has risen rapidly after a brief respite during the 1973-74 energy crisis. The cost of automobile repairs and medical and hospital care resulting from auto accidents was $36-billion in 1975, an 18.6 per cent increase from the year before.[10] As claims go up, premium rates follow. Conning & Co., a Connecticut insurance research firm, estimated that auto insurance rates nationwide increased 20 per cent in 1976, compared with a 15 per cent rise in 1975. The firm predicted an increase of from 8 to 10 per cent for 1977.[11]

State and Federal Regulation

THE BASIC idea of insurance—spreading predictable losses over an entire group whose members are exposed to risk—existed in ancient Phoenicia, Babylon, Greece and Rome. But the origins of modern insurance date from the 14th and 15th centuries when traders and shippers in Mediterranean port cities devised ways of routinely insuring their expensive cargoes and ships. As marine insurance spread throughout the maritime cities and states of Europe, the first insurance codes and regulatory procedures developed.[12]

In the United States, insurance companies began to do business in the first decades of the 18th century. But it was not until after the Revolutionary War that governmental regulation of insurance started. The first American insurance regulation came in the form of special charters granted by state legislatures to insurance companies. These charters generally contained regulatory provisions. The states depended solely on the insurance companies' honesty in reporting their financial worth and investment decisions. No state officials entered the picture until 1858 when Massachusetts named Elizur Wright and George W. Sargent as its insurance commissioners, marking the "beginning of modern supervision" of insurance.[13]

---

[10] As reported in the Insurance Information Institute's *Insurance Facts*, 1976 edition, p. 50.

[11] *The Wall Street Journal*, Aug. 31, 1976.

[12] For background on the early development of insurance, see *Insurance: Its Theory and Practice* (1969), pp. 522-537, by Albert J. Mowbray, et al.

[13] *Ibid.*, p. 525.

After a number of states set up insurance departments in the 1860s, the National Convention of Insurance Commissioners was formed in 1871 to secure cooperation among the state regulators. That group, now called the National Association of Insurance Commissioners (NAIC), continues to meet regularly to discuss mutual concerns such as disparities among the state insurance laws.

The nation's insurance industry, today comprising 4,700 companies selling some $110-billion worth of insurance a year, has continued to be regulated solely by the states.[14] This has led a critic, Philip M. Stern, to say that insurance is the only industry "of its size and national character that is wholly free of federal control."[15]

In an industry as complex and diverse as this one, there are conflicting views on the appropriateness of state regulation. Some large companies that have customers throughout the country complain of the difficulty in dealing with 51 different sets of laws and rules, those of the 50 states and the District of Columbia. Though most insurance executives stop short of calling for federal control, many of the industry's critics are not so reticent. They say that state regulatory agencies tend to be too weak and ineffective to protect the public interest and that only federal control will suffice.

Question of Federal Versus State Control

The question of federal-vs.-state regulation of insurance has been debated in the industry, in courtrooms and in Congress for more than a century. In 1865 a group of insurance companies lobbied Congress for a federal regulatory law, but Congress did not act.[16] The Supreme Court ruled in *Paul v. Virginia* in 1869 that insurance was not interstate commerce and therefore subject only to state regulation. Between 1870 and 1901 the court turned down at least seven suits by fire insurance companies and others that were aimed at obtaining federal regulation. The states' power to regulate insurance was strengthened further by a 1913 Supreme Court decision in *New York Life Insurance Co. v. Deer Lodge County*. The court held that the way in which an insurance company conducted its business and the issuance of an insurance policy were not transactions of commerce. The *Paul* decision of 1869 was thereby upheld.

---

[14] There is a Federal Insurance Administration which deals with federally assisted insurance programs for crimes, floods and riots—disasters that private insurance does not cover. The agency, a unit of the Department of Housing and Urban Development, does not have regulatory powers.

[15] Philip M. Stern, writing in *The Washington Post*, Aug. 24, 1975. Stern is a philanthropist, tax expert and the author of several books, including *The Great Treasury Raid* and *The Rape of the Taxpayer*.

[16] See Spencer L. Kimball and Herbert S. Denenberg, eds., *Insurance, Government, and Social Policy* (1969), p. 367.

But in 1944 the Supreme Court reversed itself, ruling in *U.S. v. Southeastern Underwriters Association* that restrictive agreements between insurance companies were in violation of the Sherman Antitrust Act. The court said that states could regulate aspects of the insurance business related to local welfare, but the significant portion of the decision held that the federal government had the right to be the nationwide regulator.

After that decision, the insurance companies stepped up pressure on Congress to exempt their industry from antitrust legislation.[17] With President Roosevelt lending his support, Congress in 1945 passed the McCarran-Ferguson Act, which specifically exempted the insurance business from the antitrust laws for three years. The law further provided that after 1948 the insurance industry would be subject to federal antitrust laws only to the extent that it was not regulated by state law. Since every state regulates insurance, the exemption has remained in force ever since.

Since its enactment, the act has been repeatedly challenged. Efforts to change the law continue to the present time *(see p. 152)*. The Senate Judiciary Antitrust Subcommittee and the Federal Trade Commission studied the problem of state-vs.-federal regulation in the 1950s and 1960s. Other congressional committees have been looking into various aspects of the insurance industry since then.

Criticism of State Regulatory Commissions

The economic difficulties of the 1970s have led to increasing criticism of the effects of government regulation on both businesses and consumers. And the states' regulation of the insurance industry has not been immune from the critical comment. One of the regulators' most vocal critics is Herbert Denenberg, who was Pennsylvania insurance commissioner from 1971 to 1974. Denenberg is among those who have said that state regulatory agencies generally are weak and cannot control powerful insurance companies.

One reason often cited is that the average salary of a state insurance commissioner tends to be much less than that of a company executive. Philip M. Stern said: "Any regulator of talent working constantly with higher-paid counterparts in the [insurance] industry, is constantly aware that he could instantly improve his lot by moving to the other side of the table." There is little incentive for insurance experts to stay with the low-paying state insurance commissions. Indeed, the average tenure of state insurance commissioners is around two years.[18] When

---

[17] See Congressional Quarterly's *Congress and the Nation*, Vol. I, p. 454.

[18] According to an unidentified industry source quoted in *The Wall Street Journal*, Aug. 2, 1973.

Property-Liability Insurance Companies
by State, 1976

State	Home Offices	State	Home Offices
Alabama	23	Missouri	69
Alaska	4	Montana	3
Arizona	18	Nebraska	74
Arkansas	13	Nevada	1
California	97	New Hampshire	25
Colorado	26	New Jersey	35
Connecticut	30	New Mexico	7
Delaware	26	New York	213
District of Columbia	12	North Carolina	50
Florida	25	North Dakota	40
Georgia	44	Ohio	143
Hawaii	9	Oklahoma	31
Idaho	11	Oregon	10
Illinois	291	Pennsylvania	205
Indiana	115	Rhode Island	12
Iowa	185	South Carolina	29
Kansas	34	South Dakota	59
Kentucky	36	Tennessee	40
Louisiana	8	Texas	178
Maine	30	Utah	5
Maryland	25	Vermont	14
Massachusetts	48	Virginia	46
Michigan	56	Washington	20
Minnesota	179	West Virginia	20
Mississippi	7	Wisconsin	202
		Wyoming	3

SOURCE: Insurance Information Institute, New York City

they leave the state jobs, many state commissioners move to high-salaried positions in the insurance industry.

The closeness of regulated and regulator is described by Denenberg this way: "It's one big family, with smiling and friendly lobbyists...and attorneys all holding hands and seeing eye-to-eye."[19] Denenberg was referring to the California insurance commission; similar descriptions have been applied to others. A former Washington State insurance commissioner, Karl Herman, has said, "How can you really be objective when you are wined and dined and paid by the people you are supposed to be regulating?"[20]

---

[19] Quoted by Howard S. Shapiro in *How to Keep Them Honest* (1974), p. 151.
[20] Quoted in *The Wall Street Journal*, Aug. 2, 1973.

One problem is the wide variation among the state regulators' capacity to regulate. New York's State Department of Insurance, for example, is considered one of the nation's most powerful. Its operating budget for fiscal 1976 was some $13-million and it had more than 600 employees. The District of Columbia's insurance department consists of 25 employees with a budget of about $500,000 a year. It does not have a full-time attorney on its staff. Even the best state insurance departments have been hard-pressed to keep up with computer-age complexities. Just keeping tract of statistical data has proven impossible for some understaffed insurance departments. They are forced to use unaudited annual statements prepared by the insurance companies as the basis for regulatory decisions. As the states have felt the pinch of deficit spending, the trend has been to reduce regulatory budgets even more.

Quite often the commissions are further handicapped by state laws that restrict the scope of their authority. Denenberg has said that state insurance laws "have been written by and for the insurance industry and have been administered by and for the insurance industry."[21] So-called "competitive-pricing" laws, in effect in 19 states,[22] are foremost among the critics' examples of restrictive laws.

Competitive-pricing laws were enacted in the late 1960s and early 1970s to allow insurance companies, in effect, to set rates without state approval. The rationale is that the insurers will keep prices low in order to try to win customers. Insurance commissions in some states are not required to hold hearings on rate increases or to notify customers that insurers have asked for or received permission to raise rates. In Virginia, the state insurance commission has not held hearings on insurance rates or on the effect of the state's competitive-pricing law since the law went into effect four years ago. After reading Virginia's competitive-pricing law, Denenberg told *The Washington Star:* "[T]here is really no rate regulation in Virginia.... As far as I'm concerned, it's a fantastic con job."[23]

Recent Proposals for Federal Supervision

Last year saw another revival in interest in furthering the federal government's role in insurance regulation. Sen. Edward W. Brooke (R Mass.) introduced a bill to give property-casualty insurers the option of escaping state rate regulation in exchange for federal controls on incorporation and insolvency. Brooke has announced that the bill, which died with the 94th

---

[21] Writing in *The Wall Street Journal,* Aug. 2, 1973.

[22] Alabama, California, Colorado, Florida, Georgia, Idaho, Illinois, Indiana, Louisiana, Minnesota, Missouri, Montana, Nevada, New Mexico, New York, Oregon, Utah, Virginia and Wisconsin.

[23] *The Washington Star,* Jan. 11, 1977.

Congress, will be reintroduced during the current session and that hearings will be held on the measure.

In addition, the Justice Department recommended in the last days of the Ford administration that the insurance industry's exemption from antitrust laws be rescinded. The Justice Department's Task Group on Antitrust Immunities, established two years ago by President Ford, recommended enactment of a plan similar to the one proposed by Brooke. That plan entails a dual system of insurance regulation, giving insurance companies the option of remaining under state regulation or accepting a federal charter. Insurers who took the latter action would be exempt from state regulation but would lose their antitrust immunity. The Justice Department plan also would give the existing Federal Insurance Administration *(see footnote 14)* the added job of detecting and dealing with financially troubled insurance companies. A federal guaranty fund would be set up to protect policyholders in the event their company went broke.

Reaction to the proposals has been mixed, but in general the insurers favor retaining state regulation. However, the College of Insurance, an industry-supported institution that grants degrees in business administration and actuarial science, supports proposals advocating federal regulation instead. A report by the college's Research Institute said that federal regulation would provide a "golden opportunity" for the property-casualty industry to free itself of the "unreasonable burdens of state regulation."

On the other hand, the Independent Insurance Agents of America (IIAA), a trade association of independent insurance agents, objects strongly to federal regulation. The group maintains that the present system is best for the public, the insurance agents and the industry as a whole, and that the movement by the federal government into the field would solve no problems. The IIAA Executive Committee said that federal regulation "would, at best, merely add another complicated and excessive layer of regulation on that already ably provided by the several state insurance departments."[24]

There is little likelihood that the Justice Department recommendations will be adopted in the immediate future. For one thing, the task force that studied the problem and made recommendations was set up by the outgoing administration. In addition, President Carter has indicated his support of state regulation.[25] The prospects that Brooke's bill will be enacted

---

[24] College of Insurance Research Institute report and IIAA Executive Committee statement were quoted in the *Journal of Commerce,* Dec. 2, 1976.

[25] Carter and the other presidential candidates were presented a list of questions by the Kemper Insurance Group last spring. When asked if he supported state regulation, Carter's response was: "I am in favor of the continued regulation of the insurance industry at the state level."

into law are not good, a writer said in *The Journal of Insurance,* because "the insurance industry will probably oppose the plan...."[26]

Changes in Management Practices

THIS YEAR the property-casualty insurers continue to face most of the problems that contributed to the industry's underwriting losses during the last four years. Although economic inflation has ebbed somewhat—the Consumer Price Index in 1976 recorded the slowest growth in four years (4.8 per cent)—social inflation showed no sign of abating. The crisis in product-liability insurance continued throughout 1976. Both the Commerce Department and the U.S. Senate began investigating the problem. State regulatory commissions continued to come under criticism for weaknesses in dealing with the problem, and the tort system was criticized by insurance companies as adding to the problem.

But part of the problem, as exemplified by the near-collapse of Government Employees Insurance Co. (Geico),[27] was the management of the insurance companies themselves. No other major insurance company was pushed so close to insolvency, but many of them made critical investment mistakes in the early 1970s that resulted in huge financial losses. In an effort to get more capital by attracting more customers, many insurers lowered rates by around 15 per cent. *Business Week* commented editorially early last year that the casualty insurers "have watched the stock quotes instead of the actuarial tables, and in the scramble to raise cash for investment, they have priced insurance the way a chain store prices a loss leader."[28] When the stock market dropped and the number of bad risks increased with the influx of new customers, underwriting losses climbed.

Case of Insurer's Flirtation With Insolvency

Geico, the nation's fifth largest insurer of automobiles, reported that its losses for 1975 amounted to $126.4-million and that most of these were incurred in the fourth quarter. Further losses of $26.4-million followed in the first quarter of 1976. Those figures represented the first monetary setback for Geico since its founding four decades earlier. Most observers

---

[26] Gene Kacson, "Carter's Congress," *The Journal of Insurance,* January-February 1977, p. 8.

[27] Despite its name and its location in Washington, D.C., Geico is not connected with the federal government or with any organization of government employees.

[28] *Business Week,* Jan. 26, 1976. A "loss leader" is an item sold at no profit to entice shoppers into the store.

Casualty and Liability Insurance Premium Income,* 1973-75

Type of Insurance	1973	1974	1975**
	(add 000,000)		
Auto Liability, Pvt. Passenger	$ 8,513	$ 8,666	$ 9,600
Auto Liability, Commercial	2,242	2,270	2,500
Total Auto Liability	$10,756	$10,936	$12,100
Auto Physical Damage, Pvt. Passenger	5,341	5,324	5,700
Auto Physical Damage, Commercial	1,077	1,136	1,200
Total Auto, Physical Damage	$ 6,418	$ 6,460	$ 6,900
Total, All Automobile	$17,175	$17,397	$19,000
Medical Malpractice	N.A.	N.A.	700
Other Liability	N.A.	N.A.	3,000
Total Liability (other than auto)	$ 2,701	$ 2,935	$ 3,700
Fire Insurance and Allied Lines	3,417	3,455	3,500
Homeowners Multiple Peril	3,630	3,991	4,500
Farmowners Multiple Peril	182	223	270
Commercial Multiple Peril	2,508	2,846	3,200
Workers' Compensation	4,761	5,413	6,100
Inland Marine	1,057	1,127	1,250
Ocean Marine	650	760	800
Surety and Fidelity	700	747	780
Burglary and Theft	129	128	120
Crop-Hail	192	259	312
Boiler and Machinery	136	140	155
Glass	36	33	31
Credit	84	69	50
Aircraft	160	163	175

*Stated by the insurance industry as "net premiums written"
**Estimates
SOURCE: Insurance Information Institute, New York City

attributed the financial problems to the company's miscalculation of claims and settlements. Rates were set too low and business was expanded too rapidly, most insurance analysts said. What happened to Geico is illustrative of many of the significant trends in the property-casualty business today, even though the case has some unique factors.

Geico was formed in 1936 by Leo Goodwin Sr., a Texas accountant who developed a novel method of selling insurance. He sold directly by mail—eliminating the agent and the agent's commission—to people who qualified as preferred risks. Goodwin was thus able to sell insurance premiums at rates 20 to

30 per cent lower than those of conventional insurers. In 1948, Goodwin, who owned 25 per cent of Geico, and Fort Worth banker Cleaves Rhea, who provided the capital for the firm, moved Geico from Texas to Washington, D.C. In the nation's capital they concentrated on winning a large market of preferred risk customers, employees of the federal government.

Geico went public that same year. Many of its stockholders were its policyholders. They bought into the company basically because Geico offered lower rates than most other auto insurers and the company was noted for its attentive, fast and competent customer service. It was also a model of good management, pioneering quality-control techniques ordinarily associated with manufacturing industries.[29] The company reported in 1962 that it had achieved a 53 per cent improvement in the quality of outgoing policies and other documents. This was an important achievement, because faulty insurance documents, unlike defective machinery, cannot be scrapped; they must be redrawn.

Geico's success peaked in November 1972 when its stock hit an all-time high of $61 per share in over-the-counter trading.[30] Geico began to add customers other than government employees to its rolls, and some observers say that is where its troubles started. The expansion of its policyholder base led from federal, state and municipal workers to professional, managerial, technical and administrative personnel in non-governmental activities.

Then, in 1973, Geico dropped all age and occupation restrictions and began a further expansion program. By the end of 1975, Geico had enrolled 2.8 million people nationwide. As the number of policyholders increased, so did inflation. It pushed the size of claims upward and the company was forced to draw on its capital and surplus—two elements that are a crucial measurement of an insurer's solvency. Reserves slipped to $25.9-million in April 1976. A year earlier the figure stood at $153.9-million.

Industry's Joint Effort in Bailing out Geico

As the situation worsened in 1976, Geico's problem was put in the hands of Maximilian Wallach, District of Columbia insurance superintendent. Wallach devised a plan whereby the casualty insurance industry assumed a large part of Geico's outstanding liability claims. Geico, which had long been regarded with hostility by its rivals because of its discount pricing, thus became dependent on their aid.

---

[29] See "Quality Control in Industry," *E.R.R.*, 1963 Vol. I, pp. 227-246.

[30] Geico stock has been traded in the first weeks of 1977 at around $6 per share.

Twenty-eight companies assumed the liability for losses of nearly one-fourth of Geico's outstanding policies under an agreement put into effect Dec. 2, 1976. Geico's problem thus touched the entire property-casualty insurance industry. In addition, a large portion of Geico's stockholders purchased 8.25 million preferred shares of Geico stock. These new investments in the company totaled $62-million and led Wallach on Dec. 2, 1976, to declare Geico a "financially untroubled company."[31]

The insurance companies went to Geico's aid for several reasons. They obviously believed that the bankruptcy of a firm as big as Geico would hurt public confidence in the entire industry. A more compelling reason, perhaps, is that they wanted to avoid having to pick up the full amount of Geico's claims losses. In addition, *The Wall Street Journal* observed that some insurance-industry watchers believed that a Geico collapse could have had a "domino effect"—"failures by other companies unable to meet increased assessments."[32]

Attempts to Cut Losses; Assigned-Risk Plans

To cut underwriting losses, property-casualty insurers have been raising premiums and dropping high-risk policyholders. The problem is especially apparent in automobile insurance where increasing numbers of drivers have found that no company will insure them. When someone is denied auto insurance, there is an alternative—so-called "assigned-risk" insurance pools. These are state-regulated systems, in which the automobile insurers split the burden of providing insurance to high-risk motorists. The degree of each insurance company's participation in assigned-risk pools is based on its share of the market. Assigned-risk rates generally are 25 per cent higher than traditional insurance but still do not offset the losses that are incurred. The reason is that assigned-risk drivers tend to be involved in more accidents and file more claims than others.

There are several different assigned-risk systems in effect in the states. Maryland has a unique, state-administered plan, called the Automobile Insurance Fund, which was created on Jan. 1, 1973. The Maryland plan's purpose is the same as the other assigned-risk plans: to provide insurance for motorists unable to buy it elsewhere. But the Maryland program differs in that the state administers the plan, with the insurance companies subsidizing any losses. For the first three years of the Maryland program underwriting losses were $34.5-million.

Some other state provide assigned-risk reinsurance programs in which companies are not permitted to turn down prospective

---

[31] Quoted in *The Washington Post*, Dec. 3, 1976.
[32] *The Wall Street Journal*, June 21, 1976.

policyholders. The insurers are allowed, though, to assign a portion of their high-risk drivers to a reinsurance pool that is shared with other insurers. Four states, Florida, Missouri, New Jersey and Hawaii, have a third kind of assigned-risk system, the joint underwriting pool, in which a group of insurers acts as service agents for high-risk drivers. A statewide pool of all insurers assumes the financial responsibility.

There are similar assigned-risk plans for home and property owners in high-risk areas who are unable to buy insurance in the usual way. Fair Access to Insurance Requirements (Fair) plans came into being in 1968 after riots in several of the nation's inner cities discouraged insurance companies from writing policies in those areas. Fair plans are in operation in 26 states, the District of Columbia and Puerto Rico. Like auto assigned-risk plans, Fair programs are operated under cooperative government-insurance company agreements and have been money losers. Other special pooling plans have been set up in 33 states for joint underwriting associations for medical malpractice insurance and workmen's compensation.

In the event an insurance company becomes insolvent, guaranty fund laws take effect in 45 states and the District of Columbia.[33] Under these plans, all insurance companies doing business in the state must pay specified amounts into a fund that guarantees the liabilities of any insolvent company for a fixed period of time. In most states it is 30 days. During that time, each policyholder of the defunct company is instructed to renew his or her insurance with a solvent company. The guaranty fund investigates, defends, settles and pays all claims that would have been handled by the insolvent company. In order to provide operating money for the guaranty funds, all property-casualty insurers are assessed a percentage of their premium volume.

Trends Toward the Return to Profitability

Despite its various problems, the property-casualty insurance industry made something of a comeback in 1976. Underwriting losses were cut almost to half of the previous year's level. This was due primarily to the easing of inflation and the raising of premiums. In addition, state legislatures and courts nationwide took up the question of limiting insurance liability judgments. Industry observers say that state insurance commissioners generally granted insurers' requests for higher rates in 1976.

Life insurance companies were not as severely affected by economic and social inflation as were the property-casualty in-

---

[33] Alabama, Arkansas and Oklahoma have no guaranty fund laws. Arizona's law has been declared unconstitutional. New York has another type of guaranty plan called pre-assessment funding.

surers. Although investments by the life insurers have not been totally successful, business in general has not suffered. According to *The Wall Street Journal,*[34] one problem for the nation's life insurance companies was excess cash on hand in 1976. It is estimated that the major life insurance companies had some $5-billion to invest at year's end. The excess funds were due primarily to the drop in housing construction. Mortgages and private loans usually represent a large share of life insurance company investment.

What *Forbes* magazine[35] termed a "major trend" in the insurance industry is the movement by the large mutual life insurance companies into the property-casualty field. Prudential Insurance, the largest life insurer in the United States, began selling property-casualty insurance for the first time in 1971. By the end of 1975, Prudential ranked 38th in the field. Two other big life insurance companies, Metropolitan Life and Equitable Life Assurance, also have joined the property-casualty field.

Another development of the last few years has been the selling of many new types of insurance by the property-casualty insurers. Many businesses hold policies that insure computerized records and accounts against power blackouts and computer accidents. Businesses also have begun taking policies against bombings, riots and ransom for kidnaped executives. Special types of insurance have been developed covering environmental suits, including damages from nuclear exposure.

A number of other measures designed to save money are being taken by the insurance industry. Many insurers are urging policyholders to increase deductibles. By increasing the amount the insured must pay before a claim against the insurance company can be made, the companies hope to reduce both the number of claims and the monetary amounts paid out. A side benefit is that policyholders' premiums are lowered.

The most important overall trend in the property-casualty business is the deliberate cutting back of coverage. The insurance industry, it is said, is moving back "toward the original insurance principle—the idea that every policyholder should pay for ordinary losses himself, with his insurance covering only the big risks that could destroy him."[36] The long period of ever-broadening insurance coverage peaked in the early 1970s. If underwriting losses are cut significantly in 1977, stricter limiting of coverage could become the property-casualty industry's guiding principle for years ahead.

---

[34] Nov. 29, 1976.
[35] Sept. 1, 1976, p. 69.
[36] Quoted in *Business Week,* Sept. 6, 1976, p. 50.

Selected Bibliography

Books

Denenberg, Herbert S., et al., *Risk and Insurance,* 2nd ed., Prentice-Hall, 1974.

Kimball, Spencer L., and Herbert S. Denenberg, eds., *Insurance, Government, and Social Policy,* Irwin-Dorsey, 1969.

Mowbray, Albert J., et al., *Insurance: Its Theory and Practice,* McGraw-Hill, 1969.

Articles

Adams, John F., "Consumer Attitudes, Judicial Decisions, Government Regulation and the Insurance Market," *The Journal of Risk and Insurance,* September 1976.

"Assigned Risks Vex the Auto Insurers," *Business Week,* May 31, 1976.

"Auto Industry on a Collision Course," *State Legislatures,* March-April 1976.

Bernstein, George K., "Reconsideration of Public Law 15: The Implications," *Best's Review,* April 1976.

"Insurance Costs: Burgeoning Headache for Businessmen," *U.S. News & World Report,* July 5, 1976.

Journal of American Insurance, selected issues.

Journal of Insurance, selected issues.

Loomis, Carol J., "An Accident Report on Geico," *Fortune,* June 1976.

Massery, Louis N. II, "The Regulated Cry Wolf About Insurance Rates," *Trial Magazine,* May 1976.

Perham, John C., "The Dilemma in Product Liability," *Dun's Review,* January 1977.

"Red Ink Floods the Casualty Market," *Business Week,* Jan. 26, 1976.

"Sue! Sue! Sue!" *Forbes,* Sept. 1, 1975.

"The Overload on the Nation's Insurance System," *Business Week,* Sept. 6, 1976.

"Who Is Raping Whom," *Forbes,* Sept. 1, 1976.

Reports and Studies

Editorial Research Reports, "Controlling Health Costs," 1977 Vol. I, p. 61; "Malpractice Insurance Crunch," 1975 Vol. II, p. 925; "Auto Insurance Reform," 1971 Vol. I, p. 21.

Interagency Task Force on Product Liability, "Briefing Report," Jan. 1, 1977.

Senate Select Committee on Small Business, "Impact on Product Liability," Sept. 8 and 10, 1976.

U.S. Department of Commerce, Bureau of Domestic Commerce, "Product Liability Insurance: Assessment of Related Problems and Issues," March 1976.

G ENETIC RESEARCH

by

Sandra Stencel

Mar. 25
1 9 7 7

Editor's Note: The guidelines for recombinant DNA research that are discussed on pages 168-170 are being revised by the National Institutes of Health.

GENETIC RESEARCH

M ANY AMERICANS have never heard of recombinant DNA —a gene-splicing technique which enables scientists to combine the genetic material DNA (deoxyribonucleic acid) of different species and create new or drastically altered forms of life. Yet experiments in this relatively new area of genetics could have as great an impact on our lives as the splitting of the atom. "The discovery of recombinant DNA is one of the more striking technological achievements of our century," declared biochemist Liebe F. Cavalieri of the Sloan-Kettering Institute for Cancer Research.[1]

Like atomic energy, recombinant DNA research has the potential for great benefits and grave perils. Some scientists fear that these experiments could create dangerous life forms which, if they escaped from the laboratory, might unleash uncontrollable diseases or alter the course of evolution. Others say the risks are minimal and they claim that this research could revolutionize agriculture, greatly simplify control of pollution and lead to cures for diseases like cancer. Caught in the middle is the citizen who does not know which side to believe.

Adding to the public's confusion is the fact that the concerns over recombinant genetic engineering were raised initially by the very scientists doing the work. The issue came to public attention in July 1974 after a group of prominent scientists proposed a voluntary moratorium on certain gene-splicing experiments until the potential risks could be studied and proper safety measures could be worked out. The moratorium was lifted the following February after a group of scientists met at Asilomar, Calif., and adopted strict guidelines for all future research. The Asilomar guidelines were replaced by a stricter and more detailed set issued in June 1976 by the National Institutes of Health.

The guidelines have not ended the controversy over recombinant DNA. Not all scientists are satisfied that the guidelines provide adequate safeguards against potential hazards. Furthermore, the guidelines apply only to research funded by the National Institutes of Health and other federal agencies. Concern over the adequacy of the guidelines has prompted

---

[1] Liebe F. Cavalieri, "New Strains of Life—or Death," *The New York Times Magazine,* Aug. 22, 1976, p. 8.

several communities, including Cambridge, Mass., to adopt or consider further restrictions on the conditions under which such research may proceed *(see p. 178)*.

At the federal level, a committee representing 16 government agencies issued a report on March 15 urging Congress to require federal licensing of all laboratories doing recombinant DNA research. The House Subcommittee on Health and Environment held hearings March 15-17 to consider a bill introduced by its chairman, Rep. Paul G. Rogers (D Fla.), to achieve that end. Similar bills have been introduced by Rep. Richard L. Ottinger (D N.Y.), Rep. Stephen J. Solarz (D N.Y.) and Sen. Dale Bumpers (D Ark.). The Senate Subcommittee on Health, headed by Sen. Edward M. Kennedy (D Mass.), will consider these bills and other aspects of the recombinant DNA controversy at hearings scheduled for mid-April. "Not since the congressional investigations of atomic energy in the 1950s has science sparked such heated political discussion," observed Arthur Lubow, an associate editor of *New Times* magazine.[2]

Advancing Technology of Recombinant DNA

The development of recombinant DNA technology is considered by many scientists to be the most important advance in molecular biology since the discovery of the structure of DNA in 1953. *(see p. 173)*. The analytic power of the new technology has led some scientists to compare it with the invention of the microscope. "The ability to combine genes of different species in a growth medium is the most powerful tool to come along in my lifetime," declared Dr. Frederick Neidhardt, chairman of the microbiology department at the University of Michigan.[3]

The scientific technique involved is relatively simple to understand. By using a substance called a restriction enzyme, researchers can separate DNA molecules at specific points and then recombine them with DNA segments separated from another source. The resulting hybrids are inserted into bacteria in which they reproduce. In this way, genes wanted for study can be produced in large quantities. Sometimes researchers use viruses (tiny life forms consisting largely of DNA) to carry genes into bacteria or other host cells. Another way to get foreign DNA into bacteria is to use something called a plasmid *(see p. 165)* This is a small circular piece of DNA found naturally in bacteria; it can move easily from one cell to another.

For the moment the chief value of recombination is that it provides scientists with a way of learning more about how genetic molecules function. While biologists already know a

---

[2] Arthur Lubow, "Playing God With DNA," *New Times,* Jan. 7, 1977, p. 52.
[3] Quoted in *Business Week,* Aug. 9, 1976, p. 66.

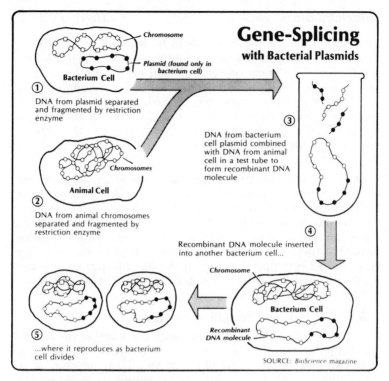

Gene-Splicing

with Bacterial Plasmids

① DNA from plasmid separated and fragmented by restriction enzyme

Chromosome

Plasmid (found only in bacterium cell)

Bacterium Cell

② DNA from animal chromosomes separated and fragmented by restriction enzyme

Chromosomes

Animal Cell

③ DNA from bacterium cell plasmid combined with DNA from animal cell in a test tube to form recombinant DNA molecule

④ Recombinant DNA molecule inserted into another bacterium cell...

Chromosome

Bacterium Cell

Recombinant DNA molecule

⑤ ...where it reproduces as bacterium cell divides

SOURCE: *BioScience* magazine

great deal about the operation of DNA in bacteria, they understand much less about its activity in higher organisms such as human beings. According to Dr. Stanley N. Cohen, a molecular geneticist and professor of medicine at the Stanford University School of Medicine, the use of recombinant DNA technology has already provided scientists with knowledge about how genes are organized into chromosomes and how gene expression is controlled. "With such knowledge," he told the Committee on Environmental Health of the California Medical Association last Nov. 18, "we can begin to learn how defects in the structure of such genes alter their function."[4] The research also could provide scientists with improved understanding of the way in which cells—including cancer cells—reproduce.

In addition to recombinant DNA's potential contributions to the advancement of fundamental scientific and medical knowledge, there are possible practical applications as well. For example, General Electric has applied for a patent on a process that will use the recombinant technique to create bacteria capable of absorbing oil for cleaning up spills. In medicine, it might be possible to "teach" bacteria to produce inexpensive and abundant quantities of human insulin, blood clotting factors, and other valuable hormones. DNA containing the genetic

---

[4] Stanley N. Cohen, "Recombinant DNA—Fact and Fiction," *Science*, Feb. 18, 1977, p. 655.

information for the hormone would be inserted into bacterial cells and, it is hoped, the cells would replicate the manufacturing process. The same procedure could eventually be used to produce vitamins, antibiotics and other drugs. Recombination could make possible a new form of medicine, gene therapy, to treat such genetic disorders as diabetes, sickle cell anemia and cystic fibrosis. By dealing with such diseases at the genetic level, researchers hope to effect a cure rather than merely treat the symptoms.

One of the most promising applications of genetic engineering is in agriculture. Researchers are using the gene-splitting technique to try to develop strains of wheat and other food crops that require no nitrogen fertilizer. Leguminous plants such as soybeans have the ability to convert atmospheric nitrogen into a form that they can use for nourishment. If the nitrogen-fixing genes from leguminous plants could be transferred to other plants, it would greatly reduce the need for synthetic, petroleum-based fertilizers.

Potenti l Health and Evolutionary Hazards

Critics of recombinant DNA research ask whether the potential benefits—many of which are purely speculative at this time—are worth the attendant risks. Their answer is a resounding no. They fear that such experiments might create Andromeda-type germs which could unleash uncontrollable diseases. For example, it is said that disease-producing bacteria like streptococci could, as a result of genetic engineering, accidently be made immune to antibiotics and other drugs used to treat them. Similarly, a bacterium that now inhabits the human body without doing harm might receive a genetic transplant that would cause it to begin manufacturing a deadly toxin. Moreover, it could spread undetected for a long time.

Harold M. Schmeck, a science reporter for *The New York Times*, wonders what would happen if some of the anticipated benefits backfired. "What if the postulated oil-gobbling bacteria got loose and became a contagious disease of automobiles, aircraft and all other machinery lubricated by oil?" he asks. "What if the insulin-producing bacteria learned to thrive inside humans and somehow sent every infected person into insulin shock? What if scientists inadvertently produced a super germ or a super weed capable of upsetting the entire balance of life on earth?"[5]

Most discussions of risks center on potential health hazards. But there is also concern about the long-range effect on the master plan of evolution. The leading spokesman for the prophets of evolutionary disaster is Dr. Robert L. Sinsheimer,

[5] *The New York Times*, Feb. 20, 1977.

Human Cloning—Next Step?

Some people maintain that current work in recombinant DNA is a first step in the direction of human cloning, or the multiplication of large numbers of genetically identical individuals. The process already is being used with other species. It has been used successfully with plants, fruit flies, and, more recently, with frogs.

Although the cloning of human beings is not yet technically feasible, a few researchers say it would be possible and desirable in the near future. Writing about cloning in *Psychology Today* in June 1974, Dr. James D. Watson said that if such technology "proceeds in its current nondirected fashion, a human being born of clonal reproduction most likely will appear on earth within the next 20 to 50 years, and even sooner if some nation actively promotes the venture."

Although most scientists—including most of those involved in recombinant DNA research—oppose the idea of human cloning, a few defend it. Dr. Joshua Lederberg of Stanford University has said: "If a superior individual is identified, why not copy it directly...?"*

*Quoted in *The Human Agenda* (1972), by Roderick Gorney, M.D., p. 222.

chairman of the biology division at the California Institute of Technology. Sinsheimer maintains that there are natural barriers to genetic interchange between cells of higher organisms (such as man) and cells of lower organisms (such as bacteria). To break down these natural barriers is to risk causing unpredictable damage to the evolutionary process. "The point is that we will be perturbing, in a major way, an extremely intricate ecological interaction which we understand only dimly," he said.[6]

Sinsheimer considers the deliberate misuse of gene-splicing a serious possibility. The problem is analogous to that of nuclear terrorism, he said. "It may well be that there are some technologies that you should not use not because they can't work but because of the social dangers involved and the repression that would be necessary to prevent social danger."[7] The 1972 treaty on biological warfare signed by the United States and 110 other nations would cover toxins or other biological agents developed through recombinant DNA research. But the Federation of American Scientists observed that "treaties are neither universal nor self-enforcing," and therefore "the world must begin to face a biological proliferation threat that might, before long, rival that of nuclear weapons."[8]

[6] Quoted by William Bennett and Joel Gurin in "Science that Frightens Scientists; The Great Debate Over DNA," *The Atlantic*, February 1977, p. 58.
[7] Quoted by Nicholas Wade in "Recombinant DNA: A Critic Questions the Right to Free Inquiry," *Science*, Oct. 15, 1976, p. 305.
[8] *F.A.S. Public Interest Report*, April 1976, p. 1.

Of special concern is the relative simplicity of the experiments. Science writer Judith Randal recounted the story of a Massachusetts Institute of Technology undergraduate who, after having read published reports, demonstrated on paper that he knew how to build an atomic bomb. "Since recombinant DNA work requires only a meager investment in equipment and can be carried out in a limited space," she wrote, "a similarly resourceful high school student could conceivably collect the necessary materials and then simply turn the experimental brew loose on the general environment."[9]

Those who support recombinant DNA research emphasize that scientists know of no hazardous agent it has ever created. Critics concede this point, but insist that until the potential risks can be accurately determined and assessed, the research should be restricted, postponed or banned altogether. Proponents find this approach unsatisfactory. They argue that no one will ever be able to guarantee total freedom from risk in any significant human activity. "All that we can reasonably expect," Dr. Cohen has said, "is a mechanism for dealing responsibly with hazards that are known to exist or which appear likely on the basis of information that is known."

Lab Rules for Genetic Altering of Microbes

At present, the principal mechanism for balancing the potential benefits and risks of genetic engineering is the set of guidelines issued by the National Institutes of Health on June 23, 1976. The guidelines provide two lines of defense against the escape of genetically altered microbes—physical and biological. There are four levels of physical containment:

P1 *(minimal):* strict adherence to standard practices.

P2 *(low):* limited access to laboratory during experiments; precautions against the release of aerosols and the prohibition of mouth pipetting.

P3 *(moderate):* laboratories equipped to ensure inward air flow; requires use of safety cabinets, the wearing of gloves by personnel, and decontamination of recirculated air.

P4 *(high):* special facilities of the kind used in biological warfare testing; requires rooms equipped with air locks, clothing changes and showers before leaving work area, and decontamination of all air, liquid and solid wastes.

Biological containment calls for the use of enfeebled strains of bacteria, as experimental hosts, which supposedly cannot survive outside the laboratory. A complex set of rules specifies which types of experiments require what combinations of physical and biological containment. Some experiments judged

---

[9] Judith Randal, "Life From the Labs: Who Will Control the New Technology?" *The Progressive,* March 1977, p. 18. Randal is a science writer for the *New York Daily News.*

especially dangerous are banned altogether. These include increasing the virulence of known pathogens or making microbes more resistant to antibiotics. No work is allowed with genetic material from organisms that produce dangerous poisons, such as botulism or snake or insect venom. No recombinant DNA molecule may be released into the environment, no matter how benign it is believed to be.

Most scientists seem satisfied with the guidelines, to judge from a straw poll conducted by the Federation of American Scientists last year.[10] The results showed that 56 per cent of the federation's members, including 64 per cent of the biologists, thought the guidelines were "probably about right." However, 7 per cent, including 12 per cent of the biologists, considered the guidelines to be overly restrictive. They regarded the potential dangers as wholly speculative and exaggerated; they were more concerned about the restraints on freedom of inquiry posed by the guidelines.

On the other hand, a substantial number of federation members—29 per cent, including 32 per cent of the non-biologists—said the guidelines did not go far enough. "The guidelines may alleviate the nervousness of some scientists but...my own view is that they will not effectively reduce the danger," said Liebe Cavalieri. "Indeed they may actually lull us into a false sense of security." Cavalieri said that in the course of 25 years of Army research with biological warfare agents at Fort Detrick, Md., equipped with the highest level of physical containment facilities, there were 423 accidental infections and three deaths.

One federal agency with serious reservations about the guidelines is the Environmental Protection Agency. The agency is particularly concerned that the guidelines permit researchers to continue using a type of bacteria that is commonly found in the human intestine, E. Coli *(Escherichia coli),* as a host for recombinant DNA molecules. Wilson K. Talley, the agency's research director, told the Senate health subcommittee on Sept. 22, 1976, that such research "should be performed on organisms...which are less ubiquitous than E. Coli." Voicing a similar concern, Dr. Erwin Chargaff of Columbia University said in a letter published in *Science* magazine last July 4: "If Dr. Frankenstein must go on producing his little biological monsters...why pick on E. Coli as the womb? Why choose a microbe that has cohabited more or less happily with us for a long time indeed?"

Other scientists dismiss such concerns. They insist that the wealth of existing knowledge about E. Coli and its genetic

---

[10] The poll was taken in April 1976 and the results made public on June 23, 1976.

makeup (E. Coli is the traditional laboratory bacterium) will make it a safer host than any other bacterium. They point out that the guidelines require the use of enfeebled strains of E. Coli that are not typical residents of the human intestine. But critics of recombinant research fear that even crippled forms of this microbe might transmit dangerous characteristics to ordinary E. Coli if they were accidently released.

Still other scientists, led by Dr. Sinsheimer, criticize the guidelines as being narrowly concerned with safety and not addressing broad moral, ethical or evolutionary questions raised by this research. In their opinion, there was not enough public participation in the process that led to publication of the guidelines. They say that those who had the greatest voice in formulating the guidelines were scientists already committed to going ahead with the research.

Industry's Freedom From U.S. Guidelines

A key problem with the NIH guidelines is enforcement. Although other federal agencies have adopted them, they do not cover private industries or laboratories with independent funding and they do not have the force of law. "As of now, there is no federal agency that is looking at research being done by private industry in recombinant DNA research," Dr. Bernard Talbot of NIH said in an interview published in *New Times* magazine Jan. 14. "[I]f private industry wants to do research, the federal government has no right to inspect or monitor the facilities...."

According to the Peoples Business Commission (formerly the Peoples Bicentennial Commission)[11] seven drug companies are engaged in or are about to begin recombinant DNA research: Hoffman-LaRoche in Nutley, N.J.; Eli Lilly in Indianapolis, Ind.; Upjohn in Kalamazoo, Mich.; Miles Laboratories in Rochester, N.Y., and South Bend, Ind.; Merck, Sharp & Dohme Research Laboratories in Rahway, N.J.; Abbot Laboratories in North Chicago, Ill.; and Pfizer in Groton, Conn. Nine other companies, the Peoples Business Commission said, are now looking into the potential applications of recombinant DNA. They are Cetus, CIBA-Geigy, DuPont, Dow, W. R. Grace, Monsanto, French Laboratories, Wyeth Laboratories and Searle Laboratories.[12] *Medical World News* reported Oct. 4 that "probably no one person in America has any clear idea of just how much recombinant research is already going on in industry or with what precautions."

---

[11] The Peoples Business Commission is a nonprofit, educational organization established to increase public awareness of corporate power and policies.

[12] See Jeremy Rifkin, "DNA," *Mother Jones,* February-March 1977, p. 23. *Mother Jones* is a national monthly magazine of news, politics, commentary and the arts published by the Foundation for National Progress in San Francisco.

Patents for New Life Forms

One problem with the current NIH guidelines on recombinant DNA is that they do not apply to private industries or independently funded laboratories engaged in such research. The Pharmaceutical Manufacturers Association, which represents the major drug companies working with recombinant DNA, has said that the pharmaceutical industry could accept the NIH guidelines with some minor modifications.

One of the drug industry's objections to the guidelines is that they require advance disclosure of research plans. That provision is considered crucial by most scientists. But pharmaceutical companies argue that it interferes with their patent rights.

The Department of Commerce announced on Jan. 10 that firms applying for patents on recombinant DNA techniques would be exempted from the advance disclosure provision. Betsy Ancker-Johnson, Assistant Secretary of Commerce for Science and Technology, said that "in view of the exceptional importance of recombinant DNA and the desirability of prompt disclosure of developments in the field," she also had recommended that the department speed the processing of patent applications that involve gene-splicing.

The department's action was widely criticized. Sen. Dale Bumpers (D Ark.) told his Senate colleagues that recombinant DNA is an area "which is entirely too dangerous to worry about proprietary information." At the request of HEW Secretary Califano, Secretary of Commerce Juanita M. Kreps on Feb. 24 agreed to suspend the order.

Concern over industry's freedom from regulation led Sens. Kennedy and Jacob K. Javits (R N.Y.) to write a letter to President Ford, dated July 19, 1976, urging him to make all recombinant research, including that being conducted by industry, subject to federal control. Responding to the letter, Ford announced Sept. 22 the establishment of an interagency commission headed by Donald Frederickson, director of the National Institutes of Health, "to review the activities of all government agencies conducting or supporting recombinant DNA research or having regulatory authority relevant to this scientific field."

Five months later, on Feb. 19, 1977, Frederickson announced that the commission had concluded that federal legislation did not completely cover the regulation of recombinant research. For example, the Toxic Substances Control Act of 1976 tightened federal regulation of all chemicals and chemical combinations, but it exempted research laboratories. In a report sent to the Secretary of Health, Education and Welfare, Joseph A. Califano, on March 15, the interagency commission recommended that Congress extend federal control to all laboratories doing DNA research. The commission recommended that a new law be enacted to (1) require registry, licensing and inspection of all laboratories where such research is conducted, (2) supersede any local rules, and (3) provide a mechanism to let private firms keep some work secret until they apply for patents *(see box, p. 171)*

While some members of the scientific community continue to oppose new legislation, most scientists attending a meeting of the National Academy of Sciences in Washington, D.C., March 7-9, appeared to support such a move. Expressing the view of many of his colleagues, Dr. Daniel Koshland, chairman of the biochemistry department of the University of California at Berkeley, said: "If there is no federal legislation then every city will make its own rules."

Some scientists and groups, including the Peoples Business Commission, have urged a more drastic step—an immediate moratorium on all recombinant DNA research. To push for such a moratorium, three scientists attending the Washington meeting—Dr. Ethan Signer of the Massachusetts Institute of Technology and Drs. Jonathan Beckwith and George Wald of Harvard—announced the formation of an international Coalition for Responsible Genetic Research. They said: "The continuation of this research without public understanding and approval and, in fact, without a full comprehension of its potential by most of the involved scientists, poses a worldwide danger which is intensified by the fact that industrial investment in the developing genetic technology has already begun."

Rise of Concern Among Scientists

THE STUDY of genetics has come a long way since Gregor Mendel's experiments with pea plants demonstrated the fundamental laws of inheritance. Mendel, a 19th-century Austrian monk, showed that for each physical trait, every individual possessed two "factors," or what later came to be known as genes.[13] Biologists had only fragmentary knowledge of the genetic process until the mid-20th century. It was known that genes were arranged in linear sequence along chromosomes, which are present in the nucleus of every living cell, but nothing was known about the molecular structure of genetic material.

In 1944, however, three biochemists at the Rockefeller Institute—Oswald T. Avery, Colin MacCloud and Maclyn McCarty—learned that genes were composed of deoxy-

[13] Mendel's findings were published in 1866 in an obscure journal, *The Proceedings of the Natural History Society of Bruenn,* and aroused little interest until 1900.

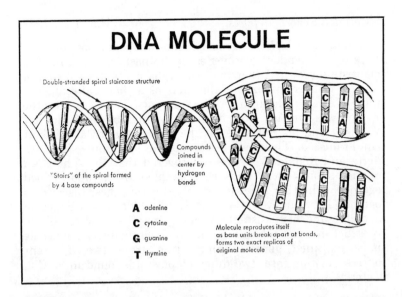

DNA MOLECULE

Double-stranded spiral staircase structure

"Stairs" of the spiral formed by 4 base compounds

Compounds joined in center by hydrogen bonds

A adenine

C cytosine

G guanine

T thymine

Molecule reproduces itself as base units break apart at bonds, forms two exact replicas of original molecule

ribonucleic acid (DNA). The next step was to determine the structure of the complex DNA molecule. This was accomplished in England in 1953 by two Cambridge scientists, Francis H. C. Crick and Maurice H. F. Wilkins, and an American colleague, James D. Watson.[14] The three scientists, employing X-ray diffraction pictures of DNA crystals, chemical analyses and their own intuition, concluded that the DNA molecule had a double-helix or spiral-staircase structure. According to their calculations, the main strains forming the backbone of the molecule are composed of long, spiral chains of sugar-phosphate units, endlessly repeated. These strands are joined together at regular intervals by small side chains, or "base" units, to complete the spiral-staircase structure.

The base units, each attached at one side to a strand unit and joined in the center by a hydrogen bond, are generally composed of one of four related compounds: adenine (A), thymine (T), guanine (G), or cytosine (C). Compound A will join chemically only with T, and G only with C. From this information, biologists deduced the method by which a DNA molecule reproduces itself. First the two main strands separate down the middle, forming a pair of templates or molds.

Thus, for instance, if it could be determined that a portion of one strand [of a DNA molecule] contains the [base] sequence AGGTCGCAT, then it would follow that the second strand would contain, at the corresponding site, the sequence TCCAGCGTA. The relationship between the two would be that between a photographic negative and the corresponding positive.[15]

---

[14] See Watson's account of their discovery in his book *The Double Helix* (1968).

[15] Isaac Asimov, "The Genetic Code," *New York State Journal of Medicine*, June 15, 1965, p. 1648. See also "Genetics and the Life Processes," *E.R.R.*, 1967 Vol. II, pp. 903-922.

Recombinant DNA, or gene-splicing, was made possible by a series of independent discoveries in the past 15 years. In 1962 scientists discovered that bacterial cells contain a substance, called a restriction enzyme, that acts as a chemical scalpel to split DNA molecules into specific segments. Ten years later the enzyme was purified from bacteria by microbiologist Herbert W. Boyer and his colleagues at the University of California at San Francisco. Then two researchers at Stanford—Janet E. Mertz and Ronald W. Davis—discovered that the split DNA fragments had sticky ends that enabled them to be joined together with other DNA fragments. Putting these discoveries together, Dr. Stanley N. Cohen of Stanford University School of Medicine and his assistant, Annie C. Y. Chang, were able to construct in a test tube a biologically functional DNA molecule that combined genetic information from two different sources—in this case, two different plasmids found in E. Coli bacteria.

Subsequent experiments by Cohen and Chang, in collaboration with Herbert W. Boyer and Robert B. Hellig of the University of California at San Francisco, showed that genes from another species of bacterium, Staphylococcus aureus, could be transplanted into E. Coli. Further experimentation demonstrated that animal DNA—specifically, ribosomal DNA from the South African toad—could be linked with plasmid DNA to form recombinant molecules that would reproduce in E. Coli. A proliferation of recombinant DNA work followed, resulting in the insertion into bacteria of animal DNA from fruit flies, toads, mice, sea urchins, slime molds and chickens.[16]

Organized Effort to Assess Research Risks

Cohen and his colleagues recognized from the beginning that the construction of some kinds of novel gene combinations might have a potential for biological hazard. At first the primary concern was that certain gene-splicing experiments might increase the risks of work with cancer viruses. One of the first scientists to voice this concern publicly was Paul Berg of Stanford, who decided to abandon plans to introduce genes from a tumor virus into E. Coli bacteria after his colleagues suggested that the resulting organism might spread cancer to humans.

Berg helped to organize a conference in New Hampshire in July 1973 to review the available information on recombinant research and to assess the potential risks. Those attending the conference—the Gordon Research Conference on Nucleic Acids—sent an open letter to Dr. Philip Handler, president of the National Academy of Sciences, warning that new organisms

---

[16] See Stanley N. Cohen, "The Manipulation of Genes," *Scientific American*, July 1975, pp. 24-33.

"with biological activity of an unpredictable nature" could be created by these experiments. They urged him to "establish a study committee to consider this problem and to recommend specific actions or guidelines should that seem appropriate."[17]

A committee was formed, with Paul Berg as chairman, and in a now-famous letter to *Science* magazine in July 1974, it recommended that certain types of recombinant DNA research be voluntarily deferred "until the potential hazards...have been better evaluated or until adequate methods are developed for preventing their spread...."[18] The types of research covered by the moratorium were (1) formation of bacteria resistant to antibiotics, (2) linkage of DNA molecules with tumor-causing viruses, and (3) introduction of toxin-formation or antibiotic-resistance genes into bacteria that did not naturally contain such genes. Berg's committee also asked the director of the National Institutes of Health, Robert S. Stone, to set up an advisory committee to evaluate potential hazards in this research, devise safety procedures and develop guidelines for researchers working with potentially hazardous DNA molecules. Finally, the Berg committee said that an international conference should be convened as soon as possible.

The Berg committee's call for a voluntary moratorium was called an unprecedented event. In fact, the American Chemical Society listed it among the most important scientific events of the last 100 years.[19] The moratorium was widely reported by the press and produced an international reaction. Stone quickly announced his intention to establish an advisory committee, as recommended, and he offered financial support for an international meeting. In England, the Advisory Board for the Research Councils, the prime source of government funding for civil research in Britain, set up a committee to assess the potential hazards and benefits of genetic engineering. In the interim, the board asked all of its units to suspend any experiments cited by the Berg committee as particularly dangerous.

In his presidential address to the British Association for the Advancement of Science in September 1974, molecular biologist Sir John Kendrew commended the Berg committee's actions and suggested the establishment of a permanent international monitoring body of molecular biologists who would assess gene-transfer experiments. On the other hand, the influential British journal *Nature,* in an editorial on Sept. 6, 1974, rejected a suggestion that it cease publication of articles on research

---

[17] The letter was published in *Science,* Sept. 23, 1973, p. 1114.

[18] *Science,* July 26, 1974, p. 303.

[19] *Chemical & Engineering News,* April 6, 1976. *Chemical & Engineering News* is the official publication of the American Chemical Society.

covered by the proposed moratorium. In October 1974, DNA recombination came under discussion at a Pugwash Conference in Austria and at an international symposium in Davos, Switzerland. Most participants at the Davos conference acknowledged the "enormous dangers" posed by recombination, but they concluded that controls would be "impractical and unenforceable."[20]

Recommendations From 1975 Conference

The international meeting proposed by the Berg committee was held in February 1975 at the Asilomar Conference Center in Pacific Grove, Calif. It was sponsored by the National Academy of Sciences and was supported by the National Institutes of Health and the National Science Foundation; 150 persons from 16 countries attended. They revealed a wide divergence of opinion in the scientific community. Nobel laureate Joshua Lederberg of Stanford expressed his dismay at the prospect that guidelines might end up "crystallized into legislation." James D. Watson of Harvard said that guidelines would be essentially unenforceable, and that therefore the best tactic was to rely on the common sense of those doing the research. Some participants argued that the risks were too remote to justify limiting the freedom of scientific inquiry. Others insisted that the moral responsibility to protect the public was more important than academic freedom or individual success.

In the end, the participants concluded that "most of the work...should proceed." They ranked the experiments by potential risk and specified safety precautions for each level. And they favored a ban on experiments that, while feasible, "present such serious dangers that their performance should not be undertaken at this time."[21]

Nicholas Wade of *Science* magazine described the actions taken at Asilomar as "a rare, if not unique, example of safety precautions being imposed on a technical development before, instead of after, the first occurrence of the hazard being guarded against."[22] Jack McWethy of *U.S. News & World Report* called the conference a landmark "because it provided for all scientists a working illustration of how specialists can examine and, when necessary, limit their research for the public good long before the issues are dragged into the...political arena."[23]

---

[20] See *Science News*, Nov. 2, 1974, p. 277, and *BioScience*, December 1974, p. 694.

[21] A report on the conference was submitted to the Assembly of Life Sciences of the National Academy of Sciences and was approved by its executive committee, May 20, 1975. See Janet H. Weinberg, "Decision at Asilomar," *Science News*, March 22, 1975, pp. 194-196, and Cristine Russell, "Biologists Draft Genetic Research Guidelines," *BioScience*, April 1975, pp. 237-240.

[22] Nicholas Wade, "Genetics: Conference Sets Strict Controls to Replace Moratorium" *Science*, March 14, 1975, p. 931.

[23] Jack McWethy, "A Move to Protect Mankind," *U.S. News & World Report*, April 7, 1975, p. 66.

Immediately after the conference, the NIH Advisory Committee on Recombinant DNA, which had been set up in October 1974, held its first meeting in San Francisco to begin translating the mandate of Asilomar into firm guidelines binding on all researchers receiving NIH grants. At a second meeting, held May 12-13, 1975, in Bethesda, Md., a subcommittee under the chairmanship of Dr. David Hogness was appointed to draft the guidelines. The first draft, made public the following July 18-19 at a meeting in Woods Hole, Mass., was widely criticized as being weaker than the rules agreed upon at Asilomar. Two Boston-centered groups, Science for the People and the Boston Area Recombinant DNA Group, organized a petition drive against the draft guidelines. Eventually a new NIH subcommittee was appointed to revise them.

The draft guidelines finally adopted by the NIH advisory committee at La Jolla, Calif., on Dec. 5, 1975, were, according to Nicholas Wade, "demonstratively stricter than the Asilomar guidelines...."[24] Although the guidelines were criticized in some quarters, they were approved by the National Institutes of Health and released on June 23, 1976.

During the months of debate that preceded the issuing of the guidelines, questions were raised about the possibility that organisms containing recombinant DNA molecules might escape and harm the environment. The National Institutes of Health pointed out that the guidelines prohibit the deliberate release of such organisms. Nevertheless it agreed to review the possible environmental impact of genetic experiments. A draft of the environmental impact statement was released for public comment on Aug. 26, 1976.[25]

Emergence of Citizen Oversight

SCIENCE TODAY is facing the equivalent of the Protestant Reformation, according to University of Chicago philosopher Stephen Toulmin. Likening the scientific establishment to the 16th century church, Toulmin said that the people are tired of being shut out of science's "ecclesiastical courts" and are demanding to be let in. The scientist "priest," he predicted, is going to be overthrown.[26]

---

[24] Nicholas Wade, "Recombinant DNA: NIH Sets Strict Rules to Launch New Technology," *Science*, Dec. 19, 1975, p. 1175.

[25] See the *Federal Register*, Sept. 9, 1976, pp. 38426-38483. The NIH guidelines were published in the *Federal Register*, July 7, 1976, pp. 27902-27943.

[26] Quoted in Barbara J. Culliton, "Public Participation in Science; Still in Need of Definition," *Science*, April 30, 1976, p. 451.

In the past, the public tended to acquiesce in the judgment of scientists in the assumption that any advance of knowledge was necessarily beneficial. But in recent years, trust and approval have given way to suspicion and apprehension among increasing numbers of Americans. Behind the public's misgivings is a litany of known or suspected hazards that were the product of scientific research: DDT, cyclamates, asbestos, PCB, vinyl chloride, radioactivity, aerosol propellants, food additives, Kepone.

The upshot of all this appears to be that "the American public is coming to regard scientific research with what might be termed a *Code Napoleon* attitude," according to George Alexander, science writer for the *Los Angeles Times*. "Just as that French legal system presumes that an individual is guilty of an alleged crime and places the burden of innocence upon the accused, so does this evolving public attitude presuppose that new research is more likely to be harmful than beneficial, that disadvantages are more likely to outweigh advantages."[27]

Nowhere is this public attitude more evident today than in the debate over the safety of recombinant DNA research. In barely five years, it already has given rise to Vietnam-type protest groups and to city council and state legislative hearings from Cambridge, Mass., to Sacramento, Calif. "Gene transplantation may be the first innovation submitted to public judgment *before* the technology had been put into widespread use and before heavy investment had given it a momentum that was hard to oppose."[28]

The first local rumblings of discontent came in Ann Arbor, Mich. Early in 1975, the regents of the University of Michigan began to consider a plan to upgrade some laboratories to the P3 level of containment *(see p. 168)*. This set off a debate which went on for over a year. At several public hearings the plan was opposed by the Ann Arbor Ecology Center and a few faculty members, notably Shaw Livermore, a professor of American history, and Susan Wright, associate professor of humanities. Despite the opposition, the regents in May. 1976 voted 6 to 1 to proceed with the research.

Community Action on Recombinant Research

The debate in Ann Arbor was largely confined to the university. A much broader public debate took place in Cambridge, Mass. The controversy over recombinant DNA erupted in June 1976 after a weekly newspaper, *The Boston Phoenix*, reported Harvard's plan to convert an existing laboratory into a P3

---

[27] *Los Angeles Times*, Feb. 27, 1977.
[28] Bennett and Gurin, *op. cit.*, p. 44.

facility. Some faculty members, led by Nobel laureate George Wald and his wife, Harvard biologist Ruth Hubbard, expressed their opposition to Cambridge Mayor Alfred E. Vellucci. He called a public meeting on the matter, saying "We want to be damned sure the people of Cambridge won't be affected by anything that would crawl out of that laboratory."

The Cambridge City Council considered the issue on June 23 at a hearing attended by nearly 500 persons and again on July 7. At the second meeting the council imposed a three-month moratorium on moderate and high-risk DNA experiments until a citizens' review board could study the problem. This was considered a precedent-setting action for involving the public in decision-making regarding biological research.[29]

The nine members of the Cambridge Experimentation Review Board met twice a week for five months (the moratorium was extended) and issued a report in January 1977 declaring that "knowledge, whether for its own sake or for its potential benefits to mankind, cannot serve as a justification for introducing risks to the public unless an informed citizenry is willing to accept those risks." The review board decided unanimously that it was prepared to accept those risks, and it recommended that the research be allowed to continue.

However, in the belief that "a predominantly lay citizen group can face a technical scientific matter of general and deep public concern, educate itself appropriately to the task, and reach a fair decision," the panel concluded that the safety guidelines developed by the National Institutes of Health did not go far enough. The board recommended some additional measures, including the preparation of a safety manual, training of personnel to minimize accidents, and inclusion of a community representative on the NIH-mandated "biohazards committees" at Harvard and the Massachusetts Institute of Technology. The review board also recommended that the city set up a permanent citizen biohazards committee to monitor the research at the universities and report violations.

On Feb. 7, 1977, the Cambridge City Council endorsed the board's recommendations after rejecting a proposal by Mayor Vellucci to ban the research altogether. "What happened in Cambridge is of major national importance," said Stanley Jones, a staff member of the Senate Health Subcommittee. "It is the first time a public community group has looked at an issue in science and made recommendations on what it thought was appropriate."[30]

---

[29] See Nicholas Wade, "Recombinant DNA: Cambridge City Council Votes Moratorium," *Science,* July 23, 1976, p. 300.
[30] Quoted in *The Christian Science Monitor,* Jan. 17, 1977.

The year-long debate in Cambridge spurred action in other communities. In San Diego, Calif., the city's Quality of Life Board acted at the request of Mayor Pete Wilson to set up a committee to review DNA work at the University of California at San Diego. After hearing an array of witnesses, the committee in February 1977 submitted a report generally endorsing the NIH guidelines. But in addition, it recommended that (1) the city council consider the desirability of confining all gene-splicing research to P3 laboratories, (2) the university refrain from experiments requiring P4 facilities, (3) it notify the city of any P3 experiment requiring the highest degree of biological containment, and (4) an ordinance be passed to bring industry and private researchers within the control of the guidelines.

In Madison, Wis., the city council recently appointed a committee to study the possible hazards of recombinant DNA research at the University of Wisconsin. A citizen review board also was set up recently in Princeton, N.J. Public hearings on the question have been held in several other university towns, including Bloomington, Ind. (Indiana University), New Haven, Conn. (Yale), and Palo Alto, Calif. (Stanford). At the state level, bills to control DNA recombination experiments have been introduced in New York and California."What all these activities represent..." Nicholas Wade wrote, "is an extended exercise in public education about the gene-splice technique and its implications.... Whatever further restrictions emerge from the present round of debate, the research will at least be proceeding on the basis of informed public consent...."[31]

Significance of Public Participation in Science

The calls to prohibit or slow down the research seem threatening and irrational to many of those scientists who first pointed to the risks. The public's response might make scientists reluctant to question the consequences of any future research for fear of generating "unjustified fears" and "opening themselves up to attack," according to Professor Mark Ptashne of Harvard.[32] Dr. Cohen writes that the public has misinterpreted the scientific community's attempts at self-regulation "as *prima facie* evidence that this research must be more dangerous than all the rest."

Because in the past, governmental agencies have often been slow to respond to clear and definite dangers in other areas of technology, it has been inconceivable to scientists working in other fields and to the public at large that an extensive and costly federal machinery would have been established to provide protec-

---

[31] Nicholas Wade, "Gene-Splicing: At Grass-Roots Level a Hundred Flowers Bloom," *Science*, Feb. 11, 1977, p. 560.
[32] Quoted in *The Chronicle of Higher Education*, Aug. 2, 1976, p. 4.

Regulation of Recombinant DNA Abroad

No matter how tough American regulations on recombinant DNA become, there is little the United States can do to control gene-splicing experiments in other countries. Some scientists have expressed concern that companies bent on avoiding federal control might set up shop in nations without strict regulations—much as oil-tanker companies use Liberia as a convenient place to register their ships. "Any accident on this globe would affect some other place," warned Dr. J. E. Rall, a research director at the National Institutes of Health.*

The only comprehensive guidelines for recombinant-DNA research outside of the United States are in Britain. The British guidelines differ from America's in that they place more emphasis on physical containment and less on biological containment. The Soviet Union is reported to be drawing up its guidelines based on the U.S. and British models.

In addition there are national committees for genetic engineering in France, Germany, Italy, Belgium, the Netherlands and the Scandinavian countries. Some of these national committees have governmental status and the authority to establish guidelines, inspect laboratories, authorize experiments, and so on; others are merely advisory.

Last October, the International Council of Scientific Unions (ICSU) voted to set up a committee to monitor research associated with recombinant-DNA and other experiments in genetic manipulation. The new body, known as the Committee on Genetic Experimentation (COGE), will conduct no research of its own. But it will attempt to monitor experiments in progress throughout the world and serve as a channel of communication among the scientific communities engaged in such research. In addition, the World Health organization has set up a committee to consider health implications of recombinant DNA.

* Quoted in *The Christian Science Monitor*, Feb. 24, 1977.

tion in this area of research unless severe hazards were known to exist.[33]

So far, the scientist's fear of citizen review seems unjustified. Most public bodies that have considered the recombinant DNA controversy have endorsed the guidelines issued by the National Institutes of Health with minor changes. The report submitted by the Cambridge Experimentation Review Board was praised by both critics and supporters of recombination. "It proved that even complex scientific issues can be understood by lay people who devote the necessary time and energy to the problem," wrote Dr. David Baltimore of the Massachusetts Institute of Technology.[34] As science increases its powers to modify all aspects of society, more and more people are taking the time to question the implications of scientific research.

[33] Stanley N. Cohen, "Recombinant DNA: Fact and Fiction," *Science*, Feb. 18, 1977, pp. 656-657.
[34] David Baltimore, "The Gene Engineers," *T.V. Guide*, March 12, 1977, p. 30.

Selected Bibliography

Books

Handler, Philip, ed., *Biology and the Future of Man*, Oxford University Press, 1970.
Watson, James D., *The Double Helix*, Atheneum, 1968.
Winchester, A. M., *Heredity: An Introduction to Genetics*, Barnes & Noble, 1961.

Articles

Bennett, William and Joel Gurin, "Home Rule and the Gene," *Harvard Magazine*, October 1976.
——"Science That Frightens Scientists: The Great Debate Over DNA," *The Atlantic*, February 1977.
Cavalieri, Liebe F., "New Strains of Life—or Death," *New York Times Magazine*, Aug. 22, 1976.
Cohen, Stanley N., "The Manipulation of Genes," *Scientific American*, July 1975.
——"Recombinant DNA: Fact and Fiction," *Science*, Feb. 18, 1977.
Crossland, Janice, "Hands on the Code," *Environment*, September 1976.
Fields, Cheryl, "Can Scientists Be Trusted on Hazardous Research?" *The Chronicle of Higher Education*, Aug. 2, 1976.
"Fruits of Gene-Juggling: Blessing or Curse?" *Medical World News*, Oct 4, 1976.
Gwynne, Peter, "Caution: Gene Transplants," *Newsweek*, March 21, 1977.
——"Politics and Genes," *Newsweek*, Jan. 12, 1976.
Lubow, Arthur, "Playing God With DNA," *New Times*, Jan. 7, 1977.
"Pandora's Box of Genes," *The Economist*, March 5, 1977.
Randal, Judith, "Life from the Labs: Who Will Control the New Technology?" *The Progressive*, March 1977.
Rifkin, Jeremy, "DNA," *Mother Jones*, February-March 1977.
Russell, Cristine, "Weighing the Hazards of Genetic Research: A Pioneering Case Study," *BioScience*, December 1974.
——"Biologists Draft Genetic Research Guidelines," *BioScience*, April 1975.
Science,, selected issues.
Weinberg, Janet H., "Decision at Asilomar," *Science News*, March 22, 1975.

Reports and Studies

Editorial Research Reports, "Genetics and the Life Process," 1967 Vol. II, p. 903; "Human Engineering," 1971 Vol. I, p. 367; "Medical Ethics," 1972 Vol. I, p. 461.
National Institutes of Health, "Recombinant DNA Research Guidelines," *Federal Register*, July 7, 1976.
——"Recombinant DNA Research Guidelines: Draft Environmental Impact Statement," *Federal Register*, Sept. 9, 1976.
U.S. Congress, Senate Subcommittee on Health, "Oversight Hearing on Implementation of NIH Guidelines Governing Recombinant DNA Research," Sept. 22, 1976.

JOB HEALTH AND SAFETY

by

Helen B. Shaffer

**Dec. 24
1 9 7 6**

JOB HEALTH AND SAFETY

I F STATISTICS on job-connected injury, illness and death could tell the whole story, there would be rejoicing in the American workplace. The latest government figures, considered alone, would indicate that the problem was lessening *(see table, p. 186)*. Unfortunately, statistics do not tell the whole story. Concern for job safety actually has increased, and for good reason.

In addition to the usual kinds of injuries or fatalities caused by falls, fires and machinery, an ominous succession of new hazards have come to light in recent years and months. Toxic substances associated with work and either imperceptible to the worker or ignored by him have been taking a terrible toll, sometimes not until years after exposure. These newer forms of occupational hazards are the byproducts of technological advance and are far more difficult to overcome than the older and more obvious kinds.

The severity of much occupational illness, which may strike robust workers in their prime years, adds an element of tragic drama to the situation. In addition, each new revelation of a hitherto-unsuspected health hazard arouses fear that there may be other harmful substances, as yet undetected.

Another factor arousing public interest is that a dangerous condition in the workplace may menace the health of the population at large. The worker may bring the unseen contamination home, possibly in his clothing, and thus spread the infection to his family and others. Or the substance that he deals with in high concentration while at work may be found in a product that is widely distributed for use by the consumer. A familiar example is an agricultural pesticide that is capable of making farm workers ill and also contaminates crops sent to market.

The link between hazards of the workplace and the general environment was demonstrated Dec. 10 when chlorine gas leaked from a tank at an Allied Chemical Corp. plant and drifted in a poisonous cloud along the Mississippi River near Baton Rouge, La. Some 10,000 persons had to leave the area to escape the threat of poisoning.

Occupational Injury and Illness in American Industry

Year	Total Cases	Rate Per 100 Workers	Number of Fatalities
1975	4,983,100	9.1	5,300
1974	5,915,800	10.4	5,900
1973	6,100,000	11.0	5,700
1972	5,700,000	10.9	5,500

Source: U.S. Bureau of Labor Statistics

Attention has also centered on occupational health because of controversy over a six-year-old government program to reduce those hazards. This program, authorized by Congress in 1970, vested enforcement responsibility in a new agency, the Occupational Health and Safety Administration (OSHA), in the Department of Labor. Never has an agency created for so benign a purpose been so persistently assailed by critics from so many sides.

Pressures for Revising Safety Provisions

Business, labor, consumer groups, politicians to the right and to the left, other government agencies, and even persons within the agency have had their say on what's wrong with the program. Critics include those who would strengthen the government's hand, those who would weaken it in favor of voluntary compliance, and those who would abolish the whole enterprise. Controversy has arisen particularly on standards of safety to be imposed on employers in regard to permissible concentrations of pollution in the workplace.

The controversy has generated many proposals for legislative reform—about 100 bills in every congressional session since OSHA was founded. Similar pressures for amending the law can be expected in the 95th Congress, which convenes Jan. 3, 1977. President-elect Carter has mentioned "safe working conditions" among his goals for the nation. A political campaign document from the Carter forces pointed out that, as governor of Georgia, Carter "took positive steps to improve working conditions and work-related health and safety programs" in his state. It added, "As President, he would continue this commitment and strengthen or extend existing OSHA legislation so that those who earn their living by personal labor can work in safe and healthy environments."[1]

---

[1] "Jimmy Carter on Labor," undated.

Organized labor and its friends often accused the Ford and Nixon administrations of helping the business community resist government regulation and especially the establishment of stringent (and costly) standards of environmental decontamination. Business interests, on the other hand, consider some of the regulatory standards unnecessary, unworkable, and arbitrary. Sen. Harrison A. Williams Jr. (D N.J.), author of the act creating OSHA and chairman of the Senate Labor and Public Welfare Committee which has kept a close watch on its activities, told a trucking industry conference[2] on Dec. 8 that he would continue to press the agency for more effective enforcement of the law.

Common Causes of Occupational Injuries

A cumulative listing of the multifarious hazards of the workplace would give so overwhelming an impression of danger that it might discourage all but the bravest to seek employment of any kind. But most of the hazards are familiar in all circumstances of modern life and the odds on being injured can be vastly reduced by taking ordinary precautions or reasonable safety measures. The most frequent causes of accidents on the job, cited in a recent comprehensive study of occupational health and safety,[3] are the following:

Fires and explosions from chemicals, pressurized containers or transmission lines.

Physical injury, possibly dismemberment, from unshielded parts of machines that saw, mold, roll, cut, mix, flatten, bend, grind, or simply move under mechanical power.

Electrical hazards from improper grounding or shielding.

Injuries to the eye from wood or metal chips discharged during cutting or grinding—or from the splashing or misting from liquid aerosols.

Crushing and mangling injuries from moving and lifting equipment, especially prevalent in construction and stevedoring.

Falls from equipment or from high places of work, most frequent in farming and construction work.

Mining has long been viewed as a particularly hazardous occupation because of the danger of underground accidents and the health-damaging effects of coal dust. Mining disasters make a particularly strong call on public sympathy and usually are followed by controversy over responsibility for the accident. Despite passage of the Coal Mine Health and Safety Act in 1969, according to a congressional report, mine accidents have

---

[2] Regular Common Carrier Conference, Orlando, Fla., Dec. 8, 1976.
[3] Nicholas Ashford, *Crisis in the Workplace: Occupational Disease and Injury, a Report to the Ford Foundation* (1976), pp. 69-70.

Occupational Injury and Illness by Industry

Type of Work	1974	1975	Type of Work	1974	1975
Contract construction	18.3	16.0	Wholesale and retail trade	8.4	7.3
Manufacturing	14.6	13.0	Services	5.8	5.4
Mining	10.2	11.0	Finance, insurance and real estate	2.4	2.2
Transportation and public utilities	10.5	9.4			
Agriculture, forestry and fisheries	9.9	8.5			

Source: U.S. Bureau of Labor Statistics

taken more than 1,000 lives and injured thousands more since that date.[4]

In the case of a mine or plant accident, the effect is instantaneous, the immediate cause not too hard to determine, and the extent of injury readily assessed. In the case of long-developing illness, it is difficult to determine the degree to which environmental pollutants contribute. Over the years, however, sufficient evidence has accumulated to implicate a number of substances in the workplace environment as factors in the incidence of serious disease.

The exact measure of the risk is beyond the powers of the experts; hence a variety of figures are bandied about. The National Institute of Occupational Safety and Health (NIOSH) has estimated that 390,000 new cases of occupational disease occur annually and cause possibly 100,000 deaths—far more than are counted by the U.S. Bureau of Labor Statistics *(see box, p. 186).* Since its establishment in 1971, NIOSH has placed some 23,000 chemical compounds on its list of toxic substances that might, in sufficient concentration, be harmful to workers. But health research is time-consuming and cannot keep pace with the rate new chemical compounds are introduced in industry. Meanwhile, new and strange illnesses sometimes appear.

The worker's first symptoms may be so vague as to be dismissed—a pervasive or recurrent spell of fatigue, dizziness, shortness of breath, loss of appetite, difficulty in sleeping, visual or hearing irregularities. Since many of those afflicted are young, healthy men with little history of prior illness, there may be a tendency to postpone medical examination until the affliction is well-established. In some cases the damage is not

---

[4] House Committee on Education and Labor, Subcommittee on Labor Standards, "Scotia Coal Mine Disaster," a staff report, Oct. 15, 1976, p. 6. The report title referred to a mine disaster in Letcher County, Ky., in which two explosions, on March 9 and 11, 1976, took 26 lives.

revealed until some time after the individual has left the contaminated workplace. The damage may be irreversible.

Job-connected illnesses of this kind are by no means a new
discovery. A British physician in the 18th century, Percival
Potts, observed an unusual incidence of cancer of the scrotum
among chimney sweeps, attributable to their overexposure to
coal tar. Half a century ago, a number of young women who
painted radium on watch dials became victims of cancer. Mme.
Marie Curie, discoverer of radium, suffered radium burns and
her death in 1936 was attributed to the cumulative effects of
radium poisoning.

Illnesses From Dust, Gas and Chemicals

Among the best-known diseases associated with dust pollution are pneumoconiosis, the "black lung" of coal miners, and
silicosis. Silicosis is prevalent among workers in mining,
quarrying, stonecutting and glassmaking who inhale silica particles. It has been estimated that 200,000 coal miners or ex-
miners suffer some degree of pneumoconiosis.[5] A study of 9,000
miners showed that the disease affected one-third of them to
some degree and threatened more than 200 with disability or
death.[6] According to OSHA, 1.1 million workers may be "at
risk" from coal dust.[7]

Other well-recognized dust-origin diseases of the workplace
are asbestosis, which afflicts miners and other handlers of
asbestos; berylliosis, affecting workers in metallurgical, ceramic
and other industries using beryllium; and byssinosis, sometimes
called "brown lung," caused by breathing cotton dust. The "risk
populations" for these conditions have been estimated at 350,-
000 for asbestosis, 30,000 for berylliosis, and 800,000 for
byssinosis.[8] Dr. Irving J. Selikoff, director of Environmental
Sciences Laboratory of Mount Sinai School of Medicine in New
York and a specialist in asbestosis research, has estimated that
400,000 of the 1 million Americans who work or have worked
with asbestos will die of cancer during the next half-century unless far better treatment is devised.[9] He cited several studies
that indicated the death rate from a rare form of liver cancer
called mesothelioma was three or four times higher than normal
among asbestos workers. In testimony before a Senate committee, Selikoff referred to asbestosis as a "hidden time

---

[5] National Academy of Engineering and the National Academy of Sciences, *Man, Materials and Environment*, a report for the National Commission on Materials Policy, March 1973, p. 75.

[6] "News from NIOSH," *Job Safety and Health* (an OSHA publication), January 1974, p. 33.

[7] Occupational Safety and Health Administration, "The Target Health Hazards" (1972), Bulletin No. 2051.

[8] Figures from public health sources cited by Nicholas Ashford, *op. cit.*, pp. 75-77.

[9] Statement at scientific conference at Cold Spring Harbor Laboratory, N.Y., Sept. 8, 1976.

bomb."[10] NIOSH said in August 1975 that garage workers who change or grind brake linings could be exposed to hazardous levels of airborne asbestos.

In matters of chemical toxicity, public attention tends to center on particular pollutants as cases of severe illness come to light. Vinyl chloride was in the news after the B. F. Goodrich Co. disclosed in 1974 that three workers in its Louisville plant had died of angiosarcoma, a rare form of lung cancer, apparently from breathing air contaminated with vinyl chloride—a colorless gas derived from chlorine and petrochemicals, and used in the manufacture of plastic products. The disclosure was followed by government efforts to impose stricter limits on permissible concentrations of the gas, and these efforts led to objections from industry that the limits were too strict. "The plastics industry has been shaken to its roots," *The Wall Street Journal* commented. The Louisville cases may constitute "only the tip of the iceberg."[11]

The next pesticide problem to capture attention involved workers at the Life Science Products Co. in Hopewell, Va. It was learned by early 1976 that 110 workers at the Hopewell plant had high levels of the pesticide Kepone in their blood. Twenty-eight were hospitalized with such symptoms as uncontrollable trembling and memory loss. All production of the pesticide ceased and the plant was razed. Allied Chemical Corp., for which Life Science was the sole supplier of Kepone, was fined $13.4-million in federal court for dumping the pesticide in the James River. Still the damage lingers on. Certain types of fishing have been banned in the James and the lower Chesapeake Bay, and civil suits by stricken workers are pending.

More recently, the spotlight has been on Leptophos, another pesticide, marketed as Phosvel. It was revealed that a number of employees and ex-employees of the Velsicol Chemical Corp. at Bayport, Texas, where the product is manufactured, showed symptoms indicating neurological damage. Leptophos has been manufactured in the United States since 1971 but for export only. It was implicated in the deaths of 1,200 water buffaloes in Egypt after the pesticide was applied liberally to crops in that country.

There appears to be no end to the succession of health hazards being reported to worker-protection authorities. Their concern is directed not only to contaminating substances but to such factors as excessive noise, heat, and vibration. A number of studies show that these conditions can contribute appreciably to

---

[10] Testimony before the Senate Commerce Subcommittee on Environment, Feb. 23, 1976.
[11] *The Wall Street Journal*, Oct. 2, 1974.

worker illness and debility. Excessive noise, according to one study, not only can impair hearing but "triggers changes in cardiovascular, endocrine, and neurological function."[12] A NIOSH official, commenting on the range of problems, said recently; "[W]e have been reacting in a crisis environment for the past two or three years."[13]

Development of Protective Laws

T HE NEED for government action to protect the health and safety of the worker became apparent as industrial activity expanded during the 19th century. The Massachusetts Department of Factory Inspection, established in 1867, was the first state agency to deal with job safety. Ten years later Massachusetts became the first state to enact a law imposing safety standards on industry; the standards applied only to the operation of spinning machinery in textile plants.

Other states followed with various types of job-safety laws. Though the protection was limited, the laws encouraged injured workers to bring damage suits against employers for negligence. This, in turn, encouraged support for proposals to establish an insurance system that would not only guarantee indemnity to an injured worker but relieve the employer of the expense of litigation and the risk of having to pay damages.

The principle of compulsory insurance was not readily accepted, however. Several early state laws to this effect were declared unconstitutional. Beginning with New Jersey in 1911, however, the states enacted workmen's compensation laws that stuck. Mississippi in 1948 became the last of the 48 states then in the Union to enact such a law.

A big argument for workmen's compensation was that it would encourage employers to maintain safe conditions in order to reduce their payment for casualty insurance. Studies over the years have not agreed on the effectiveness of the system in actually reducing work-connected injury and illness, although most studies have taken it for granted that the overall effect was beneficial. Some indicated that the accident rate dropped immediately after a compensation plan was adopted but the effect tended to level off as the years passed. Others attempted to show that the plans became increasingly effective as benefits were liberalized and worker-coverage extended.

---

[12] Nicholas Ashford, *op. cit.*, p. 75.
[13] Joseph K. Wagoner, director of field studies and clinical investigation for the National Institute of Occupational Safety and Health, quoted in the *Los Angeles Times*, June 27, 1976.

Congress, in the same act that created OSHA, ordered that a special commission be set up to look into "the fairness and adequacy" of workmen's compensation laws. Among the reasons for congressional concern, the act cited "the growth of the economy...increases in medical knowledge...[and] new technology creating new risks to health and safety." The presidentially appointed body, known as the National Commission on State Workmen's Compensation Laws, undertook an exhaustive review of the situation and issued a great deal of data and analytic material before it was disbanded July 31, 1972. It did note that accident rates were not necessarily lower in states where benefits were relatively high.

A more recent review, prepared by a research analyst on occupational health under a government grant, was even more skeptical of the supposed connection between high benefits and plant safety. While a study of available data showed the risk of serious work accidents had been appreciably reduced between the late 1920s and the early 1970s, it also showed the rate had declined for home accidents as well. Until definitive data become available to buttress their claims, he said, others should stop talking about "the beneficial effects of workmen's compensation on the occupational safety movement...."[14]

Spate of Protective Legislation in 1969-70

Until a very few years ago, the federal government was quite modest in its demands on private industry for the protection of employees. Nor was the issue of worker health and safety given prime attention by the public except briefly in the wake of a particularly sensational disaster. The Office of Industrial Hygiene and Sanitation had been established in the U.S. Public Health Service in 1914, but its work was (and remained over the years) mainly research and investigation. The agency had no enforcement duties. [15] Except for legislation pertaining to mines and railroads, the only direct intervention into private enterprise for worker safety was provided by the Walsh-Healey Act of 1936, which mandated health-safety standards for companies holding government contracts of more than $10,000.[16]

The situation changed during the 1960s. By this time the

---

[14] Lee Ellis, "Workmen's Compensation and Occupational Safety," *Journal of Occupational Medicine,* June 1976, p. 425. Ellis's research was financed jointly by the U.S. Bureau of Labor Statistics and the Kansas Department of Health and Environment.

[15] The agency underwent many changes of name and place over the years. In 1953, it became the Division of Industrial Hygiene within the newly created Department of Health, Education and Welfare. Later it became the Bureau of Occupational Safety and Health, and still later was transformed by the 1970 OSHA Act into the National Institute of Occupational Safety and Health. In 1973 the agency was transferred within HEW from the Health Services and Mental Health Administration to the Center of Disease Control in Atlanta, while still under the overall control of the U.S. Public Health Service—itself a branch of HEW.

[16] This protection was extended in 1965 to employees of suppliers of services to the government.

public had become sensitized to the issue of environmental pollution and there was general recognition that what harmed workers on the job could affect the well-being of the entire population. Meanwhile, in the 1950s, the number of reported industrial accidents had taken a sharp turn upward. This situation led to the enactment of the Coal Mine Health and Safety Act of 1969 and the Occupational Safety and Health Act of 1970. Still a third law, the Federal Railroad Safety Act of 1970, gave the Department of Transportation authority to regulate safety conditions on the railroads.

It has been said that federal laws concerning occupational health and safety now "cover virtually all of the nation's industry." And the three federal agencies chiefly involved—the Departments of Interior, Labor and Transportation—"have been given broad regulatory power and substantial appropriations with which to implement the federal law on health and safety."[17]

Coal Mine Safety; Black Lung Indemnity

Mine legislation has had a long history but one of limited protection. After a series of mining accidents, the U.S. Bureau of Mines was established in 1910 in the Department of the Interior. But the bureau did not acquire authority to inspect mines until 1941 or to set and enforce safety-health standards until 1952. A mine explosion in December 1951 that took 119 lives near West Frankfort, Ill., spurred enactment of the federal Coal Mine Safety Act of 1952. Under this law, the bureau could close a mine if conditions presented an immediate danger. But its authority extended only to mines that employed at least 15 persons, a restriction that was not lifted until 1966. In the same year, Congress passed the Metal and Non-metallic Mine Safety Act extending protection to other miners.

Another coal-mine accident, claiming 78 lives at Farmington, W.Va., on Nov. 20, 1968, spurred enactment of the most stringent of all mine safety laws, the Coal Mine Health and Safety Act. It became law on Dec. 30, 1969, establishing mandatory health and safety standards for underground mining—in contrast to surface, or strip-mining. The standards applied to fire protection, roof supports, escape ways, communications systems and permissible levels of dust.

In addition, the law required that miners be given chest X-rays when their employment began and periodically thereafter. If a miner was found to be developing black lung, he was to be given an opportunity to transfer to a job in a less dusty part of

---

[17] Frederick R. Blackwell, "Federal Safety Laws March On," *Natural Resources Lawyer*, fall 1974, p. 661. Blackwell is former chief counsel of the Senate Subcommittee on Labor.

the mine. The act also provided monthly cash payments to coal miners disabled by the disease or to their widows. Amendments to the act in 1972 liberalized these benefits to include all dependents in an afflicted miner's household as beneficiaries, extended coverage to surface as well as underground miners, and broadened the definition of black-lung disability.

Except for the black-lung-claims adjudication program, which is being transferred to the Department of Labor from HEW, enforcement of standards set by the act is in the hands of the Department of Interior. Interior in 1973 created a new agency, the Mining Enforcement and Safety Administration, to carry out enforcement duties.

The black-lung indemnity program has presented many difficulties. There were so many complaints about delays in processing claims that the House Appropriations Committee ordered a staff study of the problem. The study attributed the large backlog of cases mainly to shortages of personnel and to the complications of shifting the processing function from one department to another. "It might have been less an ordeal and less costly in the long run to have left the program with the Social Security Administration [in HEW]," the staff report concluded. But to reverse the decision now would only "create a more chaotic situation than now exists."[18]

New Principle Under 1970 Job Safety Act

The most significant development in the protection of worker health and safety was passage of the Occupational Health and Safety Act in 1970. It took effect April 28, 1971. The agency that administers the act has had several reorganizations and changes of leadership, and its activities have met with criticism and controversy. But the act did introduce something new into the governing principles of American life—that the worker has a legal right under federal law to a safe place to work. Moreover, the employer is now required, under penalty of law, to meet government-imposed standards of safety. This principle seems to have become firmly entrenched.

The act established in the Department of Labor a new agency, the Occupational Safety and Health Administration (OSHA), and created a new post of Assistant Secretary of Labor for Occupational Safety and Health to run it. In one way, the act represented a compromise between those who thought responsibility for worker safety should remain where it had traditionally been, with the states, and those who thought the time had come for the federal government to take a firm hand. The act provided that any state could develop its own occupational

---

[18] House Appropriations Committee, "Processing of Black Lung Benefit Claims," report by committee's Surveys and Investigations Staff, January 1976, pp. 7, 9.

health and safety program, but the plan and its operation would be subject to the federal agency's approval.

If a state plan is approved, the state may enforce it. But the federal office will evaluate the state effort for at least three years and may withdraw approval during that period. The act provided federal funding for 90 per cent of the cost of developing a state plan and for 50 per cent for the operation. To date, 22 states have had their plans approved, but only South Carolina has completed all steps and put its plan in effect.[19]

"The Congress declares...its purpose and policy...to assure so far as possible every working man and woman in the Nation safe and healthy working conditions..."

The Occupational Safety and Health Act
of 1970, Sec. (2) (b)

The act covers nearly all employees of companies in interstate commerce. Unlike many other regulatory functions of government, there are no exemptions by size of business.[20] The act applies even to employers of only one person, and "employee" includes everyone, including supervisors and corporation executives. Although the act applied originally only to civilian workers in private employment, executive orders from the White House extended the terms of the act to federal employees. Approximately 62 million people, 80 per cent of the nation's work force, are thus covered.

The law does not set standards but it empowers the Secretary of Labor to do so in specific situations, and it sets forth the procedures by which these standards are to be determined. The federal agency maintains a staff of inspectors who may enter a place of private business without notice to check on compliance. If a violation is found, a citation will be issued. If the citation is challenged, a hearing will be held before an administrative judge representing the Occupational Safety and Health Review Commission, another new agency established by the law.

---

[19] South Carolina's plan was certified on Aug. 3, 1976. The other 21 states are Alaska, Arizona, California, Colorado, Connecticut, Hawaii, Indiana, Iowa, Kentucky, Maryland, Michigan, Minnesota, Nevada, New Mexico, North Carolina, Oregon, Tennessee, Utah, Vermont, Washington and Wyoming.

[20] A rider on an appropriation bill in 1976 did exempt farms that employ fewer than 10 persons.

The judge's decision becomes final in 30 days unless sent for review to the full commission. Employers may appeal to the full commission or to federal court. Employees may appeal the proposed date for correcting a violation. Fines of up to $1,000 may be imposed for each violation and for each day of failure to correct the violation. Criminal penalties may be invoked if a death occurs from a willful violation.

The law also provides for research, training of personnel, and employee education on safety. The research function is a vital part of operations since standards on toxic substances are dependent on scientific findings. Responsibility for research is placed in the hands of the National Institute for Occupational Safety and Health, established by the act. The law orders the institute to develop "criteria dealing with toxic materials and harmful physical agents and substances which will describe exposure levels that are safe for various periods of employment, including...exposure levels at which no employee will suffer impaired health or functional capacities or diminished life expectancy as a result of his work experience." This standard-setting function has been the source of much controversy.

Problems in Safety Enforcement

C ONFLICT is inherent in almost any worker protection program. While everyone applauds the goal of reducing the risk of worker injury, illness or death, there are large areas of doubt as to whether some of the safety measures—actual or proposed—are worth the cost involved. Inevitably, opinion differs on what action should or should not be taken.

All regulatory agencies of government inspire a certain amount of resentment among the people upon whom the regulations are imposed. Safety regulations touch an even more sensitive nerve than most. To the businessman, a citation for a violation is at best a nuisance. It is likely to be expensive and to offend him personally for implying that he may be heartlessly indifferent to the welfare of his employees. The small businessman, in particular, is likely to bristle at the sudden appearance of a government inspector armed with authority to look around his shop.

In a study of occupational health prepared for the Ford Foundation, Nicholas Ashford of the Massachusetts Institute of Technology observed that "inherent difficulties [are] encountered whenever the law is used as the predominant mechanism for social control of science and technology." He found this to be especially true of the OSHA program which "cannot be successfully implemented if we continue to ignore the fundamental conflicts and tensions which exist between various groups of people and between various institutions in our society."[21] Ashford described five sources of conflicts:

1. Self-interest, especially between management and labor which are accustomed to dealing with each other as adversaries.

2. Lack of sufficient data on which to base an unassailable decision—as in deciding how much abatement of contaminants in the air is required.

3. Differences in perception of "what is just or fair," for "honest men will differ and argue on how much control a government should exercise to protect its citizens."

4. Overlapping functions between government agencies, as in the case of OSHA and the Environmental Protection Agency.

5. Different parts of the total problem dealt with by "various professional interests." Unfortunately "the professionals, institutions and laws related to job health in our society have been historically quite separated from those related to job safety."

Complaints Against the Regulatory Agency

It is generally agreed, even within the federal agency itself, that OSHA made a clumsy start and was ill-equipped, both in funds and qualified personnel, to deal with the conflicts cited by Ashford. It is also generally agreed that the situation improved after Morton Corn, a University of Pittsburgh professor and specialist in industrial hygiene, took over as agency director a year ago.

President Nixon, on signing the OSHA bill, praised it as "one of the most important pieces of legislation...ever passed by the Congress." Nixon said it represented "the American system at its best: Democrats, Republicans, the House, the Senate, the White House, business, labor, all cooperating in a common goal—the saving of lives, the avoiding of injuries, making the place of work for 55 million Americans safer and more pleasant." His choice of OSHA administrator, George Guenther, however, was regarded as a political appointee lacking special qualifications needed to marshal united support from the diverse forces mentioned by Nixon.[22] Guenther's problem was compounded by a small budget[23] and an inadequately trained staff.

---

[21] Nicholas Ashford, *op. cit.*, p. 39.

[22] During the Watergate hearings, a confidential memo from Guenther, dated June 14, 1972, came to light in which he suggested using "the great potential of OSHA as a sales point for the fund-raising and general support by employers" and asked for suggestions "on how to promote the advantages of four more years of properly managed OSHA for use in the campaign."

[23] Some $35.7-million in the agency's first full year of operation, fiscal 1972; in the current fiscal year, 1977, it is $130-million.

One of the most pervasive complaints raised against the agency was that its inspection and enforcement staff concentrated on job safety as opposed to job health—that is, on physical conditions in the plant related to accident prevention rather than on concerns about worker illness. The factory and shop inspector traditionally was more attuned to accident prevention than to the more subtle hazards to health. Even worse were complaints that inspectors were issuing violation citations for minor technical deviations from standards—what became known as the "broken toilet seat violation."

Some of the difficulty arose from a provision in the act that required the agency to adopt immediately, as interim measures, appropriate standards already established by other agencies. The aim was to get the program started quickly while standards for newer hazardous situations were being developed. Accordingly, OSHA issued a number of so-called "consensus standards" to prevail for two years. These were drawn from existing standards, such as those established under the Walsh-Healey Act and by the National Fire Protection Association and American National Standards Institute.

Complaints followed that some of these standards were trivial, inapplicable or outdated. A kind of folklore grew up about absurd "violations" cited against places of business. In addition, businessmen and shop owners complained about the officiousness of inspectors. Richard P. O'Brecht, director of labor law for the U.S. Chamber of Commerce, told a congressional committee that criticism of the agency reflected not an absence of commitment to worker safety but the "frustration and often outrage caused by what many employers view as the heavy-handed application of the OSHA program."[24]

Federal Efforts to Correct Shortcomings

Small businessmen in particular were in distress. Rules and regulations were often so wordy and technical that proprietors had difficulty understanding them. "How can he [the employer] determine whether his wooden ladders are properly constructed and in compliance by being referred to 11 pages of fine print on the subject which includes everything from algebraic equations to the fibre stress characteristics of more than 50 different types of wood?" O'Brecht asked.

The small businessman has no one to turn to. Unlike the big corporation, he has no technical specialists to handle such problems. If he asks the agency to send an inspector to see if he is in conformity and to advise him on correcting any deviations from the standard, he stands in jeopardy of being cited for a

---

[24] Testimony before the Subcommittee on Labor, Senate Committee on Labor and Public Welfare, April 12, 1976.

violation. The Chamber of Commerce has long demanded a system that would permit on-site consultations with OSHA experts who would inform the proprietor if anything is wrong and advise him how to correct it—and give him a chance to correct it before citing him for a violation.

The agency has been trying to meet these criticisms. It has instituted a training program in "human relations" for its inspectors to help them deal more sympathetically with the small businessman. And it has written and rewritten manuals to offer compliance instructions in simpler language. Perhaps even more important, an effort is being made to enlarge the staff on health protection, as distinct from safety protections.

Recognizing that there is a shortage of qualified occupational-health inspectors and very few places where such training can be acquired, OSHA set up its own work-study program to attract potentially well-qualified individuals to fill the needed jobs. The goal is to obtain a corps of 2,200 specialists—1,100 safety inspectors and 1,100 industrial hygienists whose concern is primarily with the illness factor. Each group of specialists will be made aware of the problems of the other so that, for example, if a safety inspector suspects the presence of an airborne health hazard, he will call on an industrial hygienist to check it.

These measures have not allayed all criticisms. They have tended to deepen suspicion among labor unions that the agency is too ready to make concessions to business at the expense of worker health. Units of the Ralph Nader consumer-interest organization in Washington, D.C., keep up a steady flow of pamphlets berating OSHA—saying that it is not fulfilling its mandate or is going soft on industry.

Organized labor has its own list of recommendations for reform and these do not conform with those of the business community. The AFL-CIO has drawn up a list of proposed reforms. "It is time the federal government lived up to the promise...of a safe and healthy workplace for every American worker," the statement said.[25] Among the "specific actions [that] must be taken":

> More money for the agency, more qualified manpower and more facilities, including a laborator *.
>
> "Full federal preemption of promulgation and enforcement of occupational safety and health standards in all states."
>
> Coverage for all workers, including state and local government employees.

---

[25] American Federation of Labor and Congress of Industrial Organizations, "Policy Resolutions," adopted October 1975.

Authority to compliance officers to issue on-the-spot orders that employees leave places of "imminent danger."

Transfer NIOSH, the occupational health research agency, from HEW to the Department of Labor and also transfer health and safety responsibility for miners and railroad workers to Labor.

To these criticisms have been added others from the General Accounting Office, an arm of Congress, in a series of reports. The GAO noted that OSHA permitted states, while developing their programs, to maintain lower safety standards than are required by the federal government. Federal agencies themselves have been criticized in these reports as having inadequate worker-protection programs. The House Government Operations Committee, after several days of hearings, issued a critical report on Sept. 27, 1976, saying: "In its five years of operation, the OSH administration has failed to provide adequate protection for the health of American workers." But the committee was "encouraged" by the commitment for improving the program that was shown by the agency's director, Morton Corn.

Cost-Benefit Issue; Dollars Versus Risks

Behind all the arguments on worker health and safety lies the basic question of cost. It has become customary to apply the concept of a cost-benefit ratio to questions of policy in this area. To some it seems crass to balance a dollar figure against the health or life of a human being. It helps to consider the balance as between cost and risk, a more acceptable frame of reference, familiar to all in the form of insurance.

Dr. Philip Handler, president of the National Academy of Sciences, told a scientific forum: "There is no escape from the need, somehow, to equate dollars and lives, to agree to the dollar value of an average human life in the population at risk...."[26] In a later extension of remarks on this subject, Handler said: "[W]hen the government contemplates regulatory activity to diminish the risk associated with some technology...an attempt is required to state both the cost and the benefits in quantitative form."[27]

Generally speaking, the employer is more interested in the cost of instituting a safety or health-protection measure and the employee is more interested in getting the maximum amount of protection. It has been pointed out, however, that if the risk is not too great, the worker may prefer to forgo a safety measure in

---

[26] Talk at a National Academy of Sciences forum, "How Safe is Safe," May 1973, reprinted in Harold P. Green's "The Risk-Benefit Calculus in Safety Determinations," *George Washington Law Review*, March 1975, p. 798.

[27] Philip Handler, "A Rebuttal: The Need for a Sufficient Scientific Base for Government Regulation," *George Washington Law Review*, March 1975, pp. 809-811.

favor of some other benefit—higher wages, for example. Some studies are critical of unions that for years pressed for other benefits as alternatives to health-protective measures.

An academic critic of OSHA complained: "[T]he basic problem with the implementation of the act is that there is no fundamental agreement on the practical methods of balancing considerations of greater safety and health against considerations of cost." He argued that "the government...should not force more safety and health on society than workers would choose for themselves if they had to pay the costs...directly." "In their private lives," he added, "...they smoke cigarettes, drive when they could walk, ski when they could read a book, and use power mowers when safer hand mowers would do."[28]

That the cost of protection will be high is generally taken for granted. Nevertheless a government program of the OSHA type appears to have become a permanent element in the nation's economic life. And some of the early suspicion of the motives of the new agency administering the program has subsided. A spokesman for the construction industry has said that "most of our original apprehension has proven groundless." He said the agency "is neither as effective as some of its advocates thought it would be nor is it the obstacle to normal operations that was originally anticipated by industry." Of one thing he was sure: "OSHA is here and working and...it is never going to go away."[29]

---

[28] Robert Stewart Smith, *The Occupational Safety and Health Act* (1976), pp. 1, 34. Smith is an assistant professor at the New York State School of Industrial and Labor Relations at Cornell University.

[29] John A. Woodhall Jr., "After Five Years an Assessment of OSHA," *Construction*, April 1976, p. 29. Woodhall is chairman of the Central States Construction Division of Central-Allied Enterprises Inc., and chairman of the National Safety and Health Committee of the Associated General Contractors of America.

Selected Bibliography

Books

Ashford, Nicholas, *Crisis in the Workplace: Occupational Health and Safety,* MIT Press, 1976.

Brodeur, Paul, *Expendable Americans,* Viking, 1974.

Page, J. A. and Mary-Win O'Brien, *Bitter Wages: The Report on Disease and Injury on the Job,* Grossman, 1973.

Smith, Robert Stewart, *The Occupational Safety and Health Act,* American Enterprise Institute for Public Policy Research, 1976.

Articles

Blackwell, "Federal Safety Laws March On," *Natural Resources Lawyer,* fall 1974.

Chelius, James R., "The Control of Industrial Accidents: Economic Theory and Empirical Evidence," *Law and Contemporary Problems,* summer-autumn 1974.

Conn, Harry, "Quieting Ear Pollution," *The American Federationist,* October 1975.

Ellis, Lee, "Workmen's Compensation and Occupational Safety: A Review and Evaluation of Current Knowledge," *Journal of Occupational Medicine,* June 1976.

Ettkin, Lawrence P. and J. Brad Chapman, "Is OSHA Effective in Reducing Industrial Injuries?" *Labor Law Journal,* April 1975.

Klein, Edward A., "Warning: The Workplace May be Hazardous to Your Health," *Journal of Occupational Medicine,* June 1976.

Job Safety and Health, selected issues.

Page, Joseph A. and Peter N. Munsing, "Occupational Health and the Federal Government: The Wages Are Still Bitter," *Law and Contemporary Problems,* summer-autumn 1974.

Woodhall, John A. Jr., "After Five Years: An Assessment of OSHA, *Construction,* April 1976.

"Why Nobody Wants to Listen to OSHA," *Business Week,* June 14, 1976, p. 64.

Studies and Reports

Department of Labor and Social Security Administration, "Processing of Black Lung Benefit Claims," report to House Committee on Appropriations, January 1976.

General Accounting Office, "Better Data on Severity and Causes of Worker Safety and Health Problems Should Be Obtained from Workplaces," Aug. 12, 1976.

U.S. Congress, House Appropriations Subcommittee on Labor, testimony of Morton Corn, 1976, pp. 534-631.

U.S. Congress, House Committee on Education and Labor, "Scotia Coal Mine Disaster," a staff report, Oct. 15, 1976.

INDEX

E

F